The Love Suicide at Amijima

Michigan Classics in Japanese Studies
Number 5

Center for Japanese Studies
The University of Michigan

The Love Suicide at Amijima

(Shinjū Ten no Amijima)

A Study of a Japanese Domestic
Tragedy by Chikamatsu Monzaemon

Donald H. Shively

Center for Japanese Studies
The University of Michigan
Ann Arbor, Michigan

Library of Congress Cataloging-in-Publication Data

Chikamatsu, Monzaemon, 1653–1725.
    [Shinjū ten no Amijima. English]
    The love suicide at Amijima : a study of a Japanese domestic tragedy
by Chikamatsu Monzaemon / Donald H. Shively.
        p.   cm. — (Michigan classics in Japanese studies ; 5)
    Translation of: Shinjū ten no Amijima.
    Reprint. Originally published: Cambridge, Mass. : Harvard University
Press, 1953. Originally published in series: Harvard-Yenching Institute
monograph series ; 15.
    Includes index.
    ISBN 0–939512–51–3 (pbk.)
    I. Shively, Donald H. (Donald Howard), 1921–   . II. Series.
PL793.4.S513 1991
895.6'232—dc20   91–318
                                                                              CIP

The paper used in this publication meets the requirements
of the ANSI Standard Z39.48–1984 (Permanence of Paper).
Printed in the United States of America

Acknowledgments

For the support and assistance which contributed to this study I wish to express my gratitude to the Society of Fellows at Harvard University, the Harvard-Yenching Institute, and the University of California. My greatest indebtedness is to Professor Serge Elisséeff who for many years has encouraged me in the study of Japanese literature and who made a careful reading of this play with me. The manuscript has also been read by Professors Edwin O. Reischauer and James Robert Hightower, both of whom offered many valuable criticisms and suggestions. I am grateful as well to Mrs. Richard N. Frye for editorial assistance, and to my wife for her patience.

DONALD H. SHIVELY

Berkeley, California
July 1951

Contents

Introduction

Translation

Notes to the Translation   99

Introduction

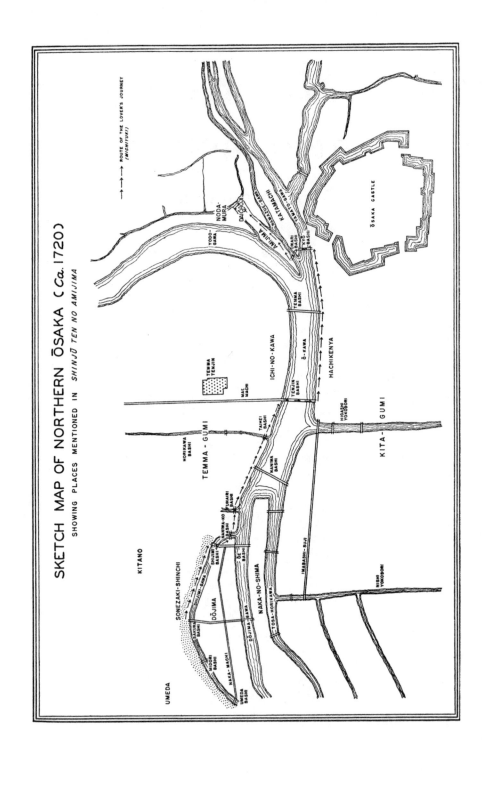

SKETCH MAP OF NORTHERN ŌSAKA (Ca. 1720)

SHOWING PLACES MENTIONED IN *SHINJŪ TEN NO AMIJIMA*

→ → → ROUTE OF THE LOVER'S JOURNEY
(*MICHIYUKI*)

ŌSAKA CASTLE

KATAMACHI

AMIJIMA

NODA-
MURA

DAICHŌJI

KYŌ-
BASHI

TENMARI
BASHI

YODO-
GAWA

TENMA
BASHI

ICHI-NO-KAWA

Ō-KAWA

TENMA
TENJIN

MAE-
MACHI

TENJIN
BASHI

HACHIKENYA

TEMMA - GUMI

NORIKAWA
BASHI

TAIHEI
BASHI

NANIWA
BASHI

HIGASHI
YOKOBORI

KITA - GUMI

KITANO

SONEZAKI-SHINCHI

SHIJIMI
BASHI

NANIWA-KO
BASHI

FUNAIRI
BASHI

Ō-
BASHI

IMABASHI-SUJI

DŌJIMA

DŌJIMA-GAWA

SHIJIMI-GAWA

NAKA-NO-SHIMA

TOSA-HORIKAWA

NISHI
YOKOBORI

UMEDA

SAKURA
BASHI

MIDORI
BASHI

NAKA - MACHI

UMEDA
BASHI

Introduction

1. *The Theater in the Culture of the Osaka Townsmen*

The leading playwright of the Japanese popular drama movement which began in the opening years of the seventeenth century was Chikamatsu Monzaemon (1653–1725). Of his many plays
none is better known today than *The Love Suicide at Amijima*
(*Shinjū Ten no Amijima*). Written in 1720, it is a mature work
of his late years and is considered by modern Japanese scholars to
be the finest example of his domestic plays, or *sewamono,* a form
which is largely his invention.[1] The esteem in which this work is
held in the history of Japanese literature is indicated by the fact
that there have been more commentaries written on this than on
any other play.

The plot concerns the ill-conceived love of the young owner
of a paper store, a married man with children, and a prostitute.
The lovers, unable to extricate themselves from their family and
professional obligations so that they may marry, escape the unsympathetic world by seeking death in a double suicide.

Westerners who read this play will find some aspects of it to be
of merit. The dramatization is often skillful. The plot as a whole
is well integrated, and the details of the story are unfolded in a
natural manner. Unexpected complications in the course of events
hold the reader's attention; variety of action sustains the pace.
The flow of events seems logical, and the main characters have a
tragic quality. In fact, the social and ethical dilemma of the lovers,
if abstracted out of their particular cultural environment, seems
to deal with a universal experience.

Yet the Western reader may be at a loss to understand why the
play or its author has gained quite such recognition in Japan. He
finds that in translation the style is undistinguished, and he may
feel that the characters are inadequately delineated, the moral con-

flict is meaningless, and the suicide unnecessary. He will probably be more convinced that the play does not merit serious attention when he learns that it was written for the puppet theater, and that in the last two centuries it has been performed only after the most extensive rewriting.

The Westerner who is critical of this play is perhaps correct in the opinion that *Ten no Amijima* is not a work of universal appeal. However, this is not to deny that it deserves its position of esteem in Japanese literature. The very fact that it has markedly less appeal to a Western than to a Japanese reader enhances its importance for the study of comparative literature. The play is appreciated by the Japanese for special characteristics of style, content, and form which are unfamiliar to the Western reader. It is the product of a culture radically different from Western cultures, and its merits can be appreciated only after the most elaborate explanations. The elements of literary style, such as meter, word-plays, and allusions, are much more thoroughly swept away in translation from Japanese than they would be if translated from an Indo-European language. Another barrier to understanding the play is the social environment, the social and moral conflicts, which made it more poignant for the Japanese audience of two centuries ago than for modern Japanese. To understand the play we must also be aware of special conventions of the Japanese drama which conditioned it, and the peculiar requirements of the puppet theater which it had to meet. At the risk of doing some violence to appreciation of the play as a work of art, it will be subjected in this Introduction to such analysis as will show the specific ways in which the play is a product of its particular environment. Our first consideration then will be the culture of the Osaka townsmen and the theater that developed in it.

The Genroku, the era name for the years 1688–1704, refers more broadly to the cultural period from about 1680 to the 1740's. This was a time of unprecedented prosperity in the cities, of extraordinary productivity in the development of new popular forms of literature and art. It followed upon the establishment of internal peace and a form of centralized political control at the opening of the seventeenth century. The first three shogun, or military overlords, of the Tokugawa family had evolved an intricate system of political and social control which ran largely on its own momentum through the two and a half centuries (1600–1867) of the Tokugawa period. During the Genroku period the authority of this central government was unchallenged at home, and was free of threats from abroad. The old problems seemed to have been settled, and the new ones were yet to develop significant proportions; thus the administration had no concerns more serious than matters of finance and succession.

Domestic peace and a stable political structure were propitious for those interdependent developments which contributed to the expansion of the economy—the improvement of the transportation system, the increased circulation of commodities, the growth of a money economy, the formation of rice exchanges and credit houses, and a rising standard of living for all classes. In this rapidly developing economy, it was the commercial centers, the cities, which gained the greatest benefits, and much of the wealth of the nation passed into the hands of the merchants. They made large profits by government contracts for construction projects, for transporting commodities, and for reminting. They made even more money by speculation in rice and other products, by wholesaling monopolies, and by lending money to the feudal lords and members of the samurai class.

The center of the new urban culture was the city of Osaka, which dominated the commercial world as the transportation entrepôt and the location of the rice exchange. It had risen to importance in the sixteenth century when it outstripped the port of Sakai which neighbored it to the south.[2] For several generations from the seventeenth into the eighteenth century it held a clear preëminence as the center of urban life over the two larger cities which had a population of over half a million.[3] Heian, the modern Kyoto, the ancient Imperial capital and center of traditional culture, was too steeped in its past glories to live fully in the present. Edo, the modern Tokyo, the effective political center of the nation as the headquarters of the Tokugawa administration, was in the process of being built, and its townsmen were still rather stifled by its rustic provincialism and military atmosphere. The chief characteristic of Osaka which distinguished it from the other two was that it was predominantly a commercial city. Under the Toyotomi family it had a brief career as a political and military center, until the fall of Osaka Castle in 1615. In the years that followed, the Tokugawa strove to gain the favor of the inhabitants by the remission of taxes and by public works, such as developing the canal system.[4] Osaka Castle was reconstructed as a bastion of Tokugawa power against any uprising of the feudal lords of southwest Japan, but it was not needed for this purpose until the middle of the nineteenth century; during the Genroku period the Castle did not cast a shadow over the civilian character of the city. Those samurai stationed in Osaka who were not in the Castle garrison were more commercial than military, since they were on duty at the commercial offices which the various feudal lords had established in Osaka to market the rice and other products of their fiefs.

It is not surprising that, at this center of commercial activity, the Osaka townsmen (*chōnin*) developed the most pronounced bourgeois spirit in Japan. Under a system of corporate responsibility they had a measure of management of their own affairs. They were responsible to a commissioner from the central government, the *machi bugyō,* for carrying out the instructions and requirements of the central government. Although the townsmen had no real opportunity for participation in political life, they were actually freer in the ordering of their lives and the conduct of their business than any other class in Japan.

By the time of the Genroku period the actual position of the Osaka townsmen was very different from their theoretical status in the Tokugawa social order. The feudal overlords, influenced by Confucian ideas of the functions and productivity of the occupations, had decreed a four-class hierarchy which placed the samurai or official class at the top, the farmers second, the artisans third, and the merchants fourth. This system did not take economic status into consideration. In the course of the economic expansion of the seventeenth century the Osaka merchants became wealthy, and the townsmen as a whole—merchants and artisans—were comparatively prosperous.[5] It is true that they had little opportunity for participation in politics or for social advancement, but anything that money could buy was theirs. Their energy and wits were channeled into making money and spending it, and these became the great satisfactions in life.

The prosperity of the townsmen created a demand for forms of entertainment and art to meet their tastes and interests. It led to the development of gay quarters in the cities, where they could divert themselves in the restaurants, brothels, and bathhouses. It led to the development of new literary genres and new forms of drama, music, and dance. Their tastes brought forth new schools of painting, the development of the techniques of multicolored woodblock prints, and advances in the crafts of the weaver and the dyer.

All of these forms reflected the buoyant spirit of the townsmen, their lack of restraint and their verve. They contrasted sharply with the simplicity of the traditional forms of entertainment and art of the samurai, who considered the culture of the upstart townsmen plebeian, gaudy, and often immoral. Yet the samurai often were attracted by its excitement and fell under its spell. In subject matter, the bourgeois art bore a closer relation to actual life than did the art of the higher classes. The new literary genres and the domestic plays dealt with the social and moral problems of the townsmen. The paintings and woodblock prints took as subject matter scenes of their daily life, often in the gay quarter. The music of the three-stringed samisen and the drama recitations caught the tempo of their energetic, emotional lives. The patterns of their clothes and the woodblock prints reflected their love of bold color and design.

This tendency of *chōnin* art to represent actual conditions of life in rather graphic terms was in part the result of its origin as popular art of a class with but rudimentary education. However, it was more than a literal-mindedness, for it also reflected intellectual changes in Japan. Coincidentally with the rise of the merchant class in the early seventeenth century, the otherworldliness of the Buddhist outlook was giving way among the educated to the more practical social ethic of Confucianism. Concepts of legal procedure were becoming dominant in business as in feudal relations. The increase of commerce contributed to the growth of a mentality among the townsmen which placed importance on facts and figures. In the world of business, abstract concepts seemed of less utility. The practical, impatient townsmen found classical culture too antiquarian, too restrained, too profound. In the forms of art and literature as modified to meet the taste of the townsmen, there was a trend from the romantic toward the realistic, from the historical to the everyday.

This is exemplified by the three literary genres which developed during the seventeenth century: the *haiku* or seventeen-syllable poems, the *ukiyo-zōshi* or short stories, and the popular plays.

The *haiku* (or *hokku*) as a simple, terse poetic form appealed to the townsmen. It derived from classical forms but was simplified and had been freed of most of the scholastic rules of prosody and restrictions on subject matter. The composing of *haiku* and the related form of "chain poems" (*haikai renga*) became popular pastimes and the object for social gatherings and contests. They were often as much games, however, as art forms, games in which humor, nimbleness of wit, or quantity of production were appreciated more than aesthetic quality.[6]

A literary form even more representative of the townsmen is the short story of Ibara Saikaku (1642–1693) and those he influenced, such as Nishizawa Ippū (1665?–1731). These men delighted in describing the life of townsmen of all professions. With keen humor and sharp insights they described how merchants made their fortunes and squandered them. They reported in greatest detail on life in the gay quarters and gave the full particulars of recent love suicides. The terse and witty style of this prose, like the subject matter, suggests the tempo of *chōnin* life.

The content of Chikamatsu's plays shows a similar trend from classical materials to those of the contemporary world dealt with in the short stories. In literary style they were similar to contemporary prose, and were characteristic of *chōnin* culture in the rhythm of the language, the bombast, and the emotionalism. The two types of theater for which he wrote were developed specifically for *chōnin* taste, and contrasted in form and treatment with the classical theater. The *kabuki* and the *ningyō jōruri*, or puppet theater, both products of the seventeenth century, are so interrelated by cross influences in their development that they must be considered together.

That the *kabuki* theater is a characteristic product of *chōnin* culture can be seen in its points of contrast to the classical *nō* drama and *kyōgen* farces of the Muromachi period (1336–1568). Like many of the townsmen's arts, it emerged from a crude, plebeian medium, and was elevated by borrowings from a classical art form of the upper classes. Its rudimentary beginnings were in shrine dances and mimes, but it was the *nō* which supplied many of the elements that made it a dramatic form. The plots of most early *kabuki* were taken from the *nō* texts (*yōkyoku*) or from that corpus of military stories (*gunki monogatari*) on which the *nō* drew so heavily. The *michiyuki*, or poetic journey of the *nō* plays, became a regular feature of the *kabuki*. Its dances and posturing were influenced by the *nō*, and the style of recitation and early techniques and terminology of staging were borrowed from it.

However, in its spirit and tempo it is as different from the *nō* as the Tokugawa townsman was from the Muromachi warrior. In contrast to the subtlety and restraint of the *nō*, the action of the *kabuki* is direct, the language bombastic, and the movements exaggerated. Historical events are unfolded in lively action on the stage, instead of being narrated in retrospect by a priest or the spirit of a samurai. The impersonal recitation in poetic diction which characterizes *nō* is supplanted in the *kabuki* by extensive use of dialogue, in rough and ready language. During the last decade of the seventeenth century, the introduction of the domestic plays about contemporary occurrences in the townsmen class made *kabuki* even more representative of *chōnin* culture. At the same time the use of more elaborate sets and staging techniques and the development of more mature acting styles began.

The early *kabuki* had developed certain characteristics, especially in acting styles, which restricted its potentiality as a serious art medium; this was probably an important reason why the puppet theater was able to rise to such popularity and compete with it during the Genroku period. The *kabuki* is said by tradition to have originated in 1603 with the appearance in Kyoto of Okuni, who was evidently a renegade Shinto priestess.[7] Her suggestive dances attracted notice, and her performances were provided with some plot content by her lover, Nagoya Sanzaburō (or Nagoya Sanzō) , who outlined farces for her from his knowledge of *nō* and *kyōgen*. In many of the *kabuki* troupes which soon appeared the women's roles were played by men, and the men's roles by women, providing the opportunity for a great deal of indecent pantomime. The acting and dancing was often calculated to advertise the actors' and actresses' secondary profession of prostitution. It is not surprising, then, that the *kabuki* theaters were established next to the gay quarter. The central government, deploring the immorality of the *kabuki* theater, began to place prohibitions on it as early as 1608. There were some troupes composed entirely of women, who performed *onna kabuki*, or "women *kabuki*." But the impersonation of men by women was considered to be especially disruptive of public morals, and women were banned from the stage in 1629, an order which remained in force for over two centuries.[8]

Even before this prohibition, at least as early as 1617, there was an all-male theater, known as the *wakashū kabuki*, or "young men *kabuki*," which was connected with homosexual prostitution. This type of drama was banned intermittently, notably in 1642. It continued without serious interference after 1652 when certain superficial reforms were made to satisfy the authorities. An example of these changes was the requirement that the boys who played female roles shave their forelocks in conformity with the masculine fashion. In compensation, the practice soon arose of wearing a purple cloth cap over the shaved portion to simulate the appearance of women's coiffure. In this modified form, known as *yarō kabuki*, or "fellow *kabuki*," the emphasis was still on sex rather than on art, as is abundantly illustrated by the *yarō hyōbanki*, the critical booklets rating the boy actors, which stressed their physical appeal more than their dramatic skill. It was probably not until the 1680's that art began to take precedence over sex in *kabuki* acting, with the development of new styles by Arashi San'emon (1635–1690) and Sakata Tōjūrō (1647–1709).[9] For some time, however, the actors continued to be idolized by the townsmen public as much for their appearance as for their acting.

The excessive popularity of the actors also inhibited in another way the development of *kabuki* into a mature drama form. The individual actor confined himself to a type of role in which he felt he excelled and demanded of the playwright a vehicle which would suit his style and rhetorical declamations which would utilize his voice to its best advantage. The written text (*kyakuhon*) was sometimes little more than an outline on which the actor improvised, and in most cases the actor's whims took precedence over the structure of the plot. This was such a restricting medium for the able writer that many of them, like Chikamatsu, turned more and more to writing *jōruri* for the puppet theater, where their literary talents would have fuller scope.

Jōruri, a style of recitation used in narrating certain romances,[10] began to be used to accompany the performance of puppets at the beginning of the seventeenth century.[11] About the same time the three-stringed samisen [12] was substituted for the *biwa* as an accompaniment to *jōruri* recitation. With the development of the puppet theater, *jōruri* came to mean the style of recitation used for puppet plays, and hence the plays themselves.

This puppet *jōruri* grew rapidly in popular favor and on certain occasions was even performed for the Imperial Court, the Tokugawa shogun, and many of the feudal lords, at a time when *kabuki* was held in contempt by the upper classes. Dozens of competing styles of *jōruri* recitation were evolved in Osaka, Kyoto, and Edo, but the style which was ultimately to overshadow the others

was developed by Takemoto Gidayū (1651–1714).[13] He established his own puppet theater, the Takemoto-za, in Osaka in 1685.
His success can partially be attributed to the fact that many of the
jōruri he performed from 1685 on were written for him by Chikamatsu, who, after 1705, worked almost exclusively as a writer for
his theater.

The principal competition of the Takemoto-za among the puppet theaters of Osaka was the Toyotake-za founded in 1702 by a
former pupil of Gidayū, Toyotake Wakadayū (1681–1764). Hiring
the able playwright Ki no Kaion (1663–1742), it staged a new
play to vie with each production of the Takemoto-za, often using
the same theme for its plot.[14] The competition between the two
theaters and the two writers was a great stimulus to the development of the art. The spur of economic competition induced Chikamatsu to put more originality into his plays, Gidayū to recite
more fervently, and the puppeteers to develop new techniques and
more artistic puppets. The result was that for several decades before and after 1700 the puppet theater seems to have actually outstripped the *kabuki* in popularity in Osaka.[15] The limitations of
the *kabuki* as a serious art form during its early development can
in part be credited for this extraordinary situation, but an important cause was the outstanding talent that the puppet theater had
assembled.

The interrelation between the *kabuki* and the *jōruri* is extremely complex, and it is often impossible to determine in which
form certain of the elements originated. During the Genroku period the puppets came to be modeled in appearance and style of
acting on certain of the more famous actors of the day. It must
have been amusing to the audience to see the familiar gestures and
stance of well-known actors mimicked by the wooden puppets, but
with a touch of exaggeration which may have made the human
actors seem a little flat. The puppet theater fell into some of the
conventions of the *kabuki,* such as the use of type roles; the movements of the female puppets were modeled on the style of the boy
actors who played the female roles in the *kabuki.* At the same
time, the puppets had an influence on the acting styles of the human actors. The articulation of the wooden arms and necks of the
puppets lacked the smoothness of the movements of humans. Also,
in order to bring puppets to life on the stage in the roles of humans, all of their movements and gesticulations had to be slightly
exaggerated. The actors, not to be outdone, adopted some of these

jerky and exaggerated movements themselves. Similarly, the necessity of heightening the emotional impact of the language in the *jōruri* to make the puppets seem human influenced the language of the *kabuki*. In time, the *kabuki* was forced by the competition of the *jōruri* to improve the dramatic structure of its plays and to subordinate the actors to the play. The *kabuki* theater adapted *jōruri* texts for its own use, and as much as half of its repertoire during the Tokugawa period seems to have been derived in this way. Some of the stories used in the *jōruri* had been borrowed originally from the *kabuki*, so that a complete cycle was sometimes formed.

This process of borrowing can be seen also in the evolution of the domestic play (*sewamono*). All earlier plays in both theaters were of the category known as "period pieces" (*jidaimono*), that is, history plays. In *kabuki* there began to appear scenes which were clearly contemporary, such as a glimpse of prostitutes and townsmen in the gay quarter, and these elements were expanded until a rudimentary *sewamono* was evolved. Such innovations were copied in the *jōruri* and were developed until finally the full-length domestic puppet play was evolved by Chikamatsu, and then readapted for presentation on the *kabuki* stage.

2. The Jōruri of Chikamatsu

Chikamatsu Monzaemon is the most famous author of *jōruri*.[16] His contribution to the development of Tokugawa drama is comparable to that of Zeami (Kanze Motokiyo, *ca.* 1363–1443) in the *nō* of the Muromachi period. In a career of fifty years he wrote a hundred *jōruri*, some forty others are often attributed to him, and he was the author of about thirty *kabuki*.

Few details of his life are known with any certainty except those connected with his career as a playwright. There are at least ten different traditions concerning his place of birth, three about his place of death, and three temples claim his grave.[17] Even the exact date of his death is in doubt,[18] and there are three versions extant of his "death message" (*jisei*).[19] Until new evidence is uncovered, it seems better not to add to the excess of speculation that now exists concerning his origins and education. It need only be remarked that it is obvious from the internal evidence of his plays that he had an extensive knowledge of Japanese literature and a wide familiarity with quotations from the Chinese classics and Buddhist writings. It is generally accepted that he was born into a samurai family and that some years of his youth were spent in the service of noble families in Kyoto.[20]

It is known that he composed *haiku* which were included in a family anthology, published in 1671, when he was eighteen.[21] As in the case of Saikaku, his experience in composing *haiku* contributed stylistic characteristics to his prose. The imaginative exercise of composing *haikai renga* contributed to his agility in turning poetic phrases in meter for sustained passages. During the first half of his productive period, he wrote *jōruri* for reciters of at least five different schools and composed most of his *kabuki*. Thereafter he devoted himself almost exclusively to writing *jōruri* for the Takemoto-za. Through this wide experience and decades of intense application he constantly improved his literary style and gained an ever deeper understanding of the problems of the theater. From the crude and monotonous productions in the "old *jōruri*" (*ko-jōruri*) style, his plays gained in stature as he developed the "dialogue,"[22] the structure of the plot, and the delineation of psychological attitudes. His most creative achievement, the domestic play, was a product of the second half of his career. Indeed, the plays written during his last decade quite overshadow those of the preceding forty years, not only in maturity of concept and polish of style, but also in originality and vigor.

Chikamatsu's career as a playwright is generally divided into four phases. The first phase (1676–1685) is normally considered as beginning with the first *jōruri* for which we have a reliable date, but there is some evidence that *jōruri* he had written were being performed as early as 1673. His earliest plays were largely adaptations of *nō* texts. The second phase (1686–1703) began with the performance of *Shusse Kagekiyo,* the first important play he wrote for Takemoto Gidayū. During this period he wrote nearly half of his *kabuki,* including about ten specifically for Sakata Tōjūrō, the greatest actor of the day and his close friend. In some of these works, such as *Butsu Mo Maya-san kaichō* (*ca.* 1693) and *Keisei Awa no Naruto* (*ca.* 1695), he began to place scenes in the gay quarter, such as those involving the redeeming of prostitutes, which foreshadowed the development of the domestic *jōruri* in the following decade.

The third phase (1703–1714) opened with the production of the first pure *sewamono, Sonezaki shinjū* (*The Love Suicide at*

Sonezaki), which deals exclusively with Osaka townsmen, dramatizing the story of a recent event. Chikamatsu did not write another domestic play for three years, but in the third month of 1705, he moved from Kyoto to Osaka where he became a permanent writer for the Takemoto-za, which thereafter performed his plays almost exclusively. Here at the center of *chōnin* culture, he turned his attention more and more to the domestic plays, and thirteen of the forty-five *jōruri* written during this period were of this type. His writings in this decade relegated almost all of his earlier *jōruri* to obscurity.

The fourth phase (1715–1724) of Chikamatsu's career, although less prolific, quite overshadowed even the preceding one in its high concentration of important plays. Among the sixteen history plays and eight domestic plays is included his most famous work in each group; *Kokusen'ya kassen* (*The Battles of Coxinga*) [23] (1715) and *Shinjū Ten no Amijima* (*The Love Suicide at Amijima*) [24] (1720). Moreover, during his last four years he wrote the history play, *Kan hasshū tsunagi uma* [25] (1724), and the domestic play, *Onna koroshi abura no jigoku* (1721), which were unsurpassed in vigor of style and originality of plot. His late plays also excelled in the sympathetic depiction of human problems. The cumulative experience of forty years as a playwright and a lifetime as an observer of human life led him to his best achievements.

According to tradition, it was the difficulties arising from the death of his friend and employer Takemoto Gidayū in the ninth month of 1714 [26] which spurred him on to his greatest efforts. The theater faced a double crisis in finances and in the question of succession. One of the young reciters, Takemoto Masadayū (1691–1744), had been selected by Gidayū to succeed him as chief reciter. Some of the older reciters of the troupe, however, believed him to be unworthy to fill his master's place, and, discouraged about the future of the theater, a number of them seceded. When word of the dissension spread, the audience began to dwindle. Chikamatsu was called upon to try to save the day by writing a daring new history play. He rose to the occasion by writing *The Battles of Coxinga*, which broke all records, running continuously for seventeen months. It assured Masadayū of his position and brought new recognition to Chikamatsu,[27] whose apparent paternal concern for the young Masadayū may also help to account for the brilliant achievements of his last years.

Other circumstances at this time contributed to the development of Chikamatsu's art. His relation with Masadayū gave him more freedom in writing than he had had under Gidayū, and he was able to give fuller scope to his literary preferences. He did have to make some changes in his style to meet the special requirements of Masadayū's voice, but this necessity proved to be fortunate, especially in the case of domestic tragedies such as *Shinjū Ten no Amijima*. Masadayū's voice was weak in volume and rather thin in tone, unsuited to the type of bombastic, thundering history plays which Gidayū had delighted in. To bring out the emotional qualities of Masadayū's voice, Chikamatsu emphasized human feeling and sympathy in his writings. He succeeded in making his characters more lifelike by revealing their human frailties and by paying greater attention to dialogue, with the result that he enhanced the dramatic situations in the plays.[28]

As a writer of *jōruri* for the Takemoto-za, Chikamatsu had, of course, to meet many requirements which limit the freedom of any dramatist. Although *jōruri* permitted him wider latitude than *kabuki*, it was nonetheless a restricted medium. He was part of a business organization which produced plays for profit. Since he was in a key position to determine its economic success, he had a serious responsibility to the entire company. Obliged to write plays which would be certain of popularity, he had at times to compromise his artistic ideals.[29]

A comparison of the two types of *jōruri*—the history plays (*jidaimono*) and the domestic plays (*sewamono*)—indicates the course of development of *jōruri* into a more mature drama form. The *jōruri jidaimono*, when contrasted with the *nō*, can be described as representative of *chōnin* culture in much the same way as are the early *kabuki*. Roughly speaking, many early *jōruri*, like the *kabuki*, appeared to be a *chōnin* variation on *nō*. Although they borrowed extensively from the *nō* in structure, recitation, and subject material, they contrast with them so sharply in spirit and tempo that they unmistakably reveal their *chōnin* origin. Yet compared with the *jōruri* domestic plays, the history plays seem to be an intermediary form between the classical and the bourgeois, for the domestic plays were not only for townsmen, but are about them exclusively.[30] Also in many lesser ways, including changes in form, the domestic plays are more characteristic of *chōnin* culture. To a greater extent than the history plays they exhibit the tendency of *chōnin* art forms to develop from the romantic toward the realistic, from the historical toward the everyday. This can be seen in the points of contrast between the domestic and the history plays.

The twenty-four *sewamono* of Chikamatsu, written during the last twenty years of his life, are concerned largely with the townsmen of Osaka and Kyoto. The plot usually revolves around a love scandal, in most cases based on an actual contemporary event. The financial problems and family conflicts that follow upon an unfortunate amour often bring the play to a tragic conclusion. The domestic plays are highly charged with emotional problems, which were perhaps too close to home to be enjoyed by the townsmen as a steady diet. The history plays by contrast seem escapist entertainment with the scene laid in the historical past, the characters military or court figures of the upper class, the events enlivened with supernatural intervention, superhuman heroes, and gaudy pageantry. But after the splendor of the long five-act *jidaimono*, the program was concluded by a three-act *sewamono*, direct and poignant, which sent the audience home choked with tears.[31]

The subject matter of the domestic plays is immediate social realities, the problems of real townsmen. If these, as presented on the puppet stage, were to stir the sympathy of the audience, they had to be presented with the greatest possible realism. An atmosphere of reality was built up by presenting familiar scenes of Osaka or the interior of a typical townsman's home. This is in contrast to the deliberately unrealistic atmosphere of the history plays, which catered to sensationalism by presenting the fantastic and the mysterious, the scene being laid in the dim past when incredible feats were possible and divine intervention was a matter of course. In his so-called history plays Chikamatsu did not strive for accuracy. He jumbled history and legends from various sources—the *nō*, military stories (*gunki monogatari*), and classical novels (*monogatari*)—to spin the most entertaining story he could. He changed names and scrambled chronology.[32] Regardless of their century the characters act according to the idealized feudal pattern of ethics which was taught to samurai in the Genroku period. Despite prohibitions against depicting contemporary historical events involving the upper classes, Chikamatsu on several occasions dealt with this material in his *jidaimono*, but he was careful to camouflage the story by dating it in an earlier century.[33]

The structure of the two types of play also reveals a marked contrast. The domestic play has a closely knit, succinct plot, so presented in the love-suicide plays, for example, as to prepare the audience for the tragic culmination. If the lovers were to suffer, the reasons had to be made clear, and all routes of escape had to be blocked. In those plays which end in suicide, the suicide psychology had to be built up by reasonable and convincing steps. There had to be a clear framework of time and space, which requirement resulted in a tendency to observe the unities within an act. The structure of history plays, on the other hand, is loose and episodic; lacking any real plot, it consists rather of a series of incidents, disjointed in space and time, often with little relation between the beginning and end and with the most chaotic chronology in between. The free treatment seems to have pleased the Tokugawa audience, but the modern Japanese as well as the Occidental finds the history play distressingly weak as a dramatic form. He is disturbed not only by the feebleness of the plot, the insertion of irrelevant elements merely to entertain, and the excessive use of the supernatural, but also by the dogged insistence on a lesson of moral edification. The greatest violence is done to credibility in the careful rewarding of good and punishing of evil which conclude each history play. When the supernatural must intervene to bring about the edifying ending, it often reduces the plot to puerility. This structural characteristic, combined with the greater emphasis on the musical element in the history play, often gives these plays an operatic rather than dramatic flavor.

The difference between the two types of play is also evident in the delineation of the characters. The domestic play centers around the mental state of the main characters, the complex dilemma in the minds of the lovers, torn between their love and their obligations. The conclusion usually is a triumph of the heart, of human frailties. The interest in the domestic play lies in human attitudes rather than in events, and the interplay between events and feelings forms a dramatic balance. In the history play, the main interest is in the events, and there is greater reliance on narrative than on dialogue. Action does not flow from character but is rather external and contrived. The characters have no real individuality but are merely types, each embodying some virtue or vice in familiar garb. These stock characters—faithful retainer, brave warrior, benevolent lord, filial son, illustrious woman, blackest villain—are so manipulated as to bring about the desired end, that is, the rewarding of good and the punishment of wrongdoing. They serve merely as agents through whom the moral of the play is pointed. In the domestic play the characters also tend to be types, but to a much lesser degree. Their actions more often betray human failings, and they have more personality than the abstract paragons of virtue who are the heroes of the history play.

The contrast between the domestic and the history play also extends to the spheres of puppetry and music.[34] The study of Chikamatsu's *jōruri* as literature neglects two major dimensions of the dramatic art—first, the puppet manipulation, and second, the musical elements of recitation and samisen—which must be conceived as interrelated elements. The dance of the puppets, a combination of puppetry and music, is also an important element in some plays. These elements are used somewhat differently in the two types of play. In the presentation of the history play there is greater reliance on the purely visual aspects, and a corresponding exaggeration and lack of realism are exhibited in the movement of the puppets. The historical heroes make great leaps in the air and effect miraculous entrances and exits. There is a certain bravura in the musical accompaniment, the action, and the language of the history play—a liveliness, vigor, and exuberance of word and deed that overshadow purely dramatic qualities. Contrariwise, in the domestic play the movement of the puppets is more restrained and natural, the intention being to create an atmosphere of plausibility, of reality. The musical elements enforce the human moods, convey in turn the lively tempo of the gay quarter and the sadness of the doomed lovers at their place of death in the suicide plays. If the history play may be said to appeal to the eyes and the ears, the domestic play appeals to the ears and the heart. In the latter there is obviously greater emphasis on the recitation to create and sustain the mood.

The contrast in the essential characteristics of the two types of play makes it clear that more mature dramatic writing can be expected in the texts of the domestic plays.

3. *The Gay Quarter and Love Suicides in the Domestic Plays*

A closer examination of the subject matter of the domestic plays is revealing of the social problems of the Osaka townsmen.

The plots of most of the twenty-four by Chikamatsu revolve about a love affair, which most often ends in tragedy. Fifteen of them have been classified as "love-suicide pieces" (shinjūmono),[35] but in some of these the suicides are not consummated. The other nine deal with illicit love, which is almost always adulterous.[36] It is typical of Chikamatsu's moralistic treatment that some of the adultery cases are merely alleged, or if they actually occurred, take place in a rather accidental manner, as if to show that there was no premeditation. In most of the love-suicide plays, the girl is a prostitute in one of the gay quarters of Osaka. The subject matter, then, is similar to that of the "amorous pieces" (kōshokumono) among the stories of Saikaku, and the works of others of Chikamatsu's contemporaries, such as Nishizawa Ippū. Three of Chikamatsu's domestic plays are based on stories which had appeared earlier in rather different versions in Saikaku's Kōshoku gonin onna (Five Amorous Women) (1686). It is probable that all of Chikamatsu's domestic plays are based either directly on an actual occurrence or on a story prevalent in the popular literature of the day.[37]

The gay quarter (irozato) and its life are the subject of a great mass of chōnin literature throughout the Tokugawa period, as they are of the ukiyoe, the paintings and woodblock prints of the townsmen. That it should be the exciting center of social life, while the home and marriage were considered subjects too un-romantic for treatment, is symptomatic of the social arrangements of the townsmen.

The outlets for the money and energy of the Osaka merchant were limited. His vigor and ability were directed into a desire for property and for pleasure. He could gain prestige within his class by spending money conspicuously and by acquiring a reputation for riotous living. When a merchant indulged too ostentatiously in luxuries, he might encounter difficulties with the feudal authorities,[38] who feared that obvious enjoyment of life by the lowest class was disrupting to the hierarchical class system. The Confucian education of the officials made them ever concerned with outward appearances, and they attempted to keep the townsmen in their place by intermittently issuing sumptuary laws. At various times these restricted the size of houses merchants could live in, the richness of their ornamentation, the use of expensive textiles in their clothes, the making of certain types of cakes, and the hiring of palanquins of certain design. However, a wide margin of license was allowed for the way the townsmen could conduct themselves in the gay quarter of the large cities. It was something of a free area, where the *chōnin* could escape the social and political inequalities of the Tokugawa system. It was a pleasure quarter for the *chōnin,* and although many of the visitors were samurai, the latter usually wore a disguise, since they went at some risk to their professional standing. They avoided attention and did not attempt to enforce their social prerogatives. Only in this quarter was class unimportant. Money was the sole index of prestige and power, and there was little that money could not buy.

The gay quarter originated from the practice in earlier centuries of restricting houses of prostitution to a certain section in the town. Originally the prostitute's sole function was probably physical, but with the development of prosperity in the cities, the character of certain of the old quarters was transformed, and new quarters were established which became centers of social and sometimes even cultural activity. As the only places where the townsmen could spend lavishly and enjoy themselves, they grew rapidly into luxurious centers of entertainment. They were areas of such wonders that they were sometimes referred to as *gokuraku,* the name of the Western Paradise of Amida Buddha.[39]

In the higher type of establishment, the primary function of the girls shifted from sexual to social intercourse. They were encouraged to develop distinctive personalities and were trained in singing and dancing, in poetry and calligraphy, in tea ceremony and flower arranging. The cultural accomplishments of the higher class of prostitute far exceeded those of the townsman's wife. Their rich dress and elaborate coiffures led the trend in fashion, and the influence of their styles reached even to the ladies of the shogun's palace. A few of the girls of the highest rank attained a position of considerable independence. They would not bestow their favors lightly, but demanded a long and expensive courtship.[40] The strong personalities and accomplishments of some won respect for their profession within the *chōnin* class. Outwardly they were treated with courtesy and were addressed in terms of respect. In their relations with their masters, of course, there were few who were treated with consideration. Most of them were little more than slaves for the term of the contracts which their masters had made with their parents. Few were fortunate enough to be redeemed by a man of wealth to become his concubine, or even his wife. The treatment of girls of lower status, who far outnumbered the privileged few, was sometimes severe. However, this is not the case in the idealized view of prostitutes in Chikamatsu's domestic plays, where even the lowly girl at a highway inn, who was a waitress by day and a prostitute by night, was always a woman with a highly developed sense of moral responsibility and an unfailingly cheerful disposition.[41]

There was a hierarchy of ranks among the prostitutes, with an elaborate scaling of the attendants and adornments which accrued to each in the custom of the particular quarter. The designations of rank differed from locality to locality, and from generation to generation, with the result that the Japanese language has accumulated a list of over four hundred and fifty terms for prostitute.[42]

By the Genroku period, the Yoshiwara in Edo and the Shimabara in Kyoto had become famous licensed quarters, but it was Osaka, the center of chōnin culture, which led the field. In addition to the officially licensed quarter of Shimmachi there were the unlicensed quarters known officially as bathhouse or teashop districts, such as Shimanouchi, Fushimi Sakamachi, Dōjima Shinchi, and Sonezaki Shinchi.[43]

The Shimmachi Quarter, which opened in the second quarter of the seventeenth century, had the highest status and the most formal organization. The houses to which the girls were indentured, and where they lived, were known as okiya. The four principal classes of prostitutes in the Shimmachi were tayū, tenjin, kakoi, and hashijorō (or misejorō). An okiya had girls of different classes, but often had none of the upper two classes. The patrons or visitors were not entertained at the okiya, but went to an ageya or to a chaya (literally, "teahouse,") where they made arrangements to have a certain prostitute or prostitutes summoned from an okiya. The ageya summoned prostitutes of the two higher ranks, while the chaya called the lower two. At the ageya or the chaya the patrons could order food and drink and demand any other type of entertainers they desired, such as singers, musicians, buffoons, or actors. In the Shimmachi there were also some lower classes of prostitutes and houses which were outside of the officially recognized system. In Chikamatsu's sewamono Yodogoi shusse no takinobori, Yūgiri Awa no Naruto, and Nebiki no kadomatsu, the heroines are tayū of this Quarter, and in Meido no hikyaku she is a hashijorō.

The largest unlicensed quarter, the Shimanouchi, or Minami, "South" (i.e., the South Quarter), prospered by its location just north of the Dōtombori theater district. It had two major classes of prostitutes, the *hakujin*,[44] and the *yuna*,[45] but in time the distinction between these two categories was largely lost. These prostitutes were also indentured to *okiya* and were summoned by visitors to *chaya* (the term *ageya* not being regularly used in the Shimanouchi). In all probability, the heroine of Chikamatsu's *Shinjū Kasane-izutsu* is a *hakujin* of this Quarter.

The Fushimi Sakamachi, a lower-grade quarter located south of the Dōtombori theaters, was opened in 1698. The prostitute in Chikamatsu's *Ikutama shinjū* is from this area.

The northern counterpart of the Shimanouchi Quarter was known as Kita no Shinchi ("Northern New Land") and consisted of the Dōjima and the Sonezaki Shinchi, which faced each other across the Shijimi River. The Dōjima area was reclaimed land which was divided into streets in 1688; it soon developed into a thriving quarter. When the rice exchange was moved into this area, the district gradually turned into a commercial district, and the houses of prostitution moved north of the river into the Sonezaki Quarter. After the Kyōho period (1716–1736), there were none left in Dōjima, and the term Kita no Shinchi came to mean only the Sonezaki Quarter. The Dōjima Quarter appears in Chikamatsu's *Sonezaki shinjū, Shinjū nimai ezōshi,* and *Shinjū yaiba wa kōri no tsuitachi.*

The Sonezaki Quarter was divided into streets in 1708 and the city officials granted permission to build *chaya* (nominally, "teahouses"), *furoya* (nominally, "bathhouses"), and *niuriya* (eating stands). Within a few years it was a thriving quarter, because of its proximity to the Dōjima rice market. Directly to the south, on the islands, Dōjima and Naka-no-shima, were located many of the commercial offices of the feudal lords. The Quarter served as a convenient location where the representatives of the lords and the merchants with whom they dealt could entertain one another, in much the same way that in modern times geisha houses (*machiai*) are the scenes of business and political transactions. The *furemai chaya*, which specialized in this type of entertaining, brought great prosperity to the Sonezaki Quarter. In *The Love Suicide at Amijima*, Chikamatsu's only play concerning the Sonezaki Quarter, it is stated that the heroine, Koharu, was originally a *yuna* in the Shimanouchi Quarter, who was transferred to an *okiya* in the

Sonezaki Quarter as a *hakujin*. The *hakujin* of the unlicensed quarters did not have the high formal status or command the prices of the higher ranks of prostitutes in the official Shimmachi Quarter. However, from the late seventeenth century on, they were much in vogue, as the etiquette in their establishments was less formal and the entertainment less restrained.

In the social mores of the townsmen class, visits to the gay quarter were not condemned on moral grounds. It was not considered disruptive to the social system for the husband to have extramarital relations in moderation so long as he confined these activities to prostitutes. The relation which existed between husband and wife makes this attitude understandable. Marriages were arranged by the parents through go-betweens, the first consideration in making a match being the business or social advantages it would bring. Even in the townsmen class the bride and groom were often strangers until the time of the wedding. Finding themselves man and wife, the couple were obliged to work out a *modus vivendi* as best they could. The prejudice against demonstrativeness in the home also militated against the growth of a romantic attitude in marriage. The relation which developed between man and wife at best was usually one of loyalty rather than of romantic attachment.

The family, according to the ethical teachings of the time, seems to have been centered not so much on the husband-wife relation as on that between parent and child. The wife's primary function was to be a mother to her husband's children, whereas the husband concentrated on bringing his son up to perpetuate the family business and to ensure the continuation of masses for the ancestors.

The importance of parent-child relations is also illustrated in the case of the parents-in-law. No matter how compatible the husband and wife, if relations with one set of parents were bad, the marriage could be destroyed. This is the theme of Chikamatsu's *Shinjū yoigōshin,* in which the young couple committed a love suicide rather than permit their parents to break up their happy marriage. In our play, *Amijima,* the wife fails in her attempt to resist the decision of her father to break up her marriage.

The attitude of the wives was conditioned by the training they received as girls. They were educated in a doctrine of service and obedience to men. They were taught that jealousy was one of the greatest of evils, that they must overlook their husband's infidelity, even to his bringing a concubine into the house or setting her up in a separate establishment. They were confined largely to household tasks and to the bearing and care of the children. With little education or experience outside the home, they were not stimulating socially or interesting romantically. Whatever excitement of social intercourse or romance the townsmen might desire had to be sought outside the home.

This excitement they found in the gay quarter. The townsmen, bound by a class and family system which caused many frustrations, found in the gay quarter a place where they could give free rein to their emotions, where they could gain a self-expression and prestige impossible elsewhere. Those who had the money to pay could command in the quarter a world of luxury and license. For those who could not afford it, this life could be disastrous. Led on by glittering temptations and sometimes by infatuation, they might plunge themselves into debt which would ruin their businesses and sometimes destroy their marriages.

Chikamatsu's domestic plays about the gay quarter deal with the family conflicts and often tragedies which were brought about by indulgence in the gay life. A prostitute was a commodity available to all, and her visitor was merely a customer. But occasionally a prostitute and one of her visitors forgot their proper roles, fell in love, and wanted each other exclusively. A practical-minded author like Saikaku would have no sympathy for such uncouth conduct which showed that the lovers did not know the proper way to act in the gay quarter. However, in the idealized account in Chikamatsu's domestic plays the hero is led into the impasse, not by unbridled sexual desire as Saikaku would suggest, but by true love. He makes the fatal mistake of losing his heart to a prostitute. This leads him into financial or family difficulties which bring about a conflict between his love and his obligations (*giri*). Unwilling to be false to his love, he either commits a love suicide with the prostitute or, more rarely, through some happy development, meets his obligations in such a manner that his life is not sacrificed.

The love suicide (*shinjū*) [46] is the more frequent outcome in Chikamatsu's domestic plays. The word *shinjū* meant "sincerity of heart" and came to be used of acts by which lovers demonstrated to each other the strength of their love. Some of the methods, prevalent especially in the gay quarter, were writing vows of undying love, inflicting burns or wounds on themselves, cutting off fingers, shaving the head, tattooing, and pulling out the fingernails and toenails.[47] In cases of a hopeless love, when the couple could not remain together in this life, they might perform the supreme act of sincerity by committing suicide together, and such love suicides were called *shinjū-shi*, or "*shinjū* death," and later, merely *shinjū*. This practice was a reflection of the tradition in the samurai class of committing suicide by disemboweling oneself (harakiri or *seppuku*) when one failed to meet some obligation.

By the end of the seventeenth century the love suicide had become so frequent among the townsmen that it became something of an institution, with its own conventions and formal procedures. In 1695, when Sankatsu and Hanshichi committed suicide, they are said to have left letters which stressed the importance of love as the highest principle of conduct, overriding all others. Their story, dramatized as a *kabuki* play with the title *Akane no iroage*, was the first love-suicide play to be a hit, running one hundred and fifty days.[48] When a love suicide occurred, it was greeted as the most exciting news item of the day. It was described in greatest detail in scandal sheets and short stories, with particular attention to such points as the conflict of family obligations, the weapons that were used, and the content of the suicide notes, which were usually only apocryphal.

The *Shinjū ōkagami* (*Great Mirror of Shinjū*), published in 1704, is one of the many works which deal with this subject. It tells the story of seventeen incidents which it implies are true. The preface suggests the prevalence of this practice: "Yesterday there was a love suicide, today there was also a love suicide, tomorrow with the vicissitudes of fortune, [such] strange things will again occur." [49] The sensational and romantic treatment of love suicides in contemporary literature seems to have been suggestive to frustrated lovers of the Genroku period. Rash young men and women could anticipate that their suicides would be publicized if not immortalized in prose and drama. Love suicides became so frequent that in 1722 the officials for a time prohibited the performance of plays on this theme. They also attempted to discourage the acts by imposing punishments on those who survived unsuccessful attempts and by heaping dishonor on the corpses of those who had been successful—according them the treatment given executed criminals and exposing them to public view for three days.[50]

The most important early *jōruri* about a love suicide is Chikamatsu's *Sonezaki shinjū* (1703), which set the pattern for the host of others that were written for the *kabuki* and puppet theaters.[51]

The high point in his love-suicide plays is always the "Journey" (*michiyuki*), the poetic description of the walk of the lovers to the place of suicide, in which passage he touched on their feelings toward the familiar places they were leaving behind, the loved ones they were deserting, the conflicting obligations which had rent their lives. The report may indeed be true that such narratives, glorifying the act in a brilliant literary style, did incite other lovers to suicide.

These passages in Chikamatsu also made an impression on the audience because he placed more emphasis than other writers on the theme of religious salvation. He made the most of the tradition of popular Buddhism, derived from the *Lotus Sūtra*, that lovers who died together would be reborn on the same lotus calyx on the lake before Amida's throne in the Western Paradise. In Chikamatsu's domestic tragedies, as the lovers went hand in hand to the place of death, they seemed to be guided by Amida. At the moment before their death, Chikamatsu indicated that the lovers would be immediately reborn in Paradise. With few regrets, the lovers gained release from their unfortunate lot in this world, to gain perpetual bliss together. Although the incident on which the play is based must usually have been the imprudent act of an immature couple, Chikamatsu beautified it with a religious aura, which seemed almost to justify it. He achieved for his audience what seems the impossible. Just as he kept the illicit relations of the lovers from seeming immoral, he kept the suicides from being tragedies.

Chikamatsu's view of love suicides suggests the projection into the *chōnin* class of the feudal attitudes of the samurai. The townsmen in the domestic plays, like the samurai in the history plays, held their lives lightly, and they sacrificed themselves with so little consideration that they hardly seemed like real people. The townsmen died for love with no more hesitation than the feudal samurai died for his lord, at least in fiction. The townsmen in some domestic plays were also as quick to commit suicide as the warrior when they feared they would lose face.

The greatest shame a townsman could suffer was the failure to meet one of his many obligations. It was this sense of obligation which Chikamatsu relied on so heavily as the determinant of human action. *Giri* could be an obligation to any relative or simply to a fellow man or fellow woman. It was the obligation to meet faithfully all business agreements. It could also be the obligation to conform to certain moral principles, traditions, and laws. The system of obligations in social relations was so comprehensive that it served as the basis for the ethical code, rather than an abstract concept of good and evil. *Giri,* in its broadest sense, could encompass the total social environment of the individual. Chikamatsu pictured it as a tyrant which oppressed the individual. When a high-spirited townsman would not conform to it, but acted according to his human desires, his obligations closed in upon him and crushed him.[52]

The townsmen's ethical code was composed largely of elements of the samurai code, which had been derived primarily from Confucian principles for the governing of feudal relations. Their attitude toward parents, children, employer and employee, and women, took on the aspects of the samurai view. Modifications were made to suit their needs in accordance with the requirements of their professions. Some business agreements concerning contracts and the payments of debts took on the terminology and rigidity of feudal obligations of fealty. The problem of financial difficulties arises constantly in the *sewamono,* and in some twelve of the fifteen *shinjūmono* it is a contributory factor in the suicide decision. In some cases the fear of failing to meet financial obligations is the primary factor which leads to crime or suicide.[53]

It is, of course, impossible to reconstruct in adequate detail either the ethical system of the *chōnin* or their level of conformity. The mass of contemporary literary material which we have too often presents an ideal pattern, or a satire on it, rather than the actual pattern of behavior. However, it provides a sufficient basis for two general conclusions. It is obvious that the Genroku townsmen were guided to a greater extent by concepts of obligation than Japanese in more recent times have been.[54] On the other hand, it is impossible to accept the pattern in Chikamatsu's domestic plays as an accurate representation of the ethical behavior of the townsmen. At best it might be called the ideal. Chikamatsu, who is believed to have come from a samurai family, was a great admirer of the samurai code. He took the feudal concepts about meeting obligations, which he had applied so rigidly in the history plays, and applied them in the domestic plays to the townsmen. *Giri* often seems to be the determinant of behavior which guides the actions of the characters, especially the female ones, in mechanical fashion. It is an important element in the plot of every play, often causing some act of extreme sacrifice, which to modern Jap-

anese, as to Westerners, seems farfetched. The hero in Chikamatsu's domestic play seems to be born in a world of *giri*, but he lacks
the will or reasoning power to try to resist the unreasonable conventions which confine him. He submits to environment not by
conformity in behavior, but by suicide, and he does this so com-
placently that he hardly seems human. When *giri* is applied me-
chanically for the sake of plot it must be considered a major flaw
in Chikamatsu's writing.

Although Chikamatsu uses the conflict between the individual
and his social environment as a sort of formula, there is no doubt
that it reflects a real problem of the period. The ethical system
of the newly risen townsmen of the Genroku was inadequate to
enable many of them to resist excessive indulgence and dissipation. They admired and emulated the strict code of the samurai,
but lacked the feudal discipline which, in theory at least, enforced
it so harshly in the samurai class. The townsmen failed to meet
the standards, which of course were not designed for their civilian
needs. This disparity between theory and practice, between expected standards and levels of conformity, was probably the cause
of personal conflicts, and sometimes of tragedies.

In Chikamatsu's domestic plays the oppressive social system under which the characters are made to suffer is softened in the end
by a Buddhist solution. Despite the prominence of the Confucian ethic among the *chōnin*, the influence of Buddhism had survived far more strongly among them than in the military class.
Lacking the self-discipline of the samurai, they often failed to
measure up to the code they emulated and sought refuge in the
compassion of Buddhism, which made allowances for human
feelings (*ninjō*) in a way that Confucianism did not. In popular
Buddhism, human weaknesses were expected and salvation was
promised for all. In Chikamatsu, as in most subsequent Tokugawa literature, there is the painful collision of *giri* and *ninjō*.[55]
The heroes suffer under the ethical system and are destroyed by
it, but in the end Chikamatsu pours out upon them his Buddhist
sympathy for human failings. He does not justify their weakness,
but he indicates that their failure is not entirely their fault. He
does this by relying on a sort of popular predestination, using the
Buddhist term *inga*, originally "cause and effect," hence "karma"
or "fate." The good or bad that comes to all individuals in this
life is reward or retribution, according to their *inga*, determined
by their acts in earlier lives and in the present existence. Because

of their *inga* some individuals are predestined to suffer. The rack on which they are broken, according to Chikamatsu, is *giri*. A few can be helped by human love, but most cannot be consoled in this world. By the strength of Buddha's compassion and by the prayers of the believers, they will be saved, that is, they will attain Buddha-hood and reach the Western Paradise. Particularly in the *shinjū* plays his Buddhist love makes of death a salvation.

4. *Content of* Ten no Amijima

In entering upon a discussion of the play, *Shinjū Ten no Ami-jima*, a synopsis of the plot is essential. The developments ex-plained in the first two acts, which occurred chronologically be-fore the opening of the play, are as follows:

Kamiya Jihei, aged twenty-eight,[56] is the proprietor of a paper store which he inherited from his father. His wife, Osan, is his cousin, the daughter of his paternal aunt, and they have two chil-dren, aged six and four. For over two years he has been in love with the prostitute Koharu, aged nineteen, a *hakujin* in the estab-lishment Kiinokuniya in the Sonezaki Quarter. He has been spending so much money to visit her that it has taken all the re-sources of his business, and he is hard pressed to pay the bills from the wholesale paper houses. Osan, a compliant wife, does not com-plain of his neglect of her and the business, but her father, Goza-emon, a rigid, narrow-minded man of the old school, is intensely annoyed with Jihei. The situation for Jihei and Koharu becomes desperate when a wealthy young blade, Tahei, although unsuccess-ful in winning Koharu's favor, decides to buy her out of Kiino-kuniya and make her his concubine or wife. Koharu would rather commit suicide than be separated from Jihei. Jihei does not have the means to redeem her, and even if he could, to make her his concubine would create intolerable family relations, because Osan is his cousin and he has special obligations to her mother, his aunt. In despair over their hopeless love, Jihei and Koharu decide to commit suicide together at the earliest opportunity. Koharu's owner, the proprietor of Kiinokuniya, suspects that this is their intention and he has been taking precautions against Jihei's seeing Koharu by requiring identification of her visitors. Osan, also fear-ing the worst, has secretly written a letter to Koharu, begging her to give up Jihei and save his life. Pressed by "*giri* to a fellow woman," Koharu agrees to try to save Jihei, although she herself still intends to commit suicide.

Act 1 takes place at a *chaya* in the Sonezaki Quarter. Jihei's elder brother, Magoemon, a flour dealer, is greatly concerned about him. Although a prudent man, the model of an upright merchant, he takes the dangerous step of masquerading as a samurai to go to visit Koharu, hoping in this way to hit upon some means by which he can sever her from Jihei. Koharu sees in the sympathetic attitude of this supposed samurai a way to save Jihei and she implores him to visit her constantly so that Jihei will not have the opportunity to carry out the love suicide. Meanwhile, Jihei, hoping that the opportunity might come this very evening, is eavesdropping outside the window. He is so enraged by Koharu's apparent unfaithfulness that he draws his sword and attempts to stab her through the paper-covered sliding window. He is caught by the samurai, who shortly reveals that he is really Magoemon. He points out to his younger brother that Koharu is unfaithful to him and admonishes him about his family duties. Jihei, furious with Koharu, breaks off his relation with her. He requires her to turn over to Magoemon the written vows of undying love which they had exchanged and promises never to return to the Quarter. As the brothers leave, the impetuous Jihei curses Koharu and kicks her to show his contempt.

Act 2 takes place ten days later at Jihei's paper store. Jihei's aunt and Magoemon come to the shop because they have heard rumors that Koharu is about to be redeemed, and they believe that it is to be by Jihei. They hope to find some way of saving the situation before Osan's father, Gozaemon, breaks up the marriage. Jihei denies that he has returned to the Quarter, Osan corroborates his story, and they conclude that it must be Jihei's rival, Tahei, who is redeeming Koharu. Jihei agrees willingly to sign a vow to convince Gozaemon that he has severed relations forever with Koharu, and the others rejoice that he has truly reformed. After the aunt and Magoemon leave, Jihei weeps with mortification that Koharu is so unfaithful as to be redeemed and that he has been outdone by his rival and thus will lose face with all his business associates. Osan realizes from a remark Jihei makes in this conversation that Koharu still intends to commit suicide. Because of *"giri* to a fellow woman" Osan says that Koharu must be redeemed at once before she kills herself. With no regard for her own interests, she would let Koharu become Jihei's concubine or even wife rather than fail to meet the obligation she feels she has to save Koharu's life. She convinces Jihei that they can raise enough money to make the down payment on Koharu by pawning their clothes and using some money she had set aside to pay a bill. As Jihei is about to leave the house with the clothes to be pawned, Gozaemon bursts in. Having no confidence in Jihei's vow to reform, he has come to demand the return of Osan at once, anticipating that Jihei might pawn her clothes. He sees before him the evidence that this is precisely what was about to happen, and, against Osan's will, he drags her away from Jihei and her two children.

Act 3. Jihei, on learning of Osan's letter to Koharu, realizes that Koharu has been faithful to him. He visits Koharu that night at a *chaya* in the Sonezaki Quarter. The lovers hear that Tahei has completed the last arrangements to redeem Koharu and they resolve on suicide. Magoemon comes looking for Jihei, fearing that with his marriage broken there is nothing to deter him from suicide, but Jihei evades him. Koharu then makes her escape from the *chaya*, and the lovers, in the "Journey" passage, walk across the northern part of Osaka to Amijima. Here they commit suicide, confident that by the power of Amida's love they will be reborn on the same lotus calyx in his Western Paradise.

In earlier chapters of this Introduction the attempt has been made to give the general environment in which Chikamatsu's love-suicide plays were developed. Now in making a close examination of the best known of these plays, it will be shown how representative it is of its type and also of its environment. The play revolves about social and ethical conflicts with which the audience could sympathize. That the play was tailored to a particular clientele is evident also in the elements of local color, in the allusions to local history and geography. The play contains many stock situations which had become the conventions of *chōnin* drama. The characters in the play can be recognized as typical townsmen, even though they tend to be type roles. In short, the play has a large degree of convention and localization. A degree of these elements is essential to any popular play; and excess of them would be tedious. While a modern audience might feel that these elements in *Amijima* are excessive, evidently the Osaka audience of the day did not. The repetition of stock elements to be found in other contemporary plays was probably especially appreciated because of Chikamatsu's knack of giving them new twists. A premium seems to have been placed on the novel treatment of the familiar.

The play is centered on a social problem which, according to the evidence of contemporary literature, was not uncommon in the Genroku era—that of a husband torn between love for a prostitute and his obligations toward his family and business. In a society where the individual was subservient to the decisions of the family council, the effort of an individual to gain some measure of free expression, especially in a matter of love, was greeted with sympathy by the audience. They could feel pity for a man like Jihei. He did nothing illegal, as did the heroes of many of the domestic plays, whose love led them to commit theft or fraud. Jihei's only offense was his failure to meet family responsibilities. This they could forgive, for he was romantic and emotional, a man who was too human and who broke under the burden of the oppressive social system which afflicted them all.

Jihei's arranged marriage to his cousin had enmeshed him in a family situation which made the system of controls unusually tight. In Act 1 his family relationships are twice explained in detail so that they will be well impressed on the minds of the audience. They can be diagrammed as follows: [57]

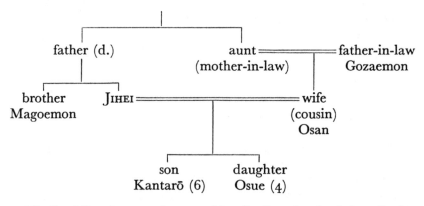

Jihei's obligations are increased by the fact that he is heavily indebted to members of his family for the love they have shown him. His aunt is not only his mother-in-law; since the death of his father, he has a filial obligation toward her because she has also acted as a parent to him. His indebtedness to her is increased by the fact that she is constantly interceding for him with her husband, the rancorous Gozaemon. Also constantly concerned about his welfare and attempting to assist him is his elder brother, Magoemon, to whom he owes respect and obedience in accordance with the family system. A third person whose love for Jihei is constantly being demonstrated is his wife, Osan, always uncomplaining and self-sacrificing. She is truly devoted to him and attempts to shield him from her father. These three exert themselves to save Jihei, and, although he feels affection as well as obligation toward them all, he forsakes them for Koharu.

His children are also introduced to emphasize the conflicting loves in the play, particularly in Act 2, the homey scene in Jihei's household.[58] In the late afternoon, while Jihei is napping, Osan is busily tending the shop at the same time that she is taking care of the household. She is greatly concerned about her two children, who have not yet returned although the evening has grown cold. Then at the conclusion of the act, when Osan's father drags her away from her home, she stumbles over the two sleeping children, waking them. These two episodes are obviously calculated to develop the dimension of mother love and to deepen the pathos of the broken home. The calculated use of the children to excite pity is most crudely handled in the last act, when Magoemon brings the six-year-old son, Kantarō, into the Gay Quarter during the early hours of a winter morning in an attempt to dissuade Jihei from suicide. Scenes such as these serve to accentuate the many loves pulling at Jihei—loves between man and woman, husband and wife, father and children, younger brother and older brother—and heighten the domestic tragedy.

Most of the domestic plays emphasize one particular type of obligation, such as *giri* toward parents, toward the wife, or toward society. *Amijima* emphasizes most strongly "*giri* to a fellow woman." That Osan and Koharu, the two women who love Jihei, should act toward each other with such extreme self-sacrifice because of their sense of *giri* gives the entire play a logic which seems artificial to the modern reader. They show remarkably little jealousy, and are motivated largely by *giri,* as if they were models of how the wives of samurai should act. When Osan writes to Koharu pleading with her, because of the "mutual sympathy" which exists between women, not to let Jihei commit suicide, Koharu agrees, replying: "He is my precious man, worth more to me than my life itself, but, being caught in an inescapable obligation (*giri*), I shall give him up" (translation, p. 81). Osan's display of *giri* to Koharu comes when she realizes it is Koharu's intention to commit suicide alone rather than allow herself to be redeemed by Tahei. She is then willing to make the most extraordinary sacrifices to try to save Koharu's life. She intends to redeem Koharu, although to do this she will have to deceive her father, pawn the rest of her clothes and those of her children, put the business into debt, let Koharu become her husband's concubine, and perhaps even demote herself to the status of nurse or cook. "If I let this woman die, I shall not be meeting my obligations (*giri*) to a fellow woman" (p. 81).

Osan is motivated by *giri* not only toward Koharu, but also toward Jihei—that is, by the necessity of maintaining her husband's face. "Even if I and the children have nothing to wear, what is important is my husband's [reputation in] society. Redeem Koharu and save her life, and please maintain your honor in front of this Tahei fellow" (p. 83). That she was combining these two kinds of *giri* in her decision is made clear in the text: ". . . she wraps together into one bundle her husband's shame and her obligation, and includes in it her devotion" (pp. 82–83).

The most farfetched exhibition of *giri* is afforded by Koharu near the conclusion of the play in making the arrangements for the suicide. The logic of her argument is not entirely satisfactory. She says that if their dead bodies were found side by side she would not be meeting her obligation to Osan because of her promise not to let Jihei die. Yet she feels that this obligation will be met if they commit suicide in two different places. Jihei argues that she no longer has an obligation to Osan because her father has forced their separation, which amounts to a divorce. Then, as if more thoroughly to obliterate the obligation, Jihei and Koharu cut off their hair, making themselves a Buddhist monk and nun with no worldly commitments. This also frees them of the obligations to each other, established by a vow they had made, to die in the same place. They then proceed to kill themselves, though they are careful to meet their no longer existing obligations by dying at places not far apart but yet separated by category—one spot symbolizing a mountain, the other a river—and by using different methods of suicide.

It is typical of Chikamatsu's attitude toward women, whether wife or prostitute, that it is they who exhibit the greater virtue and uprightness. Jihei, however, is not without his sense of obligation. In Act 3, before setting out to his place of suicide, he gives the proprietor of the *chaya* detailed instructions about the payment of his bills in the Sonezaki Quarter. Even though he fails to meet all of his business and family obligations earlier, at least those in the gay quarter are squared handsomely. Jihei is also conscious of his obligation to repay his debt of gratitude (*on*) to Osan when she decides to redeem Koharu to save his honor. As Jihei says to her father: "I have a great debt of gratitude (*dai-on*) [which obligates me] to remain with her" (p. 84). Jihei is torn between Osan and Koharu, who symbolize the conflict between obligation (*giri*) and human feelings (*ninjō*).[59] However, when the plan to redeem Koharu is frustrated, and Osan's father tears Osan away from Jihei, the latter apparently feels that his debt of gratitude is canceled, his *giri* toward Osan is removed, and he can proceed once more with the love suicide.[60]

The main themes in the play are love and *giri,* but there are also many other elements which made it of interest to the Osaka audience. One is the scenes in the gay quarter, which provide glimpses of the exciting life there with no additional expense to the spectators. To build up local color Chikamatsu uses the special slang vocabulary of the Quarter and the polite verb endings typical of the speech of prostitutes and proprietresses.[61] Act 1 and Act 3, laid in two different *chaya* in the Sonezaki Quarter, form an interesting contrast. Act 1 shows an early evening scene when business is getting into full swing and indicates the variety of pleasures and diversions that are to be found there. The voices are loud and cheerful, the mood is gay and bustling, and one can feel the verve of townsman life in the Genroku period. The men are out in search of fun, and some, like the swaggering Tahei, are high-spirited and cocky.

In the first part of Act 3 the scene is late at night, the streets are deserted, all is quiet except for the drowsy night watchman making his rounds. The voices that are heard from the Quarter are faint and inhospitable. The mood is melancholy, and the scene ends with a strong impression of the hollowness of the gay life, as Koharu and Jihei slip out of the Quarter to make their way to the place of suicide.[62]

Among the other touches of Osaka are a number of local allusions, such as those worked in about Sugawara no Michizane (845–903), apotheosized as Temma Tenjin, one of the patron deities of the city.[63] Also, in the "Journey" (*michiyuki*), twelve local bridges along the lovers' route are mentioned, as well as rivers and other

landmarks of Osaka familiar to the audience.[64] These "guided
tours" of famous spots, written in a most florid, poetic style, were
often the high point of the history play. In the domestic play they
were also part of the expected pageantry, being found in nineteen
of the twenty-four pieces. They satisfied vicariously the Japanese
fondness for excursions to famous scenic spots.[65]

In *Amijima* the audience found some of the other stock situations which they looked forward to encountering in the various
domestic plays, and especially in the love-suicide pieces. That they
could be anticipated did not detract from their interest, for it was
from the original, imaginative treatment of situations which occurred in other plays that the audience derived special pleasure.
One such stock episode was the escape scene from the house in the
gay quarter; in most of these plays the girl was under strict sur-
veillance by her proprietor, who usually suspected that she was
planning a love suicide. Often an ingenious stratagem was used,
but in *Amijima* the escape is relatively simple. The unexpected
appearances of the night patrolman and of Magoemon provide a
little excitement, but the escape episode is more distinguished
for the use of onomatopoetic effects in the recitation (see translation notes 206 and 203). The audience also waited with interest
to see what unusual treatment the author could give the circumstances and methods by which the love suicide was effected. In
Amijima Chikamatsu worked out one of the more elaborate
preparations, on the excuse that this was necessary so that Koharu
could discharge her obligation toward Osan. Another almost necessary ingredient in a domestic play was a fight scene between the
high-spirited young townsmen. In Act 1 there is a representative
instance of this, when Jihei is shamed and kicked by his rival in
love, winning him the sympathy of the audience. They are grati-
fied when, later in the act, Jihei has the opportunity to worst his
rival in the same form of abuse. Another necessary ingredient of
a domestic play is a long speech of admonition (*iken*) delivered
to the wayward hero by one of his relatives or friends. Although
these now seem dull and moralistic to us, they doubtless had
strong emotional overtones for the contemporary audience. In
Amijima the admonition is not so long and formalized as in many
of the plays, and it appears in two parts, one speech by the elder
brother in Act 1 (pp. 73–74), the other by the aunt in Act 2
(p. 78).

Not only do the domestic plays have these stock scenes, but

other elements as well are used over and over, such as the breaking of vows, the failure to pay debts, arbitrary behavior by a parent or older relative, and the redeeming of the prostitute. A limited set of ingredients is used repeatedly in somewhat different arrangements to form the plot. Although *Amijima* has many of the usual plot elements,[66] the play is put together so convincingly that it seems less stereotyped than most of the domestic plays. How the story was handled was of great importance to the audience. Before they went to see the play they were already acquainted with the gist of the story and could anticipate many of the elements which could be used in dramatizing it. It was the novel and smooth treatment of the familiar which won their applause, and in this Chikamatsu excelled.

In the delineation of characters *Amijima* is one of the most successful of Chikamatsu's plays, perhaps second only to his next domestic play, *Onna koroshi abura no jigoku*. The characters in the domestic plays have far more personality than the usual characters in history plays, but they still tend to be types which can be found in other domestic plays. It is sometimes even possible to recognize them as derived from the *kabuki* roles of a famous actor. Judged by the standards of Western drama, the failure of the Japanese theater to delineate distinctive personalities is disappointing, but it in part reflects the differing role of the individual in the two societies. In Chikamatsu's domestic plays even the same names are sometimes used for characters in play after play. It should be pointed out, however, that Chikamatsu was probably attempting to draw sympathy for his characters by making them typical townsmen, and this effect would have been reduced if he had developed individual eccentricities in them. Furthermore, the difficulties of portraying a convincing human role with a puppet are sufficiently great without trying to develop special individual personalities in each play. Thus although the characters in *Amijima* tend to be types, they at least were representative of Genroku townsmen.

Jihei, as a young Osaka merchant, is not the model tradesman his elder brother is. Rather he is one of the unsuccessful members of a profession which demanded an uncompromising standard of industry and application. Indolent and irresolute, he neglects his business and devotes his time and energy to a passionate but ill-conceived and therefore hopeless love. Both his wife and his paramour have a more highly developed sense of honor and responsibility than Jihei. He is not deficient, however, in the intense pride of his class which makes it unendurable for him to be outdone by a rival in love. In his quickness of tongue and his impulsiveness, as well as his dread of being shamed in public, he is probably typical of many Osaka townsmen. His nature is impetuous and changeable, in contrast to the steadfast and dependable character of the two women. His most significant trait for the plot of the play is that he is weak-willed, a characteristic which he shares with the heroes of many of the other domestic plays.[67]

A more colorful Genroku type is his love rival, Tahei, a playboy with a reputation as a great spender in the Quarter. Tahei states brazenly that money is the supreme power, but by the time of the late Genroku this ostentatious attitude of the *nouveau riche* was considered unrefined even among the townsmen, and Chikamatsu took care to prove Tahei wrong. In his cocky attitude and his contempt for the samurai, however, he expresses the high spirits of the newly risen townsmen. He is overbearing, always ready to pick a fight, or at least to talk a big fight. In these respects he resembles many of the heroes' rivals in other domestic plays who, through either their wealth or their refusal to pay a debt to the hero, are able to frustrate his love.[68] This play has no real villain, but Tahei, as an unsympathetic character, partially fills this role.

Osan is the model wife according to the Confucian ideal of the samurai class. Chaste, compliant, and self-effacing, she is devoted to her wayward husband and considers no sacrifice too great in order to maintain his reputation in the community. She is a better merchant than her husband; hard-working and efficient, she manages both the home and the business without complaint. Yet she is not without spirit. When the interests of her husband are at stake, she is capable of taking the initiative. She pawns some of her clothes to raise money to pay the wholesaler so that Jihei's business reputation will not be ruined. She subdues her pride to write to Koharu and plead for her husband's life. She also makes the decision that Koharu be redeemed and finds the necessary means. This is much more than the passive obedience which was expected of women according to the feudal code. Yet she acts without self-consciousness. She is a townsman's wife idealized to the point of incredibility.[69]

The personality of Koharu is less clearly delineated, and one is left with the impression that she is quite colorless. She does little more than embody the virtues of faithfulness and the sense of obligation which the prostitutes in Chikamatsu demonstrate as strongly as other women. She is faithful in her love to Jihei and would kill herself rather than be redeemed by his rival. In speaking of her, Osan says: "All we women are constant and do not change our minds" (p. 81). When Jihei believes her to be unfaithful, he curses and kicks her, but she makes no attempt to explain her conduct.[70] At the moment of performing the suicide, when Jihei is hesitant, it is Koharu who steels him to act.

The personality of Jihei's aunt is not developed in the play; hers is a familiar type role, that of the older woman who is saddled with the serious family responsibility of interceding for a wayward young relative. She is greatly worried by the conflict in her obligations, in this case between those to her nephew and to her husband. This role is common in other domestic plays and was built by Chikamatsu into the main character in *Nagamachi onna harakiri*.

Magoemon is the model Osaka merchant, in contrast to his younger brother, Jihei, who is easily distracted from his business. He is prudent and upright, full of concern for the dissolute Jihei. His part is especially interesting in that it represents the conversion into a merchant's of a feudal role, that of the faithful old retainer or admonishing loyal minister.[71]

Gozaemon, Osan's father, as an ill-tempered, narrow-minded old man, is something of a new role in Chikamatsu's domestic plays. Most of his old men are good-natured, like Magoemon in *Meido no hikyaku*. He is perhaps not an uncommon type of the Genroku period, an old-fashioned man who dislikes the verve and immorality of the younger generation. He is a believer in a strait-laced family system and sound business, who places more emphasis on his own financial interests than on human values.[72]

Sangorō, the simple-minded apprentice, is used to relieve the tension in Acts 2 and 3. Most domestic plays have such a simpleton part, often played by a maid, as in *Meido no hikyaku* and *Ikutama shinjū*.

Now that some of the ingredients of the play have been examined, we may turn to a consideration of its structure. Although the three unities did not become a self-conscious convention of the Japanese theater, it is interesting to see a strong trend toward them in Chikamatsu's domestic plays. In the five-act history plays there are often many changes of time and place within an act,[73] with a heavy reliance on the narrative to explain the transitions. In the three-act domestic plays, where there is a greater need for realistic representation on the stage, there is more unity of time and place within an act. In *Amijima*, a late domestic play, these unities are rigidly maintained in the first two acts. The first half of the third act is also restricted to one place, but in the second part, the "Journey," the scene shifts from one spot to another as in the *nō* and history *jōruri*, as the principals make their journey across Osaka to their place of death. This walk, with some references to the road to Hades and rebirth into the Western Paradise, has an appropriately unreal quality. It is not realism but the poetic language and music which carry the audience along until the place of death is reached.

Chikamatsu made deliberate contrasts between the acts in the mood and in the location of the action. Yet each act leads into the following one, various devices being used to tie them together. Act 1, which begins as a lively scene in the Gay Quarter, turns to high emotions and violence. It ends with Jihei's renouncing Koharu and the Quarter forever and leaving for his home. Here Act 2 takes place, a typical family scene contrasting sharply with the Quarter. This act ends with Osan's being forced to leave her husband and home forever. Act 3 takes place in the Quarter again, but this time the mood is melancholy, in contrast to the mood of Act 1. The literary references to the Quarter which begin and end the first part of the act are similar to those which begin Act 1, but with certain changes which give it a different tempo (translation notes 173 and 210). Each act ends on a tragic note, to stress the pathos which underlies the whole play.

The action takes place in the autumn, which is the season associated with sadness. The tragic mood of the play is reiterated by the frequent mention of different kinds of tears throughout the play, and by the repetition of words such as "pathetic," "pitiable," and "sad."

One device used to sustain the interest of the audience was to make the plot, like Jihei's family relations, complex. The element of surprise was also used repeatedly to carry the play along, as when the letter from Osan to Koharu is revealed or when Gozaemon appears at such an inopportune moment. It also added interest that the characters were represented initially as something other than they were—Magoemon as a samurai and Koharu as unfaithful. There are also the sudden reversals of mental attitudes, as when Jihei twice changed his opinion of Koharu so completely, and when Koharu and Osan both took unexpected steps because of their *giri* toward each other. The play, then, is full of sudden twists and turns in events and in the attitudes of the characters, which help to hold the attention of the audience.

The moral theme which runs through the play, and which is suggested in the title, also contributed to its structure.

In the title of our play the phrase *Ten no Ami* 天の網, "Heaven's Net," is a double reference. The first carries the hint that the lovers will receive Heaven's retribution for their sins, the second that they will be saved by Amida in accordance with his vow.

The phrase consists of the first two characters of a line in the Taoist canon, the *Tao-te-ching:* [74]

天網恢恢疎而不失
"Heaven's net is wide;
    Coarse are the meshes, yet nothing slips through."
This quotation has come into Japanese as a popular saying: *Temmō kai-kai so ni shite morasazu,* which may be translated the same way. The same meaning is also understood in another saying derived from the same passage: *Ten no ami ni kakaru,* "to be caught in Heaven's net." These sayings are interpreted to mean that Heaven's net is vast, and although the meshes are coarse, yet good will infallibly be rewarded with good, and evil with evil. The use of the phrase "Heaven's net" in the title, then, suggests that Koharu and Jihei cannot avoid suffering and death in retribution for their acts. The theme that retribution in the form of divine punishment (*bachi*) awaits Jihei runs through the play.[75]

The second allusion contained in the title is clarified by a phrase in the last line of the play: *chikai no ami,* literally "the vow's net." This is a Buddhist phrase which can be found in Japanese classical poetry and the *nō*.[76] It likens to a net the vow of the Buddha that he will save all of mankind. Thus as the play closes, Chikamatsu gives the comforting assurance that the lovers will be saved by the grace of Amida, and enjoy eternal bliss together in Paradise.[77] It makes no difference that they die for blind passion and desire, the antithesis of the Buddhist way of life and that at their moment of death their renunciation of worldly desires and family ties is a mockery of monastic vows. It matters only that they observe the proper forms, and that they have faith that they will be saved.

This salvation seems to work automatically, like the *giri* which determines the action of the women, and the *inga* which predestines the lovers to commit suicide. The characters do not seem to act on the basis of their own will or reason, but are led on by formulas. Although Chikamatsu does succeed in making the characters in *Ten no Amijima* human enough to win the sympathy of the audience, in the final analysis they are what they appear on the stage—puppets of his idealized ethic.

5. *Style of* Ten no Amijima

In considering style, the requirements of *jōruri* writing should be kept in mind. We have already seen that Chikamatsu, as the writer for the Takemoto-za, had to write plays which would be assured of financial success and that he was, therefore, obliged to compromise to a certain extent his artistic standards. *Jōruri* is much more than a literary genre. It must be written so that it can be recited musically, and it must interpret the movements of the puppets. The playwright has to work in close collaboration with the reciters and the puppeteers in order to write successfully for the puppet theater. It has been noted that the special requirements of Masadayū's voice had a marked effect on Chikamatsu's writing. Such technical restrictions on *jōruri* as a literary medium should be taken into consideration in evaluating Chikamatsu as a literary figure.

In judging his style, it must be remembered that the first consideration is not that the play should read well, but that it should sound pleasing when recited. This placed special emphasis on meter and euphony, a requirement which distinguishes it from the other prose of its day. Chikamatsu's *jōruri* follow the conventions of the texts of the *nō* drama, or *yōkyoku,* with the recited narrative sections known as *ji* generally in poetic meter of alternating phrases of five and seven syllables, while the spoken parts or "dialogue," called *kotoba,* normally have no regular meter. For the most part they are recited or sung in clearly distinguishable styles. However, since the entire text is read by the reciters, the distinction between the narrative and the dialogue is sometimes blurred. Particularly in the "Journey" (*michiyuki*), in reading the play there are sentences which cannot be clearly classified either as narrative or as the "thoughts" or "speech" of the puppets. The shading off from one to another of these makes the narrative more personal and permits the more rapid and effective depiction of the mental attitudes of the characters. In general, however, there is no difficulty in distinguishing between narrative and dialogue. On the other hand, in reading the play it is not always clear which character is "speaking," as this is sometimes made apparent to the audience only by the intonation of the reciter or the movements of the puppets. It is also obvious from reading the play that certain actions must be taking place, such as entrances or exits, which are not mentioned in the text, because these are seen by the audience.

Since *jōruri* were written and performed solely as popular entertainment, it is inappropriate to judge them by the same criterion as formal prose. The necessity of satisfying the audience influenced not only the form and content, as we have seen, but also the style. The elements of style—the various types of wordplays and allusions—although much the same as those found in classical poetry and prose, were often exaggerated or even burlesqued to amuse the audience. The deluge of puns and associated words which Chikamatsu could weave into a sentence as a tour de force was most entertaining, but it meant the introduction of many words and phrases which were not essential to the meaning and which often beclouded it. These redundancies and excursions, although usually indulged in with moderation, when overdone give the text a facetious tone.

In the dialogue passages, where a realistic effect is sought, the language is straightforward and undistinguished, and fewer stylistic devices are resorted to than in the narrative parts. It is in the "Journey," which contain Chikamatsu's most beautiful prose, that we also find him going to extremes. In those sections the principals are seen on their trip; the scenic wonders of the route are described in a flowing, poetic style,[78] which contains many literary allusions and wordplays in the best traditions of Japanese writing.[79] When the author attempts to weave in an excessive number of place names in wordplays, however, these sections become mere ornate showpieces. In this section of *Amijima* he works in the names of twelve bridges and some other local allusions, but this exercise is kept relatively well in hand. Although much of the "Journey," with its description of the walk and its wordplays, is unessential to the plot, there is often woven into it some important information about the past and future of the principals. Among the most beautiful sentences in Chikamatsu are those in these sections which describe the mental anguish of the lovers as they make their way to their place of suicide.[80]

Other parts of the narrative passages which are of special interest from the stylistic point of view are the opening sentences and sometimes the closing ones of each act. Though interlarded with wordplays and allusions, these lines make general statements about the scene and often hint at the outcome, at times even containing some moralistic implications. These lines in Chikamatsu are quite similar to the opening sentences of Saikaku's stories, especially those in his townsmen pieces, or *chōnin-mono*.

The stylistic devices which Chikamatsu uses to ornament his prose are mainly those which had a long tradition in classical poems (*tanka*) and later in *haiku*. His use of these devices, however, resembles the most popular form of comic *haiku*, which had scant respect for the formal rules of classical prosody. It is not surprising that Chikamatsu, who had composed *haiku* since early youth, should develop many of the stylistic characteristics of Saikaku, who had made a wide reputation as a prodigious composer of *haiku* before he turned to prose. In fact, in *Amijima*, Chikamatsu uses a wordplay which had appeared earlier in Saikaku (translation note 17), indicating that he had borrowed this either directly or from a common reservoir of stock puns which writers drew on in this period. In general, the wordplays of the nimble-witted Saikaku are the more intricate, but are for this reason less suitable for *jōruri*, which has to be comprehensible orally.

Like Saikaku, Chikamatsu strives for terseness. He achieves a rich concentration of words by using pivot words and puns to contract the sentences, by dropping verb inflections or even the verbs themselves, and by omitting some postpositions.[81] In Chikamatsu some of the postpositions are omitted for the purpose of maintaining the meter of alternating five- and seven-syllable phrases, but he strongly opposed the practice of adding postpositions merely to fill out the lines.[82] It is a tribute to his technical mastery that in *Amijima* there are remarkably few lines in the narrative sections which do not fall into exact meter. On the other hand, Chikamatsu was often not concise, as when he introduced words unessential to the meaning for the sake of euphony or elaborate wordplays.

Without attempting to deal exhaustively with all of the technical devices used by Chikamatsu to ornament his style, it would be helpful as a guide to the translation notes to discuss briefly some of the more common usages, such as puns, pivot words, associated words, alliteration and assonance, onomatopoeia, and popular and classical allusions. Other elements which appear, but which are not of sufficient importance to require separate discussion, are similes, metaphors, parallelisms, metathesis, and pillow-words (*makura-kotoba*). Most of these many devices are completely lost in translation, but for illustrative purposes the more notable examples of each type are pointed out in the notes to the translation.

The simple pun, in much the same usage as it appears in Shakespeare, is frequently used in Japanese prose and poetry as a serious, as well as comic, stylistic device. A few representative examples of the many uncomplicated puns which appear in this play are pointed out in translation notes 20, 37, 117, 172, 199, and 238.

A more complex type of pun is the pivot word (*kakekotoba* or *iikakekotoba*). In its classical form, as used in *tanka, yōkyoku,* and *haiku,* it is used in one meaning for the first phrase and in a second for the phrase which follows, as if the sentence pivots on that word and heads off in an unexpected direction. The first phrase, then, has no grammatically logical ending, nor the following one a logical beginning, and this gives a certain ambiguity which pleases the Japanese. A simple example from the play is the use of *ki* as the verb "comes" and as the first part of the name of the establishment, Kiinokuniya:

uchikara   hashiri   ki-   no-kuniya no Sugi

"from her establishment running comes/Kinokuniya 's Sugi." There are more complex examples in the play, such as a phrase of thirteen syllables which serves as a pivot (note 165) and an astonishing one of fourteen syllables which must be translated on three levels (note 229). Chikamatsu often uses them in series so that the sentence is constantly twisting and turning. In some cases an entire line or even more will contain so many puns and pivot words that it must be translated twice to supply all the implications of the original. The pivot word is by far the most frequent type of wordplay used by Chikamatsu, and there are usually several to a page of text. A few of the more important are pointed out in notes 9, 37, 53, 119, 165, 212, 229, 247, and 248, as well as others which will be mentioned in discussing associated words. In the translation of the play, when a word in the text must be interpreted dually, the second translation appears in parentheses. Most of these are examples of pivot words.

Associated words (*engo*) are introduced into the text because they bear some association of meaning to a word which has already been used. They may be associated to it because of various types of relation such as form, color, sound, some characteristic quality, or, more commonly, simply because they are of the same general category of object. One of the simplest examples is:

momi no kosode   ni mi o   kogasu

"[to pawn] the red silk padded robe made her being burn." Here "burn" is an associated word to "red silk," because "burn" and "red" are related words. Chikamatsu uses this device more freely than it was used in classical poetry, and he is sometimes carried away in his effort to introduce as many *engo* as possible. In cases where there is a long series of them related to one word, they are called *-zukushi*, from the verb *tsukusu*, "to exhaust, to use up," as if the series of *engo* exhausts the possibilities for that word. Examples of this are the two *kami-zukushi* which appear in the play, the six *engo* which follow the word *kami*, "paper" (note 51), and the eight which follow a homonym, *kami*, "god" (note 67). The title of the "Journey," *Nagori no hashi-zukushi*, "Farewell along all the Bridges," suggests that the names of all twelve of the bridges (*hashi*) along the route will be woven into the text as associated words, or pivot words (note 218 *et al.*). Among the many *engo* in the play, there are a number of extremely complex combinations of associated words and pivot words which can be translated on two levels (notes 15, 33, 51, 58, 67, 80, 84, 106, 109, 131, 140, 141, 146, 172, 209, 217, 228). There are also instances of the repetition of numbers or use of numbers in series, which might be classified as associated words (notes 37, 240, 244).

The phonetic characteristics of the Japanese language make it well adapted to the use of alliteration, assonance, and onomatopoeia. The more interesting examples of alliteration are indicated in notes 251 and 131, and of assonance in notes 109, 172, 178, 184, 207. In some instances onomatopoeia is used in combination with assonance, as:

hagiri kiri-kiri

[He] gnashed [his] teeth *kiri-kiri*

and:

kuroro kottori to

[He fastens] the cross-bar *kottori*

Other usages of onomatopoeia are mentioned in notes 27 and 206.

Chikamatsu uses a great many literary allusions, ranging from classical Japanese poetry and the Chinese classics to passages from his own plays. In most cases they consist of quoting a familiar phrase which is nimbly twisted or parodied to give it quite a different meaning. Examples of utilizing parts of famous classical poems are pointed out in notes 17, 106, 173, 222, 223, and 261. One of the most witty uses of classical literature is a parody on a passage from a *nō* play (note 9). The borrowing of phrases from literary sources gave Chikamatsu the opportunity to amuse his audience by mixing among the elegant, classical words vernacular or even vulgar expressions of the day. He also quoted fragments of current popular songs (notes 133 and 146).

Popular sayings (*kotowaza*) are usually worked into the text only in part, the audience being allowed to supply the rest (notes 85, 109, and 209), or else popular sayings are twisted to give them quite different meanings (notes 161 and 172). An even wittier device is the combining into one sentence of parts of two sayings (notes 4 and 208). Most of these sayings stemmed originally from ancient Chinese historical or philosophical works but had become current in Japan. Many of them appear in Kamakura period poetry, or in prose of the Kamakura and Muromachi periods such as the *Gempei seisuiki* and *nō* texts (notes 4, 29, 48, 76, 79, 85, 109). A few of the sayings probably originated in Japanese literature (notes 165 and 172). In some cases Chikamatsu uses a saying which he had employed in complete and proper usage in an earlier play, but in *Amijima* he uses just part of it, or twists it into a different meaning (notes 76, 79, 165).[83] Finally, we have noted that part of the title, *Ten no Ami*, was itself part of a popular saying, woven into the place name *Amijima*.

The allusions to his own works were a sort of self-advertising. It seems probable that the Takemoto-za had a rather restricted and faithful clientele who were familiar with many of Chikamatsu's plays. Also passages of his plays had become known to the public through the recitation of fragments as entertainment in restaurants and in the gay quarters. In *Ten no Amijima* there are references to his earlier plays which the audience was expected to recognize (notes 35, 37, and 40), and in one case he elaborates on a wordplay which was a well-known passage in one of his earlier works (note 58).[84] The height of this sort of publicizing of his own works is reached in *Amijima*, when a mendicant monk recites two famous passages from earlier successes of his (notes 29 and 33).

Another important element of style is change of tempo and

rhythm, which lends variety to his style. The most notable examples are at the opening, where there is a display of different styles of *jōruri* recitation. The play begins with the following short, contrasting sections: a lively passage of *jōruri* jargon, a flowery introduction in phrases of five and seven syllables to suggest the festive atmosphere of the Quarter, a short conversation, the recitation by a mendicant monk of three passages of *jōruri* in three different styles and tempos, a snatch of dialogue, and then a piece of improvised *jōruri*.

Thus in many ways, through the clever use of wordplays, allusions, and changes of tempo, the literary style of the play was calculated to entertain the audience. It was intended to have popular appeal and did not pretend to be formal prose.

6. *Textual History of* Ten no Amijima

This play differs from most of the domestic plays of Chikamatsu in that its source, whether fact or fiction, has never been identified. It is probable, however, that like the others it is based either on an actual incident or on a current story. A number of traditions sprang up in later years concerning the details of the original incident, but there is no reason to place confidence in them, since they are typical of the apocryphal anecdotes which surround many works of Japanese literature.

A guide to the Osaka area, the *Setsuyō kikan* (compiled before 1833),[85] contains what purports to be an account of the incident, complete with reproductions of the traditional farewell note and a sketch of the lovers' joint grave at Daichōji (Temple) in Osaka. However, from the details it gives concerning the suicide, it is obvious that this account is based not on a first-hand source, but on Chikamatsu's play. The same is true of an account in another work, a miscellany about Osaka entitled *Naniwa hyakuji dan* (published *ca.* 1892–1895).[86]

The *Wasure nokori* (preface dated 1824)[87] claims that the actual event took place in Edo, but that in dramatizing the play Chikamatsu changed the scene to Osaka. It gives the address of Jihei in Edo, but provides no supporting evidence for its claim.

An anecdote about the writing of the play which appears in the *Okina gusa*[88] is typical of the stories which have sprung up about popular writers of the Tokugawa period:

In the winter of 1720 the old master Chikamatsu was enjoying himself in a restaurant at Shinke in Sumiyoshi,[89] when suddenly someone from the theater arrived from Osaka. He reported that the night before at Daichōji on Amijima a man and woman committed a love suicide, and that, if Chikamatsu would be so good as to return quickly to Osaka to write a *jōruri,* there could be one day of rehearsal the next day, and on the day after that it could be performed. This request was so earnest that he immediately got in a palanquin and returned to Osaka. When he alighted from the palanquin he took up his brush at once and began writing [with the phrase] *hashiri-gaki,* because he began writing immediately after running back by palanquin.[90]

The phrase *hashiri-gaki* can be interpreted as a compound verb meaning "run and write" or as a noun "running-writing," that is, a cursive, flowing style of calligraphy. It appears in the play, as the first word of the "Journey," in a double sense—the *hashiri,* "run," as a pivot word which serves as a verb to conclude the last sentence of the preceding section of Act 3, and the whole expression *hashiri-gaki* as "running-writing." There is no basis in the text of the play for the meaning "run and write."

As has been pointed out by Nishizawa Ippō (1802–1852)[91] and by many since his time, this anecdote is obviously inaccurate, since the suicide was on the fifteenth day of the tenth month, while the first performance of the play was not until the sixth day of the twelfth month, or some fifty days later. Sassa has suggested that the anecdote might refer only to the "Journey," (*michiyuki*),[92] for it was not uncommon to perform just this part of a play as a short offering. With the emphasis of the "Journey" on poetic language, music, and puppetry, it formed a showpiece which could stand alone if the audience were already acquainted with the story. Sassa's suggested explanation seems unlikely, but it is within the realm of possibility.[93]

The only reliable information about the first performance of the play is that it opened at the Takemoto-za on the sixth day of the twelfth month in 1720.[94] The chief reciter at the performance was Takemoto Masadayū. The next year it was performed on the *kabuki* stage at the Morita-za in Edo, with Ichikawa Danjūrō the Second (1688–1757) as Jihei and Sodesaki Miwano (1690–1736) as Koharu.[95]

In later years *Amijima* was frequently performed in the *kabuki* and *jōruri* theaters, but only with the most drastic changes of plot and rewriting of lines. The necessity for extensive changes to adapt the *jōruri* play for the *kabuki* stage can be easily understood. In the case of *jōruri* performances, the reason Chikamatsu's plays have been so extensively rewritten is less evident. Many explanations have been suggested, such as the preference in later *jōruri* for less narrative and more dialogue, new developments in puppetry and staging, and the demand for a clearer, less ornate literary style. Perhaps most important of all was the constant demand of the public for new treatments of familiar themes, which could be satisfied by making unexpected changes in the plot.[96] All of the revisions fall far below Chikamatsu's play in literary style. Japanese scholars who have read them shudder at the desecration of Chikamatsu's texts.[97]

The first major *jōruri* revision of *Ten no Amijima* was by Namiki Eisuke (d. 1771) and others, entitled *Futatsu ōgi Nagara no matsu,* performed at the Toyotake-za in 1755. The next was performed at the Takemoto-za in 1769 and was called *(Koharu Jihei) Chūgen uwasa no kake-dai.* This revision by Miyoshi Shōraku (1696–?) and others is so extensive that it is hardly recognizable as the same play.[98] The suicide is even eliminated in this version.

The next two revisions are of greater importance, since they provided elements of the play as it appears in the present repertoire of the *jōruri* and *kabuki* theaters. A revision by Chikamatsu Hanji (1725–1783) and others, entitled *Shinjū Kamiya Jihei,*[99] was first performed at the Takeda Manjirō-za in Osaka in 1778. A new act was added at the beginning of the play, and the original Act 3 was eliminated. The version used in the puppet theater so frequently after this date is this play under the title *Zōho Ten no Amijima.*[100] The other important revision, made in the opening decades of the eighteenth century by an unknown author, was called *Ten no Amijima shigure no kotatsu.*[101] The version in the modern repertoire, which goes by the title *Shinjū Ten no Amijima,* consists of Act 1 of the original play as revised by Chikamatsu Hanji (in whose play it was Act 2) and Act 2 of the original play as it was even more extensively revised in *Ten no Amijima shigure no kotatsu.* These acts are also performed as separate plays under the titles of *Kawashō* and *Kamiji* respectively.[102]

Although the play appears frequently in revised form on the puppet and *kabuki* stage in modern times, there have been extremely few revivals in the *kabuki* theater which have attempted to be faithful to Chikamatsu Monzaemon's version. The first was performed by the pioneer actor of the Shimpa movement, Ii Yōhō (1871–1932) in the Masago-za in Tokyo in March 1902.[103] Another revival was as a bicentennial memorial of Chikamatsu's death. It opened in Osaka in October 1922 with the troupe of Nakamura Ganjirō (1860–1935), and subsequently went on tour.[104]

Chikamatsu's original version has been translated freely by Miyamori Asatarō, with the English revised by Robert Nichols.[105] This translation has many omissions, frequently of a line or more, in the narrative sections, which had the most elaborate style. The explanatory notes also are inadequate. Since the publication of this translation in 1926, many passages in the play are now interpreted differently, thanks to the subsequent work of Japanese commentators.

The best edition of the text is contained in *Chikamatsu zenshū* (*Collected Works of Chikamatsu*) edited by Fujii Otoo.[106] The use of the *kana* syllabary and characters is exactly as it appeared in the Tokugawa printed edition authorized by the Takemoto family and published in Osaka by Yamamoto Kyūbei. This edition is known as "forty-three double pages of seven columns [a page]," and Fujii collated this text with the edition known as the edition of "twenty-four double pages of ten columns [a page]."

The other commentaries and annotated editions which have proved most useful for understanding the text and identifying allusions are:

Itō Masao, *Shinjū Ten no Amijima shōkai* (1935, 435 pp.);

Higuchi Yoshichiyo, *Kessaku jōruri shū* 1.441–490, in (*Hyōshaku*) *Edo bungaku sōsho* (1935, 11 vols.);

Sassa Masakazu (*Chikamatsu hyōshaku*) *Ten no Amijima* (1906, 162 pp.);

Fujii Otoo, *Chikamatsu sewamono zenshū* (1944, 3 vols.) 3.263–328; [107]

Wakatsuki Yasuji, *Zenshaku Chikamatsu kessaku shū* (1930, 3 vols.), 1.393–471;

Kawatake Shigetoshi, *Chikamatsu meisaku shū* (1938, 2 vols.), 2.141–201 and 2.557–558, in *Gendaigoyaku kokubungaku zenshū* (26 vols.);

Kitani Hōgin, *Dai Chikamatsu zenshū* (1922, 16 vols.), 1.549–632;

Mizutani Yumihiko (gō, Futō), (*Shinshaku sashizu*) *Chikamatsu kessaku zenshū* (1907, 5 vols.), 2.741–806.[108]

Notes to the

Introduction

1. Kuroki Kanzō, for example, considers *Ten no Amijima* to be Chikamatsu's greatest play both in form and in content. See his book, *Chikamatsu Monzaemon* (1942, 298 pp.) , p. 102.

2. Osaka's location near Sakai, the leading port in the preceding two centuries, contributed to its rise as a commercial city. Osaka expanded rapidly at the close of the sixteenth century when the Toyutomi family made it their base, and much of the new population came from Sakai. Osaka also had a cultural debt to Sakai, where printing and new musical styles flourished well into the seventeenth century.

3. Kurita Mototsugu, *Edo jidai shi* (1937, 2 vols.) , 1.809–813 (vol. 9 in *Sōgō Nihonshi taikei,* 12 vols.) .

4. Tokutomi Iichirō, *(Genroku jidai) Sesōhen* in *Kinsei Nihon kokuminshi* (1918–1939, 61 vols.) , 19.11–17.

5. A factor which contributed to the attainments of the townsmen class was the movement into Osaka of thousands of *rōnin,* or unemployed samurai, whose masters had discharged them because they themselves had been dispossessed of their fiefs or simply as an economy measure. Many of the *rōnin,* better educated than the *chōnin,* became teachers, physicians, writers, or painters. A few who were able to turn their education to practical advantage became successful merchants. Kurita, *op. cit.,* pp. 690, 697–700.

6. The *haiku* appreciated by the townsmen was represented first by the Teimon school of Matsunaga Teitoku (1571–1653) , and later by the Danrin school of Nishiyama Sōin (1605–1682) . This popular tradition served as the basis on which Matsuo Bashō (1644–1694) could develop the Shōmon, a *haiku* school of high literary merit. He was a samurai by birth, a Buddhist in his philosophy, and a scholar of classical poetry by education. By combining the attitudes of the samurai, monk, and townsman, he had a wide appeal, but his art was too subtle for some *chōnin* who found the earlier schools more to their taste.

7. On the development of the early *kabuki,* see Aleksandre Iacovleff and Serge Elisséeff, *Le Théâtre Japonais (Kabuki)* (Paris: Meynial, 1933) , pp. 6–11, 15–19.

8. See Serge Elisséev (Elisséeff) , "Un nouveau livre sur le Théâtre Japonais," *Japon et Extrême-orient* (Paris) , No. 1 (December 1923) , 77–84, a review of Sekine Mokuan (1863–1923) , *Kabukigeki to sono haiyū* (1923, 120 pp., vol. 4 in *Bunka sōsho*) .

9. The date of Tōjūrō's death, given by Miyamori as 1704, is incorrect; Miyamori Asatarō, *Masterpieces of Chikamatsu, the Japanese Shakespeare,* revised by Robert Nichols (New York, 1926) , p. 22. So is the date 1705 given by Kenneth P. Kirkwood in *Renaissance in Japan, A Cultural Survey of the Seventeenth Century* (Tokyo: Meiji Press, 1938, 414 pp.) , pp. 225–228. Tōjūrō's date of birth is sometimes given as 1645.

10. During the late Kamakura period (1185–1333), various styles of metric recitation had been developed for the narration of martial and romantic stories. One of the romances which had gained great popularity by the middle of the sixteenth century was known as *Jōruri monogatari* or *Jōruri jūnidan zōshi,* the love story of a girl named Jōruri and Minamoto no Yoshitsune (1159–1189). The particular melodic style used in the recitation of this story came to be called *jōruri,* and was used for other stories as well.

11. Puppets are known to have been used in popular performances as early as the Kamakura period. At the end of the seventeenth century, the type of puppet most commonly used was about two feet high and was held and manipulated from the rear. In the next century, some of the principal puppets were as tall as three and a half feet, and required three manipulators. On the development of Japanese puppets, see Utsumi Shigetarō, *Ningyō shibai to Chikamatsu no jōruri* (1940, 610 pp.), pp. 43–251, and Watanabe Yoshio, *Bunraku, Japanese Puppet Play* (Tokyo: Japan Photo Service, 1939). For a description of the technique of manipulation now used, see Miyajima Tsunao, *Contribution à l'étude du théâtre japonais de poupées,* (Osaka: Société de Rapprochement Intellectuel Franco-Japonais, Institut Franco-Japonais du Kansaï à Kyōto, 3rd ed., 1931, 109 pp.), pp. 9–12.

12. The samisen (or *shamisen*) had a squarish soundbox and was played with a large plectrum. It was introduced into Japan via the Ryukyu Islands from China in the middle of the sixteenth century.

13. His style became so dominant that *gidayū* became another term for *jōruri* recitation.

14. Tokutomi, *op. cit.* 19.241–242.

15. This opinion, held by Japanese scholars, is based on a statement in a work on the puppet theater by Nishizawa Ippū entitled *(Imamukashi) Ayatsuri nendaiki* (1727, 2 *kan*), *kan* 2, in *Shin gunsho ruijū,* 6.518 in *Kokusho kankōkai,* Series 1 (1909).

16. His original name was Sugimori Nobumori, and his principal literary name (*gō*) was Sōrinshi, but he had many others: Heiandō, Fuisanjin, and Sanjinfuishi.

17. Kitani Hōgin, *Dai Chikamatsu zenshū* (1922, 16 vols.), 1.11–12; Wakatsuki Yasuji, *Chikamatsu ningyō jōruri no kenkyū* (1934, 900 pp.), pp. 41–42; Kuroki, *op. cit.,* pp. 5–6; Kirkwood, *op. cit.,* pp. 225–228.

18. Whether it was the 21st or the 22nd day of the 11th month of 1724 (which according to the Western calendar would be January 5th or 6th, 1725). Kitani, *op. cit.* 1.44–45.

19. *Ibid.,* 1.48–52. The *jisei* is a formal message composed before death, usually in poetry, but sometimes, as in this case, in prose.

20. Shuzui Kenji, *Chikamatsu* (1948, 191 pp.), pp. 27–29.

21. This anthology was an appendix to a book on *haiku,* the *Takaragura,* by Yamaoka Genrin (*gō,* Jiunsai) (1631–1672). Kitani, *op. cit.* 1.13–14; Miyamori, *op. cit.,* p. 31. Kobayashi Zenhachi reads the title of the anthology *Hōzō* in his study, *Shinjū Ten no Amijima* (1924, 102 pp., vol. 1 in *Chikamatsu kessaku shū*), p. 47.

22. The entire *jōruri* was narrated by the reciters, but for convenience, the "speeches" of the puppets, as opposed to the description of the action, will be spoken of as dialogue.

23. A synoptic paraphrase of part of the play under the title "The Battles of Kokusenya" appeared in Miyamori Asatarō's *Tales from Old Japanese Dramas,* revised by Stanley Hughes (New York, 1915, 403 pp.), pp. 359–403. A complete translation and critical study of the play by Donald Keene entitled *The Battles of Coxinga, Chikamatsu's Puppet Play, Its Background and Importance* (London: Taylor's Foreign Press, Cambridge Oriental Series No. 4) was published in August 1951, but was not yet available to the present author when his manuscript was being prepared.

24. Translated under the title "The Love Suicide at Amijima," by Miyamori in *Masterpieces of Chikamatsu,* pp. 221–263.

25. Translated under the title, "The Tethered Steed," *ibid.*, pp. 311–359.
26. Miyamori (*ibid.*, p. 39) twice gives the date of Gidayū's death as 1724, but he has the correct date, 1714, on p. 28.
27. Kitani, *op. cit.*, pp. 41–42.
28. *Ibid.*, pp. 42–43.
29. Utsumi, *op. cit.*, pp. 8–12.
30. There were, to be sure, *rōnin* and even some samurai in the audience, but the domestic plays seem to have been written neither for them nor about them.
31. The first domestic plays were not regarded as full-scale plays, but rather as interludes performed often after the third act of a history play. Not until about 1717 were they accorded the status of full plays. Maejima Shunzō, *Chikamatsu kenkyū no johen* (1938, 305 pp.), p. 153. Kuroki, *op. cit.*, pp. 86–89, advances the theory that the domestic play originated in form from the third act of the history play, the act in which the central conflict or tragedy of the play is usually developed. The three acts of the domestic play, he explains, were derived from the three subdivisions which usually constitute the third act of the history play. The theory has also been advanced that the domestic play was derived by omitting the first and fifth acts of the history play, and using the three middle acts. See Sonoda Tamio in *Jōruri sakusha no kenkyū* (1943, 443 pp.), pp. 109–110. Either theory would explain why the domestic play seems to begin in the middle of the story, as is so notable in *Shinjū Ten no Amijima*. The five-act history play itself did not develop until the 1670's, and is thought to have been derived from the form of five plays which constitute a *nō* program. Earlier in the *ko-jōruri* style the six-act history play was the most common, and after Chikamatsu's death longer plays began to appear.
32. Wakatsuki, *op. cit.*, pp. 75–80, 85–86.
33. *Ibid.*, pp. 81–85.
34. *Ibid.*, pp. 78–80.
35. As classified in the *Nihon bungaku daijiten* (1933, 4 vols.), 2.1022a, edited by Fujimura Tsukuru, the fifteen *shinjūmono* are the following: *Sonezaki shinjū* (1703), *Shinjū nimai ezōshi* (1706), *Uzuki no momiji* (1706), *Uzuki no iroage* (1707), *Shinjū Kasane-izutsu* (ca. 1708), *Shinjū mannen-gusa* (1708), *Tamba Yosaku* (1708), *Shinjū yaiba wa kōri no tsuitachi* (1709), *Imamiya shinjū* (1710), *Meido no hikyaku* (1711), *Nagamachi onna harakiri* (1712), *Ikutama shinjū* (1715), *Hakata Kojorō nami-makura* (1718), *Shinjū Ten no Amijima* (1720), *Shinjū yoigōshin* (1722). There are of course other systems of classification, as for example Takano Tatsuyuki's in his *Edo bungaku shi* (1935, 3 vols.) 2.461–491 (vol. 8 in *Nihon bungaku zenshi*).
36. The nine are: *Satsuma uta* (1704), *Horikawa nami no tsuzumi* (1707), *Yodogoi shusse no takinobori* (ca. 1708), *Gojūnenki uta-nembutsu* (1709), *Yūgiri Awa no Naruto* (1712), *Daikyōji mukashi goyomi* (1715), *Yari no Gonza kasane katabira* (1717), *Nebiki no kadomatsu* (1718), *Onna koroshi abura no jigoku* (1721).
37. This is typical of virtually all of the domestic plays in Tokugawa *jōruri* and *kabuki* literature. For numerous examples see Mitamura Engyo, *Shibai to shijitsu* (*The Theater and Historical Fact*) (1911), and Sakamoto Kizan's work of the same title (1947).
38. Many of the wealthiest merchants were ruined during the latter part of the seventeenth century when their property was confiscated, or when feudal lords refused to repay loans. Famous cases were those of the merchants Yodoya Tatsugorō, Ishikawa Jian, Tsuji Jirozaemon, and Nawaya Kuroemon. See Tokutomi, *op. cit.* 19.24–42; and Takekoshi Yosoburo (*sic*), *The Economic Aspects of the History of the Civilization of Japan* (London, 1930, 3 vols.), 2.251–255, 258–261.
39. Other terms used for the gay quarter tell the other side of the story, as for example *akusho*, "evil place."
40. Tokutomi, *op. cit.*, 19.139–140.
41. Koman in *Tamba Yosaku*, Acts 2 and 3.

56   INTRODUCTION

42. The most complete compilation of these terms is in an amateurish study by a Miyatake Gaikotsu entitled *Baishunfu imei shū* (1936, 125 pp.).

43. See Takano Tatsuyuki, "Chikamatsu jidai no Ōsaka no irozato oyobi yūjo" ("Osaka's Gay Quarters and Prostitutes in the Age of Chikamatsu"), an article written in 1906 and published in his *Nihon engeki no kenkyū* (1916, 2 vols.), 1.163–216. Another Osaka quarter, the Horie, opened in 1698, is mentioned in Chikamatsu but is not the locale of any scene.

44. For a discussion of this term see translation note 122.

45. For a discussion of this term see translation note 13.

46. *Shinjū* is frequently translated "double suicide," which is inappropriate only when one of the lovers survives the attempt. The two characters for *shinjū* 心中, if combined 忠, form the character *chū*, "loyalty," the cardinal feudal virtue. For this reason it is said that the Tokugawa officials evolved another word to use as a legal term for love suicides, calling it *aitaishi* or *aitaijini*, "mutual death." The modern term, *jōshi*, did not gain wide currency until after the Meiji Restoration (1868). See Miyamori Asatarō, *Chikamatsu to Shēkusupiya* (*Chikamatsu and Shakespeare*) (1929), p. 74.

47. These methods are described in the chapter on *shinjū* in the *Shikidō ōkagami* (*Great Mirror of the Way of Sex*), by Hatakeyama Kizan (1628–1704), (date unknown, 18 *kan*, of which 9 are lost), *kan* 6, in *Zoku enseki jisshu*, 2.509–522, in *Kokusho kankōkai*, Series 1.

48. Shuzui, *op. cit.*, p. 48.

49. An extended pun in the last phrases of this quotation contains the meaning that these tragedies will occur "in the Asuka River's deeps and shoals." The *Shinjū ōkagami*, a work of 5 *kan* by Shohōken (pen name, otherwise unidentified), is in *Kinsei bungei sōsho* 4.181a, in *Kokusho kankōkai*, Series 2, 1911. Another work which contains descriptions of love suicide is the *Nansui man'yū* (1810's, 15 *kan*), *kan* 2, by Hamamatsu Utakuni (1776–1827), in *Shin gunsho ruijū*, 2.483, *Kokusho kankōkai*, Series 1.

50. On the development of *shinjū* as an institution, see Serge Elisséev, "Le double suicide (Shinju)," *Japon et Extrême-orient*, No. 9 (September 1924), 107–122; Ōmichi Waichi, *Jōshi no kenkyū* (1911, 526 + 92 pp.); and Tanaka Kagai, *Edo jidai no danjo kankei* (1926, 340 pp.), pp. 86–151.

51. *Shinjū* had been dramatized in *kabuki* as early as 1674, but the first important play on the subject was written about 1695. (*Nihon bungaku daijiten*, 2.668d.) As *jōruri* love-suicide plays became more common, the theaters vied to be the first to open a performance of a play based on a recent suicide. According to one tradition, the Toyotake-za began the performance of *Shinjū niharaobi* on the 5th day of the 4th month, 1722, only four days after the suicide was committed. See Fujii Otoo, *Chikamatsu Monzaemon* (1904, 288 pp., vol. 1 in *Kinsei bungaku sōsho*), p. 88. An even faster staging of a love-suicide play, (*Oriku Jūbei*) *Amayadori beni no hanagoza* (1751), is reported by Kobayashi, *op. cit.*, p. 98.

52. Wakatsuki, *op. cit.*, pp. 88–89, 129, 139.

53. For a discussion of suicide motives in Chikamatsu's *sewamono* see Maejima, *op. cit.*, pp. 173–202, and Fujimura Tsukuru's chapter, "Chikamatsu sewa-jōruri kenkyū," in Katō Junzō, Kuroki Kanzō, and Fujimura Tsukuru, *Chikamatsu kenkyū* (1936, 137 pp.), pp. 124–128 (in the series *Shinchō bunko*, No. 174).

54. Ruth Benedict in *The Chrysanthemum and the Sword* (Boston: Houghton Mifflin, 1946) has attempted to deal with the role of obligations in modern Japanese life. Her description of the ethical system might be considered to be better as the ideal pattern of the late nineteenth century than as the behavioral pattern of the twentieth century.

55. The conflict of *giri* and *ninjō* was not used as the dominating theme by Chikamatsu, however, to nearly the extent it was by later popular writers of the Toku-

gawa period. In general, Chikamatsu placed more emphasis on *giri* in his history plays, and on *ninjō* in his domestic plays. See Fujimura Tsukuru's booklet, *Chōnin bungaku* (November 1934, 47 pp.), p. 21 (in *Nihon rekishi, Iwanami kōza*, Booklet 4 in Box 14).

56. All the ages mentioned in the play and in the discussion of it are according to the Sino-Japanese method of reckoning age. A child's age is one year (*sai*) upon birth, and another year is added each New Year's Day instead of on the birthday anniversary. As the action of the play is in the tenth lunar month, the characters by Western count are between two and fourteen months younger than the ages given.

57. Adapted from Itō Masao, *Shinjū Ten no Amijima shōkai* (1935, 435 pp.), p. 106.

58. This act, laid in the atmosphere of a typical merchant's home, illustrates the attention that Chikamatsu gave during his late years to depicting relations on the domestic scene. This element is further developed in his next two and last domestic plays, *Onna koroshi abura no jigoku* (1721) and *Shinjū yoigōshin* (1722).

59. See the article by Tsubouchi Shōyō (Yūzō) (1859–1935), "Ten no Amijima," reprinted in *Shōyō senshū* (1925–1926, 15 vols.), 8.686. This article is also found in Tsubouchi Shōyō and Tsunajima Ryōsen (1873–1907), *Chikamatsu no kenkyū* (1900, 486 + 83 pp.), pp. 205–224.

60. *Ibid.*, 8.686–687.

61. In *Ten no Amijima* there is hardly a trace of indecency in these scenes, although in some of the other *sewamono* Chikamatsu did insert suggestive words.

62. These two acts are separated, as we have noted, by another scene typical of Osaka—the shop and home of a merchant, with the household engaged in its usual activities.

63. See translation notes 219–223 *et al.*

64. For the lovers' route and place names which occur in the "Journey," see p. 2, "Sketch Map of Northern Osaka (*ca.* 1720), showing places mentioned in *Shinjū Ten no Amijima.*"

65. Such tours appeared also elsewhere than in the "Journey," like the tour of the thirty-three Kannon temples of Osaka at the beginning of *Sonezaki shinjū*, and Act 1 of *Tamba Yosaku*, where Chikamatsu introduces a game of Tōkaidō, or "Eastern Sea Road" backgammon, giving him the opportunity to weave into the text the names of the fifty-three stages of the road in addition to oblique mention of dozens of names of local products and famous historical sites along the route. These excursions, like the references to the twelve bridges in *Ten no Amijima*, often had not the slightest bearing on the plot.

66. *Ten no Amijima* bears a close parallel in plot and characterization to Chikamatsu's *Shinjū Kasane-izutsu* (*ca.* 1708). For a discussion, see translation note 33.

67. In this he does not differ greatly from such young heroes as Tokubyōe in *Sonezaki shinjū*, Tokubei in *Shinjū Kasane-izutsu*, and Chūbei in *Meido no hikyaku*, and he has some similarities to Kaheiji in *Ikutama shinjū*, Heibei in *Shinjū yaiba wa kōri no tsuitachi*, and several other Chikamatsu characters. They belong to the category of *iro-otoko* or "amorous men," whose susceptibility in love undoes their application in business, whether they be the young proprietor of a paper store, the heir, the chief clerk, or an apprentice in one of the other trades of Osaka *chōnin*. See the article by Kieda Masuichi, "Chikamatsu sewamono no ruikei," in the Chikamatsu number of *Waseda bungaku*, 250 (November 1926), pp. 44–45.

68. For example, Hikosuke in *Nebiki no kadomatsu*, or Kyūhei in *Sonezaki shinjū. Ibid.*, p. 44.

69. Osan's personality is quite similar to that of Otatsu in *Shinjū Kasane-izutsu* and Okiku in *Nebiki no kadomatsu*. It seems quite possible that her role was influenced by the parts of samurai's wives played in the *kabuki* by Yoshizawa Ayame (1673–1729) of plain, brave, chaste women. Kitani, *op. cit.*, 1.26.

70. Koharu's part as the upright prostitute is similar to that of Umekawa in *Meido no hikyaku*, and may have been influenced by the *kabuki* roles of Ogino Yaegiri. *Ibid.*, 1.26.

71. The feudal role from which Magoemon's was derived might have been the type of Kanki, the paragon of *bushi* ethics in *Kokusen'ya kassen*. This was similar to the *kabuki* parts of the actor Shibasaki Rinzaemon (d. 1722).

72. This part, with those of Jihei, Tahei, and Magoemon, are examples of four contrasting types of Osaka merchants. Kitani Hōgin, *Watakushi no Chikamatsu kenkyū* (1942, 269 pp.) pp. 73–74.

73. There are exceptions among the late history plays such as *Soga kaikeizan* (1718). Miyamori, *Chikamatsu to Shēkusupiya*, pp. 101–102.

74. *Lao-tzu tao-te-ching*, Sec. 73, *Ssu-pu ts'ung-k'an* edition, 18a line 2. The translation is by Arthur Waley, *The Way and its Power* (Boston: Houghton Mifflin, 1935), p. 233.

75. Magoemon says to Jihei: "You do not even realize your debt of kindness [to your aunt] for hiding your shame. On just this one count alone you will be a target for divine punishment wherever you go" (translation, p. 74). In another place Jihei says: "The divine punishment [awaiting] me is too fearful. Even if I should escape punishment [for my offenses against my] parents, Heaven, and the Buddhist and Shintō deities, just the punishment [for my offenses against my] wife alone means that my future will not be good" (p. 83). In the narrative section there is a passage: "The god of death (if there is one among the gods,) entices him along, and he resigns himself to this retribution for neglecting his business" (p. 91).

76. This phrase appears in at least four *nō* plays. See *Yōkyoku taikan* (1931, 7 vols.) by Sanari Kentarō: *Yoroboshi* 5.3321, *Sanemori* 2.1247, *Shunkan* 3.1429, and *Hōjōgawa* 4.2459.

77. The first of the four universal vows of the Buddha and Bodhisattva was "to save all living beings without limit." William Edward Soothill and Lewis Hodous, *A Dictionary of Chinese Buddhist Terms* (London: Kegan Paul, 1937), p. 174b. For the other functions of *ami* in the title, see translation note 1.

78. The "Journey" is a conventional feature of Japanese literature which may have been derived from the early poetic diaries. It is found in full form by the Kamakura period in the *Heike monogatari* and later in the *Taiheiki*, and is a feature of most *nō* texts.

79. For an article comparing the use of certain words in the "Journey" of *Ten no Amijima* with the *yōkyoku Kakitsubata*, see "Sōrinshi to yōkyoku to no kan; 'Shinjū Ten no Amijima' chū no 'Nagori no hashi-zukushi,'" by Iida Yutaka, in *Yōkyoku kenkyū* (November 1919), pp. 36–38.

80. Katō Junzō, *Chikamatsu gikyoku shin kenkyū* (1922, 190 + 90 pp.), pp. 147–148.

81. Among the many instances of omitting unessential postpositions in this play are the following: *Jihei manako oshi-nogoi* for *Jihei* [wa] *manako* [o] *oshi-nogoi;* and *Jihei shindai ikitsuite no* for *Jihei* [wa] *shindai* [ga] *ikitsuite no.*

82. This is according to the only reliable account of Chikamatsu's view of his art, a conversation recorded by Hozumi Ikan (1692–1769) in the second part of his preface to his *Naniwa miyage* (1738, 5 *kan*) in the edition edited by Ueda Mannen, *Naniwa miyage* (1904), p. 6.

83. Chikamatsu also indulges in twisting idiomatic expressions to give an amusing effect (translation notes 60 and 143).

84. There are, of course, many instances in *Ten no Amijima* of figures and word-plays which he had used in earlier plays, where he is being repetitive rather than making an allusion. A few examples are to be found in translation notes 85, 91, 253, and 261.

85. By Hamamatsu Utakuni (1776–1827) (60 *kan*), *kan* 25a. 35–41, in *Naniwa*

sōsho (16 vols.) 3.205–211. It is obviously in error as to the year when it states that the incident took place in the 10th month of 1722 (3.205).

86. Anonymous (9 *kan*), *kan* 3, in *Shin enseki jisshu* 1.418, Kokusho kankōkai, Series 3.

87. By Shihekian Mochō (pen name) (2 *kan*), *kan* 2, in *Zoku enseki jisshu*, 1.463, Kokusho kankōkai, Series 1. For more on such traditions, see the chapter "Shinjū Ten no Amijima," in Mitamura Engyo's *Shibai banashi* (1926, 2 vols.) 1.72–85.

88. A miscellany by Kanzawa Tokō (Teikan) (1710–1795) in 200 *kan*. Passage quoted in Kitani, *Dai Chikamatsu zenshū* 1.590–591.

89. Sumiyoshi is about five miles south of the center of Osaka.

90. Kirkwood, *op. cit.*, p. 273, gives a garbled account of this anecdote.

91. In the *Denki sakusho* (*ca.* 1850) (18 *kan*), *kan* 5, in *Shin gunsho ruijū* 1.107–108, Kokusho kankōkai, Series 1, 1907.

92. Sassa Masakazu, (*Chikamatsu hyōshaku*) *Ten no Amijima* (1906, 162 pp.).

93. This anecdote smacks rather too much of the prodigious feats often ascribed to Tokugawa writers, such as the fantastic claim that Saikaku in the course of a *haiku* contest composed 23,500 poems in a single day. That would mean one every four seconds for twenty-four hours!

94. According to the Western calendar it would be January 3, 1721.

95. Higuchi Yoshichiyo, *Kessaku jōruri shū* 1.443, in (*Hyōshaku*) *Edo bungaku sōsho* (1935, 11 vols.).

96. For a discussion of this problem, see Wakatsuki, *op. cit.*, pp. 816–822.

97. Itō, *op. cit.*, pp. 5–9; Higuchi, *op. cit.*, p. 443; Kitani, *Dai Chikamatsu zenshū*, 1.597–600.

98. Higuchi, *op. cit.*, p. 443.

99. A play of this title has been translated into English in Frank Alanson Lombard, *An Outline History of the Japanese Drama* (Boston, 1929), as "The Death-Love of Kamiya-Jihei," pp. 297–351. He describes it as "A *Kabuki* by an unknown author of the early nineteenth century, based upon a *Joruri* by Chikamatsu-Hangae, 1770." The *jōruri* is presumably Hanji's version of 1778.

100. Kuroki, *Chikamatsu Monzaemon*, p. 241.

101. Higuchi, *op. cit.*, p. 443; Itō, *op. cit.*, pp. 5–9.

102. These titles are respectively contractions of the name of the *chaya* in Act 1 (see translation note 22) and of the hero, Kamiya Jihei.

103. Shuzui, *op. cit.*, pp. 137–147.

104. *Ibid.*, p. 10. For photographs of this performance, see Miyamori, *Masterpieces of Chikamatsu*, plates facing pp. 228, 238, 240, 250, and 258.

105. Miyamori, *Masterpieces of Chikamatsu*, pp. 221–263. In Miyajima Tsunao's *Contribution à l'étude du théâtre japonais de poupées*, pp. 50–106, there is a retelling of *Ten no Amijima* which is evidently based on Chikamatsu's *jōruri*, but which is not close enough to the original to be called a paraphrase or a translation.

106. (1928, 12 vols.), 12.267–318.

107. It contains the same excellent text as Fujii's *Chikamatsu zenshū* 12.267–318.

108. In addition to the standard dictionaries and the works cited in the notes to the translation, the following specialized dictionaries and glossaries were especially helpful in the study of the text: Ueda Mannen and Higuchi Yoshichiyo, *Chikamatsu goi* (1930, 770 pp.) ; Satō Tsurukichi, *Genroku bungaku jiten* (1928, 704 pp.) ; Kitani Hōgin, "Dai Chikamatsu zenshū chūshaku jiten," which is vol. 16 of Kitani's *Dai Chikamatsu zenshū;* Yuzawa Kōkichirō, (*Tokugawa jidai*) *Gengo no kenkyū* (1936, 650 pp.)

The bibliography on Chikamatsu which has appeared since 1880 is extremely large. The fullest list, though not complete, lists over 600 books and articles. This is Inagaki Tatsurō's "Chikamatsu kenkyū bunken nempyō nōto," in *Bungaku*, vol.

19, No. 7 (July 1951), pp. 72–85. Other significant lists are in the following books: Itō Masao, *Shinjū Ten no Amijima shōkai*, pp. 391–435; Shuzui Kenji, *Chikamatsu*, pp. 167–191; Wakatsuki Yasuji, *Chikamatsu ningyō jōruri no kenkyū*, pp. 894–900; Suzuki Yukizō (*Gikyoku shōsetsu*) *Kinsei sakka taikan* (1933, 666 pp.) 1.662–664; Shigetomo Ki, *Chikamatsu* (1939, 302 pp.; vol. 11 in *Nihon koten tokuhon*), pp. 291–302; Ueda Mannen and Higuchi Yoshichiyo, *Chikamatsu goi*, pp. 734–735.

Translation

The Love Suicide at Amijima

(Shinjū Ten no Amijima) [1]

GUIDE TO THE TRANSLATION

Brackets [ ] are used to designate words not in the original text which have been supplied by the translator.

Parentheses ( ) enclose the second translation of words in the original which must be interpreted dually because they are pivot words or some other form of pun (see Introduction p. 45).

A virgule / is used to indicate alternate characters, readings, or translations.

The original Japanese text is written continuously without paragraphing, punctuation, quotation marks, or any indication in the margin as to which character is the intended speaker. Any of the divisions, signs, or guideposts which appear in the translation have been supplied by the translator. For clarity, the names of the speakers have been inserted, in italic; the speeches have been printed in roman type and the narrative passages in italic.

Act 1

*Sanjō bakkara fungoro nokkoro
chokkoro fungoro de
mate tokkoro wakkara yukkuru
wakkara yukkuru ta ga
kasa o wanga ranga ra su
sora ga kunguru kunguru mo
renge rengere bakkara fungoro.*[2]

The prostitutes of the Shijimi River [3] *[Quarter] have deep affections. This Shijimi River is indeed an ocean of love which cannot be ladled dry.* [4] *[As men walk along] singing songs of love full of recollections, their hearts stop them, as if the characters on the lantern at the entrance [of their favorite house] were a barrier.* [5] *Sauntering in good spirits about the Quarter, they chant improvised jōruri, imitate the intonation of actors, and sing the popular songs of the riverside pavilions.* [6] *Some visitors are enticed in by the music of the samisen coming from second-floor rooms. Other guests are trapped unwittingly, like the one who, wishing to avoid festival days* [7] *so that he will not be obliged to spend more than he can afford, hides his face and assumes a concealing guise. But Kiyo, the maid* [8] *[from one of the houses], recognizes him [as a patron of her establishment] who is trying to evade her. She clutches again and again at the neck-flap of his cap, and, although he slips away from her two or three times, she is determined not to let this expected lover escape, and, throwing herself upon him, she holds him close.* [9] *"What a mean trick. Now come along inside," this female Kagekiyo says, and by his cap and neck-flap she plunges him into extravagance against his will.* [10]

[In this Quarter] even the names of the bridges like Plum and Cherry [11] *enumerate flowers. Among the flowers* [12] *there is Koharu of the house, Kinokuniya, who has changed her dishabille* [13] *of a "bathhouse" in the South [Quarter]* [14] *for a love garment of this [Sonezaki] Quarter. Is her name, Koharu, an omen that in this tenth month she will leave in this society a scandalous reputa-*

tion? [15] *Who has sent for me tonight, Koharu [wonders] uneasily [as she walks toward the* chaya], [16] *and then by the dim light of a lantern* [17] *a prostitute coming from the opposite direction recognizes her and turns back to say:*

Prostitute. Isn't that Koharu? How have you been? We have not been in the same company at all lately. I've not only not seen you, but I also haven't had any news of you. Aren't you feeling well? Your face looks thin. According to what I heard from someone, because of Kamiji, [18] your master has your guests scrutinized very carefully and you are not sent out just anywhere. Indeed, I have even heard that you will be redeemed by Tahei, [19] and that you are to go somewhere in the country or to Itami. What is the truth?

Koharu. Oh, please don't say Itami, Itami. It has caused me much trouble. [20] It is such a pity, [21] for the relation between Kamiji and me isn't that serious, but that loudmouthed Tahei has spread such scandalous rumors that my good guests have left me. My master says this is all because of Kamiya Jihei and he has completely prevented us from seeing each other, and now we cannot even exchange word by letters. Strangely enough I am being sent this evening to Kawashō [22] for a samurai, I'm told, but I am anxious lest I should meet Tahei on my way there now. I feel like a person who has a revengeful enemy. Say, isn't that he I see over there?

Prostitute. Oh, then get away quickly. There, from the first block [of the Quarter] comes a chanting monk, [23] reciting his comic invocation. [24] In his audience there is a dissolute-looking man with his hair done up in a foppish style, [25] who looks showy and vain. That certainly is Tahei. Oh, oh, they're heading this way. *Almost as she speaks, along comes the impious novice in his large flat cap* [26] *and ink-black robe with tucked-up sleeves, surrounded by merrymaking onlookers. Beating time on his gong* gon-gon ten-ten [27] *in rhythm he mouths gibberish into his waggish incantation:*

Monk. * [Coxinga:] "Han Kai's style is not unique.
　　　　For crashing down gates
　　　　watch the style of Japan's Asahina."
　　　　Then hauling down the gate's crossbeam
　　　　and the entanglement of felled trees,
　　　　he slays Uryōko and Saryōko,

　　　　　　* *Dōguya* [28] [style of recitation].

and without difficulty passes through the barrier,
as [irresistible as] the sun and moon.²⁹
Namamida namaida, namamida namaida.

* [Wankyū] wanders bewildered,
lamenting that in this transient world
he can find no one resembling his Matsuyama.
He weeps and weeps,
ē ē wā wā wā,
and laughs and laughs.
How base it is to end life in madness [he grieves],
lying down on the mattress of turf,
a wretched sight.³¹
Namamida namaida, namamida, namaida.

† *Ei ei ei ei ei*
The dyer Tokubei's fortune
has been deeply stained with love by Fusa,
and this cannot be bleached out
even with lye/ (satiation) .³³
Namamida namaida, namamida namaida
namamida namaida, namaida.

Sugi. See here, monk, *says Sugi [the maid accompanying Ko-
haru].*
Monk. What is it? ³⁴ *[he asks].*
Sugi. That's unlucky. And just when reports of love suicides in
this Quarter have subsided.³⁵ Quit that song, and let us hear an
incantation of the Journey from *The Battles of Coxinga,* and
from her sleeve pocket she draws a coin as remuneration.
Monk. ‡ For a mere one or two pennies
to make the long journey
of over three thousand *ri* to China
doesn't pay, doesn't pay,
doesn't pay, doesn't pay,³⁷
he grumbles, and walks on.
*Mingling with the crowd, Koharu scurries along and dashes
agitatedly into the Kawachiya.*
Proprietress. Well, well, you came quickly. I haven't even

spoken your name for a long time. Koharu, Koharu, it is a rare treat to see you; Koharu, you've been so long absent,[38] *The proprietress* [39] *shouts in her hearty [professional] voice. [Sugi departs.]*

Koharu. Say, you can be heard to the entrance. Please don't say "Koharu, Koharu" in a loud voice. Out in front is the detested Ri Tōten.[40] Speak quietly, I beg of you, *she replies, but she is overheard, for suddenly in come three companions.*

Tahei. Koharu-dono, you've given me the fictitious name of Ri Tōten. First, I wish to thank you. Comrades, this is the Koharu-dono I've told you about privately, the most sincere, the most openhearted, and the best in bed. Will I soon have her as my wife, or will she be redeemed by Kamiya Jihei? She's a prostitute who puts men in competition. Make her acquaintance, *he says, approaching arrogantly.*

Koharu. I don't want to hear about it. If you consider it a feat to give without knowledge a scandalous reputation to people,[41] you may busy yourself in that, but I don't want to hear about it, *she says, drawing away a little, but he edges up to her again.*

Tahei. Even if you don't want to hear about it, I'll make you listen by the clink of my gold coins.[42] You certainly have a fine karma.[43] With so many men in the three districts of Temma and Osaka,[44] [you get] Kamiya no Jihei, father of two children, whose wife is his cousin, whose father-in-law is his aunt's husband.[45] He has a business which is hard pressed every sixty days [46] even by the payments due the wholesale houses. For him to pay close to 10 *kamme* [47] as the ransom to redeem you would be a preposterous undertaking.[48] As for me, having no wife or children, I have no father-in-law; nor do I have parents or uncles. I'm called Tahei the Independent. Although I can't rival that Jihei in talking big in the gay quarter, when it's just a matter of wealth, this Tahei will win. When it comes to applying pressure with the power of money, eh, men, I don't know anything I can't overcome. Koharu's guest tonight is that Jihei, but I'll "take" [49] her from him, I'll "take" her, this Independent [Tahei] will "take" her. Proprietress, serve some sake, serve some sake.

Proprietress. What are you talking about? Her guest tonight is a samurai, and he'll probably be here soon. Please go somewhere else to enjoy yourself, [*the proprietress*] *says, but he continues with a waggish expression:*

Tahei. A guest's a guest, whether he's a samurai or a townsman, with the mere difference of whether or not he wears a sword. If it's a matter of the number of swords he wears, still he can't wear five or six. When he's fully equipped, the long and the short sword [50] make only two. I'll "take" Koharu with the samurai thrown in. Even though you try to escape me and hide from me, we meet because it is our destiny. We've met just now thanks to the babbling chanting monk. How blessed is the efficacy of the incantation. I'll recite an incantation also. Here, I'll use this firepan as a gong, and this pipe as a mallet. This will be amusing:

> *Chan chan, cha chan chan*
> *ei ei ei ei ei*
> The paper-dealer Jihei,
> excessively infatuated with Koharu,
> has scattered about his prestige and money
> until his fortune is holey paper,
> like wastepaper unfit even to blow his nose on.[51]
> *namamida butsu namaida*
> *namamida butsu namaida*
> *namaida namaida.*

While he is thus kicking up a row and shouting, there appears at the entrance a woven hat,[52] worn even at night for concealment.
Tahei. Ah, Toilet-paper has come! My, what an extreme disguise! Why don't you come in, Toilet-paper? If you're afraid of Tahei's incantation, [say] "Praise Ami [da Buddha]" [and worship me]. Let's have the (woven) hat,[53] *he says, pulling him in, but only then does he see that it is a genuine samurai, wearing two swords and severely dressed and glaring intensely at him through [the slits in] his woven hat with round eyeballs bulging like gongs. Tahei, unable now to utter* nen *or* butsu,[54] *gasps* haa, *but he manages to keep his face from flinching, and continues:*
Tahei. Koharu, I'm a townsman, and I've never worn a sword, but the glitter of the great amounts of "New Silver" [55] at my place, I believe, can twist and deflect mere swords. It is the most extreme insolence for that Toilet-paper dealer, with his capital as thin as paper for filtering lacquer juice, to try to compete with this Independent [*Tahei*]. If we saunter from Sakura Bridge down to Naka-machi,[56] somewhere or other along the way we'll trample and crush that Wastepaper. Come along, men, *and as if gesticulations alone make the man they swagger off filling the whole street.*

Because of where he is, the samurai guest takes no notice of the fool, and endures him [in silence].[57] *These various unpleasant remarks about Kamiya go to Koharu's heart, dejecting and distracting her so that she fails to greet her guest. At this moment, Sugi comes running back from (Ki)nokuniya, and says with an uneasy expression:*

Sugi. But a moment ago when I accompanied Koharu here, just because I left before the guest arrived, I was severely scolded [by my master] for not having waited to make certain of the guest. Excuse the discourtesy, *she says, pushing up his woven hat and examining his face. She adds:* No, it isn't he. There is nothing to be concerned about. Have him keep you all night, and have a deep intimacy, Koharu. Talk to him captivatingly. Proprietress, I'll see you later, *and with this succession of puns she leaves.*[58] *The most upright* [59] *samurai is greatly displeased. [They enter and sit down.]*

Samurai. What's this all about. My face is judged as if you take me for a tea caddy or a tea cup.[60] (Is it to make a fool of me?) I did not come here to be trifled with.[61] It is difficult even during the day for me to leave the residency [62] where I serve, and in order to remain out overnight I have to give notice to the chief official and sign the register. These are difficult regulations, but, because I had heard of you and longed for you, I hoped that I would be able to have a meeting with you, and, unaccompanied by any attendant, I came earlier to make arrangements with this *chaya.*[63] I hoped at any rate that by entrusting myself to your affection I would gain something worth remembering always, but you haven't smiled at all or given me a word of greeting. You've kept looking down as if you were counting your coins in your bosom.[64] Aren't you going to get a sore neck? What about it, proprietress? This is something novel to come to a *chaya* and be [made to feel like] a night nurse in a maternity room, *he grumbles.*

Proprietress. You've reason [to be annoyed]. It's natural that you should think it strange since you are not acquainted with all the circumstances. This girl and a visitor of hers called Kamiji are deeply in love. It is Kamiji only day after day and no one else can lay a hand on her, until her other visitors have scattered like leaves in a storm. When an infatuation reaches such a pitch, it might lead to a mishap both to the visitor and to the girl. First of all, because such affairs interfere with business, it is the practice of proprietors everywhere to thwart them. That is why you were examined. And of course Koharu has reason to be in low spirits. The visitor also has reason [to be annoyed]. Reasons, reasons. I'm caught between all these reasons as the proprietress, and I would say that the very essence of reason would be to take this in good spirits. Come on, have something to drink and be cheerful and gay, I ask of you, Koharu, Koharu. *She does not answer, but raising her tearful face she says:*

Koharu. Samurai, is it true that those who die during the Ten Nights [65] attain Buddhahood, simply by the fact that they die?

Samurai. How would I know that? Ask the priest at your family temple.

Koharu. Yes, that's what I should do. Then there is something else I should like to ask you. In committing suicide either by the sword or by hanging oneself, probably it would be much the more painful to cut one's throat, wouldn't it?

Samurai. I've never tried it to see whether it would hurt or not. Ask more normal questions. What an uncanny feeling this girl gives you, *and samurai though he is, his expression betrays displeasure.*

Proprietress. Koharu, that's no way to greet a visitor you're meeting for the first time. Cheer up, now. Well, I'll go find my husband, and then let's have some sake, *and she goes out the entrance. Outside, the evening moon is already low, the clouds have scattered, and there are few people still strolling by.*[66]

In Temma for many years [there has been enshrined] an efficacious deity (kami). (There is also in Temma a long-established, virile) Kami-sama (Kamiya Jihei) who is not a deity (kami). He is the talk of [gay] society, so deeply is he in love with Koharu. They are bound together in an unlucky liaison. Now, in the tenth month, they have been forsaken by the god of marriage.[67] *They are thwarted [by Koharu's master] and have been reduced to the condition of being unable to meet. They have pledged in farewell letters that, if they have an opportunity to meet, it will be the day of death for them both. Every night [Jihei sets out] ready to die and trudges distractedly as if his spirit has already left [his body]. He burns with anticipation.*[68] *At an eating house,*[69] *he gets news of Koharu, when he overhears that she has gone to Kawashō for a samurai guest. Immediately he thinks: Ah! It will be tonight. [Reaching Kawashō,] he peers in through the lattice [on the window],*[70] *and in an inner room he can see the guest wearing a hood.*[71] *He can see only his chin moving and cannot hear his voice.*

Jihei. How pitiful she is. Koharu keeps her face turned away from the lamp. How thin it has become! Her heart is full of thoughts of me. Would that I could secretly inform her that I am here. If she could fly with me, would it be to Umeda or Kitano? [72] I'd like to let her know. I'd like to call her. *As his heart calls to her, his spirit [flies] ahead to her, and his body [remains like] a cicada's castoff skin, clinging to the lattice. He weeps agitatedly. The guest within yawns widely:*

Samurai. Keeping a worried prostitute company makes me depressed. It's quiet now around the entrance. Let's go into the front room and at least gaze at the lanterns to clear away our [gloomy] spirits. *Come along, he says, and they go out into the front room. [Jihei], with a "good heavens," [73] squeezes his shoulders and body into the small shadow cast by the lattice. [The couple] inside do not know that he is hiding there and listening.*

Samurai. Koharu, by observing your behavior and some of your words this evening, I see that it is your intention to commit a love suicide with this Kamiji, or whatever he is called, of whom the proprietress spoke. That's right, isn't it? I know that ears which have heeded the god of death will not listen to advice or reason, but such action would be extremely foolish. The man's family and relatives would not blame him for his rashness, but would blame you and hate you. There would be the shame of your dead face being exposed to [the gaze of] countless people. You may not have parents living, but if you do, there would be divine punishment for being unfilial. Of course [you will not attain] Buddhahood, and the two of you will not be able even to descend smoothly to hell together. This is pathetic, this is saddening. This is only our first meeting, and although I am a samurai by profession, I cannot stand by and see you die. [74] Perhaps this can be resolved by money. I should like to help you if five or ten gold pieces will be of use. [I swear by] the God, Hachiman, [75] by the divine protection of samurai, not to tell anyone. Confide in me everything that is in your heart, *he says softly.*

Koharu puts her hands together [as if in prayer]:

Koharu. I am so grateful, so obliged to you. That you, who have not had a long intimacy or friendship with me, have spoken so sympathetically and have even [been willing to] take an oath, makes me shed tears of gratitude. It is indeed true that one's face reveals [what is in one's thoughts]. [76] To be sure, I have promised to die with Kamiji. We are thwarted by my master and have no opportunity to meet. The difficulty is [that Jihei hasn't the money] so he cannot redeem me immediately. Between my former master in the South [Quarter] and the one here, I still have five years of service [77] [to complete]. During this period, if I were redeemed by someone else, it would bring dishonor to me, of course, and to my lover. [When he asked:] "Rather than that, won't you die [with me]?" "Yes, let's die," I promised on the spur of the moment, under the pressure of unavoidable obligation. [We planned to] watch for an opportunity, we decided on our signals, and [waited only for me] to slip out. In this way, as if any time might be the hour of my death, my life has been unreal, as I live from one day to the next. My mother, who is dependent on me alone, lives in the Southern district and does some piecework. My only regret is that, after I die, she might become a beggar outcast [78] and starve to death. As for myself, I have but one life. Although I am ashamed that you must consider me a shallow woman, I would rather put aside this shame, because above all I do not want to die. I ask you, please, please, settle this affair so that I shall not die, *she says, and he nods with a thoughtful expression.*

[*Jihei,*] *listening outside, starts with astonishment. This is so unexpected, that he feels like [a monkey which] has fallen from a tree.*[79] *He is beside himself with agitation.*

Jihei. Then were all [her promises] lies? How infuriating! For these two years I have been deceived. That rotten-hearted fox! Should I rush in and cut her down with one blow, or should I heap shame on her to her face, to vent my anger? *he says, gnashing his teeth and shedding tears of regret.*

Inside, Koharu sobs and weeps:

Koharu. Although it is a cowardly request, [I must throw myself] on your sympathy and ask you please to come to see me through this year and until about the second or third month of next spring. Then whenever he comes to ask me to die with him, would you interfere, and thus keep postponing my hour of death? If our relation can be severed naturally, he will not kill himself, and my life will be saved. Because of what karma did I promise to die [with him]? As I think about it now, I regret it so, *and leaning on her knee, she weeps.*

Samurai. I consent. I have a plan. The breeze is coming up, and also people can see in, *he says, rattling shut the sliding windows inside the lattice [casement].*

Jihei, who has been listening, is in a frenzy.

Jihei. That's a prostitute, and a cheap prostitute! I misjudged her bad nature, and she stole my heart, the thieving whore.[80] Should I cut her down or shall I stab her? What should I do? *The silhouettes of their two faces are reflected on the sliding window.* I'd like to beat her, I'd like to trample on her. What are they blabbing and nodding about. Koharu is beseeching, whispering, weeping. I press my chest and rub it, but I cannot contain myself, I cannot stand it. *His heart leads him on impetuously, he draws his one-foot-seven [sword],[81] [made by] Magoroku of Seki,[82] and aiming it through an opening in the lattice at where he judges Koharu's side to be, he makes a thrust, but she is sitting too far away. She is startled, but unharmed. The visitor instantly leaps forward, and grasping both of Jihei's hands, jerks them in, and with the cord from his sword, quickly binds them to a post of the lattice and ties them firmly.*

Samurai. Koharu, do not be alarmed. Do not look out. *At this moment the proprietor and his wife return.*

Proprietor and Wife. What's happened? *they ask agitatedly.*

Samurai. It is nothing serious. A rowdy thrust the blade of his sword through the sliding window, and I bound his arms to the lattice.[83] I have a plan, so do not untie the cord. If a crowd gathers there will be a row in the Quarter. Let us all go into the inner rooms. Koharu, come along, let us go and sleep together.

Koharu. Yes, *she answers, but she recognizes the sword, and her breast, which it had failed to stab, feels suddenly pierced.* Excesses caused by drinking are common occurrences in the Gay Quarter. I think it would be best to let him go without taking any action, don't you, Kawashō?

Samurai. Certainly not. Leave this to me. Everyone go in [the inner rooms]. Koharu, this way.

Jihei can see their shadows in the inner room. He is tied in such a way that the lattice [serves as] a manacle, but when he struggles, the bonds draw tighter. He feels fully the living shame [84] of having fallen as low as a dog tied to worldly desire.[85] He weeps bitter tears. How pitiful is this sight!

The Independent Tahei comes sauntering back:[86]

Tahei. Say, that man standing by the lattice in front of Kawashō is Jihei. I'll throw him down, *and grasping his collar, he pulls down.*

Jihei. Ouch, ouch.

Tahei. You are a coward to yell "ouch." Oh, you have been tied up. Then you must have been stealing. Pickpocket! pickpocket! [87] *he says, striking him.* You robber,[88] you criminal! [89] *he adds, kicking him.* Kamiya Jihei has been stealing, and he has been tied up, *he calls, making such a row that passers-by and people from the neighborhood come running up. The samurai comes flying out of the house.*

Samurai. So it is you who have been calling "thief." What has Jihei stolen? Out with it, *he says, grasping Tahei and hurling him forward onto the ground. When he tries to get up, he tramples him and kicks him down. Then seizing him, he says,* Now, Jihei, trample on him and vent your anger, *and he throws Tahei at his feet. Jihei, bound though he is, tramples and tramples on his cheekbones, and tramples him all over until he is covered with dirt.*[90] *As Tahei gets up, he glares about him:*

Tahei. You fellows around here did a lot of looking on, and let me be trampled, eh? I have memorized each of your faces. I shall get my revenge. Remember that! *and, unhumbled in speech, he runs out.*

The crowd bursts out laughing:

Crowd. Even after he has been trampled, how he jaws! [91] Let's throw him from the bridge and make him swallow some water. Let's do it, *and they dash out in pursuit.*

After the crowd disperses, the samurai approaches and unties Jihei's bonds, and then taking off his own hood, reveals his face.

Jihei. Magoemon! my elder brother! I have no face, *and he throws himself on his knees, prostrates himself on the ground, and remains weeping there.*

Koharu. Then this is your elder brother? *says Koharu running out. Jihei seizes her by the bodice* [92] *of her dress and pulls her up in front of him:*

Jihei. You beast, you fox. I want to trample you even more than I do Tahei, *and he raises his foot, but Magoemon [shouts]:*

Magoemon. Hey, hey, hey! That is the sort of foolishness that has been causing trouble. It is a prostitute's business to deceive people. Do you realize that now? I, Magoemon, met her just now for the first time, and I could see through to the bottom of her heart. You are a blunderer not to discover during over two years of intimate friendship with this woman what her true nature is. With that foot with which you would trample Koharu, why don't you trample your own confused nature? You are impossible. You are my younger brother, and nearing thirty,[93] father of Kantarō and Osue, children of six and four, and responsible for an establishment with a frontage of thirty-six feet,[94] and yet you do not realize that you are ruining your fortune, and you will not heed your elder brother's advice. Your father-in-law is your aunt's husband, your mother-in-law is your aunt and is just like a mother to you. Your wife, Osan, is also my cousin. We are bound together, we are bound together, over and over, in relationships of marriage and blood.[95] Even at family meetings the only [topic of discussion] is the complaint that you frequent Sonezaki. It is [especially] regrettable because of our aunt. Her husband, Gozaemon, is an unfeeling, old-fashioned man. He becomes angry and says: "I've been done in by my wife's nephew and have thrown away my daughter. I shall take back Osan and cover Jihei with shame throughout Temma!" Our aunt alone bears the anxiety. [She humors him] by acting [sometimes] as your enemy and as your ally [at other times]. She suffers such worry that she is on the verge of illness. You do not even realize your debt of gratitude to her for hiding your shame. On just this one count alone you will be a target for divine punishment wherever you go.[96] [I realized that, going on] in this way, you cannot maintain your household, and, wishing to set our aunt's mind at ease, I came to see Koharu's real nature for myself, in this way hoping to hit upon a plan. I arranged with this proprietor so that I could see for myself the cause of your weakness. [Now I see that] you have good reason to forsake your wife and children. What a faithful prostitute she is! What a conquest this is! What a fine younger brother I have! I have made something of a name for myself as Koya no Magoemon,[97] [but now for your sake I find myself looking like] a fancy-dressed participant in a festival procession,[98] or else a lunatic. I am wearing a long and a short sword, which I have never done before, imitating, like a bit actor,[99] an official of a storehouse residency.[100] These swords are the height of foolishness, but I can't get rid of them here. I am so angry and feel so ridiculous that I am sick at heart, *he says, gnashing his teeth and grimacing, trying to hide his tears.*

Koharu, the entire time choked with tears, can only say:

Koharu. You have good reason for everything [you say], *and her words are drowned out by tears.*

Striking the ground, Jihei [cries]:

Jihei. I have done wrong. I have done wrong, elder brother. For three years I have been bewitched by that old badger. I have neglected all my relatives and family,[101] even my wife and children, and my business is in confusion, all because I have been deceived by this housebreaker,[102] Koharu. Ten million regrets. Since I no longer love her, of course I shall never even come here again. You badger! Fox! Housebreaker! As proof that I have broken with you, see this! *and [he draws out] his amulet bag* [103] *which he wears next to his skin.* These are the vows [104] we exchanged, one at the beginning of every month, twenty-nine in all. When I return these to you, there is no love or sympathy left. Take them, *and he flings them at her.* Elder brother, would you verify the number of the vows of mine that she has and take charge of them and burn them at your house? Now, [Koharu,] give them to my elder brother.

Koharu. As you say, *she says, and weeping, she draws forth her amulet bag. Magoemon throws it open.*

Magoemon. One, two, three, four . . . ten, twenty-nine. The number is right. In addition there is a letter from a woman. What is this? *he says, opening it.*

Koharu. Oh, that is an important letter which I cannot show you, *and she reaches out for it, but he brushes her aside. By the lantern he looks at the address, and [almost] before he has finished reading, "To Koharu-sama from San at Kamiya," he slips it in his bosom without betraying any expression.*

Magoemon. Now Koharu, a moment ago [I swore by] the divine protection of samurai. Now, as Koya no Magoemon, [I swear by] the divine protection of merchants that I shall show this letter to no one, not even to my wife. I alone shall read it, and put it in the fire with the vows. You can count on this pledge.

Koharu. Oh, I am grateful. Then I can keep my honor, *and she sinks into tears again.*

Jihei. Oh, ho! You [talk about] keeping your honor or not, as if you were human. Elder brother, I do not want to see her face another moment. Come, let us go. Yet I cannot bear this resentment and regret. As something to remember always, I will trample once on this woman's face. Permit me that, *and coming up to her suddenly, he tramples the ground like a foot-bellows.* I've blundered. For about three years [I have thought you] beloved, charming, darling, adorable, but this very day I am bidding you farewell with just this one foot, *and he kicks her on her temple. She cries out, and as the brothers leave together, how pathetic they too look. [Koharu] sees them off, raising her voice and grieving, and how pitiable she is.*

Is she unfaithful or faithful? [105] *Her true heart is [hidden] deep in that letter from [Jihei's] wife. Until this letter has been read by someone, her love will not be known. [Jihei,] (parting from his love,) goes home.* [106]

Act 2

Auspiciously, the name of Amamitsu-kami [107] is given to the nearby Tenjin Bridge, and even the busy street (which runs directly) [between the Bridge and the Shrine] is called Deity's Front Street.[108] A business is carried on [here], a paper store, under the name of Kamiya Jihei, and it is [conducted] vigorously so that customers practically rain on it. The paper is genuine, (and this brings prosperity). The business [profits by] its location, and because it is a long-established shop.[109] The husband is dozing by the covered brazier,[110] and [Osan] sets up a pillow screen [111] to protect him from drafts. Outside people are going by to the Ten Nights [services],[112] while the wife, Osan, singlehanded, takes care of both the shop and the house.[113] She says to herself:

Osan. These days are short and now it is time for supper. [The maid], Tama, went to Ichi-no-kawa [114] on an errand, but what has become of her? Why doesn't that [apprentice] Sangorō come back? The wind is cold, and the two children must have become chilled. This is the time when Osue wants my breast, but the fool doesn't even know that. What can be done with such a fool? What an annoying fellow!

Kantarō. Mama, I have come back alone, *calls her son, running home.*

Osan. Oh, Kantarō, you've returned. What has become of Osue and Sangorō?

Kantarō. We were playing at the Shrine,[115] but Osue said she wanted her milk, and did a lot of crying.

Osan. Of course, of course. Your hands and feet are [as cold as] nails. Warm yourself at the covered brazier where your father is sleeping. What shall I do about that fool? *and impatiently she runs out into the shop, and [sees] Sangorō dawdling home alone.* See here, you fool, where did you leave Osue?

Sangorō. Well, sure enough, I guess I did drop her somewhere or other. Someone may have picked her up, so shall I go and look for her [back there] somewhere?

Osue. You . . . If any harm has come to my precious child, I'll beat you to death, *she shouts, but at that moment the maid, Tama, carrying Osue on her back, returns home calling:*

Tama. Oh, how pathetic. She was down at the crossing crying. Sangorō, when you are minding the children, do it properly.

Osan. Oh, how pitiful, how pitiful. You must want my breast, *and going to the covered brazier like the others, she nurses her.*[116] *Then she adds:* Now, Tama, give that fool a beating he will remember. *But Sangorō shakes his head:*

Sangorō. No, no. Just now at the Shrine I gave each of them two tangerines to eat, and I ate five, *and, like the fool that he is, he makes such a pun* [117] *that they have to laugh in spite of themselves.*

Tama. I got involved with this fool and almost forgot. Osan-sama, Koya no Magoemon and [his] aunt are coming this way from the west.

Osan. Well, well. In that case I must waken Jihei. Husband, please get up. It seems that Mother and Uncle [118] are on their way over here. They will probably be annoyed again if they see a merchant taking a nap during one of these short days.

Jihei. All right, here goes, *and he rises with a grunt, and, taking his abacus in one hand, he draws his account book toward him:* 2 [into] 10 makes 5, 9 divided [by 3] is 3, 6 divided [by 3] is 2, 7 [times] 8 is 56 *-year old Aunt comes in with Magoemon.* Ah, elder brother, and Aunt. Welcome. Come this way. I was just now engaged in some urgent accounting. 4 [times] 9 [is] 36 *momme.* 3[times] 6 is 1 *momme* 8 *fun,* with 2 *fun* short. (Kan) tarō! Osue! Grandma and Uncle have come. Bring the tobacco tray. 1 [times] 3 is 3. Here, Osan, serve some tea,[119] *he jabbers.*

Aunt. No, no. We did not come to drink tea or have a smoke. Even though you are young, you are the mother of two children. There is no merit in just being amiable about this. When a man is dissipated, it is entirely because his wife is negligent. When the business is ruined and the husband and wife separate, the shame is not just the man's. Why don't you pay more attention and be more resolute? *she says.*

Magoemon. Aunt, that is in vain. He is so impudent that he even deceives his elder brother. [He wouldn't listen] meekly to the admonitions of his wife. Yes, Jihei. You fooled me shamelessly, didn't you? You even let me see the returning of the written vows, but, before ten days are passed, you are redeeming her. What are you doing—calculating Koharu's debts? Stop it, *and snatching away the abacus, he hurls it clattering into the vestibule.*[120]

Jihei. This is extremely annoying. Since the other day, I have not crossed my threshold except to go twice to a wholesaler's at Imabashi [121] and once to Tenjin [Shrine]. To say nothing of redeeming her, I have not even been thinking of it.

Aunt. Don't say that, don't say that. Last night at the Ten Nights chanting [service] the talk among the congregation was the great gossip that a prostitute [122] known as Koharu of the Sonezaki *chaya*,[123] Kinokuniya, is deeply loved by a great spender [124] from Temma who has driven away her other guests, and that soon, in fact, any day now, this great spender will redeem her. And there was much other talk, such as that even in this time of high prices, there seems to be an abundance of money and fools. My husband, Gozaemon, who has heard her name often enough, [said to me after we returned home]: "This great spender from Temma who is involved with Koharu of Kinokuniya is definitely that Jihei. He may be my wife's nephew, but he is no relative of mine. My daughter is more important to me. He probably intends to redeem the *chaya* woman and then sell his wife to a *chaya*. I shall take her back before he gets his hands on all her clothes," [125] and he was halfway out of the house before I could soothe him by saying: "You're too violent. This can be settled quietly after first looking carefully into the good and bad of the case." [For this purpose] I have now come here with Magoemon. According to what Magoemon has been saying: "The Jihei of today is not the Jihei of yesterday. He has broken off his connection with Sonezaki and is the most respectable of men." But what kind of disease is this, which recurs again. Your father was my elder brother. How sad it was when your father, Kōyodōsei,[126] on his deathbed, raised his head from his pillow to say to me: "Jihei is your son-in-law and your nephew. Take care of him." I have never forgotten these words, but, your nature being what it is, his request was in vain, *and prostrating herself, she weeps bitterly.*

Jihei claps his hands and says:

Jihei. Ah, I understand, I understand. The Koharu mentioned in this gossip is Koharu, but the great spender who is redeeming her is very different. That is Independent Tahei—elder brother knows him also—who became rowdy the other day and got trampled on. This fellow does not have a wife and children or any relatives, and he sends home to Itami for money [at will]. For some time I have been preventing this fellow from redeeming her. It is clear that he believes that now the opportunity has come to redeem her. I haven't even thought of doing that.

At that, Osan's face brightens:

Osan. Even if I were [as amiable as] Buddha, I wouldn't have to sympathize with my husband's ransoming a *chaya* woman. In what my husband has just said, there is not a particle of falsehood. Mother, I will be a witness of that. *The words of the husband and wife match like [the two halves of] a tally.*¹²⁷

Aunt and Magoemon. So that's it, *say the aunt and [her] nephew, clapping their hands and feeling relieved.*

Aunt. This is something we must be careful about. Above all I am very happy, but, in order that we may be reassured and that my obstinate husband will have no further doubts, would you consent to write a vow?

Jihei. Certainly. I'd write a thousand of them.

Magoemon. This is most satisfying. I bought this on the way here, *and Magoemon [draws] from his breast a charm from the Kumano [Shrines] [on which vows are written].*¹²⁸ *[But what Jihei writes] now reverses his [previous] vows of eternal love, [suggested by] the clusters of crows [on the charm],*¹²⁹ *for on [an identical form entitled] "Divine Punishment Vow," [he writes]: "[I promise to] sever my relations with and cease thoughts of Koharu. If this is a falsehood, [I should be punished] by Brahma and Indra and by their subordinate Four Great [Devas]." To this text,*¹³⁰ *in which are enumerated [other] Buddhist and Shintō deities, Kamiya Jihei [writes] his name boldly, (firmly) affixes his seal in blood, and presents [the vow].*

Osan. Thanks to you, Mother and Brother, I am also reassured. Since we have had children, I have never received such firm [assurances from him]. Do rejoice at this.

Aunt. Indeed. Since he is in this spirit, he will settle down [in his conduct], and the business will probably prosper also. The whole family have concerned themselves about this only for the good of Jihei and out of pity for the grandson and granddaughter. Come, Magoemon, let us return quickly, for I should like to relieve my husband's mind. It is becoming cold. Don't let the children catch cold. This has been because of the help of Buddha [during] the Ten Nights. Shortly, [I shall offer] prayers of thanks. Praise Amida Buddha, *and they leave for home. Her state of mind is [as blissful as] Buddha's.*

Jihei sees them to the door, and hardly have they crossed the threshold when Jihei throws himself down by the covered brazier and pulls the grill-striped [131] *quilt up over his head.*

Osan. So you still have not forgotten Sonezaki? *she says in disgust, and coming up to him, she pulls off the quilt. He is crying so [freely] that a waterfall of tears is pouring over his pillow, enough to float his body. She pulls him upright, leans him against the frame of the covered brazier, and peers searchingly into his face.* You are the limit, Jihei-dono. If you are so reluctant to part with her, it would have been better not to write the vow. Year before last, on the second day of the Boar [132] in the tenth month, at the covered-brazier warming ceremony, right here we placed our pillows side by side. Ever since then, for two years, I have been left alone in the nest, as if in this wife's bosom there dwells a demon or a serpent.[133] At long last, thanks to Mother and Brother, it seemed that we would have intimate, conjugal talks in bed, and I had no sooner begun to rejoice . . . You are cruel, you are heartless. If you regret it that much, go ahead and cry and cry. Your tears will flow down to the Shijimi River, and Koharu will probably scoop them up and drink them. Oh, you are unfeeling, you are hateful, *and embracing his knees, she throws herself down, pleading and lamenting.*

Jihei wipes his eyes:

Jihei. Tears of sorrow flow from the eyes, and therefore if tears of mortification would issue from, say, the ears, then you could tell my feelings without my telling you. But since all tears come from the eyes and are not of different colors, it is natural that you cannot perceive my feelings. I have no longing or anything else for that beast-woman with a human skin. But against that Independent Tahei I do have a grudge. He has plenty of money and has no wife and children. He has been making arrangements to redeem her, but until that time [when I left her] she would not submit to Tahei's wishes. She said to me time and again: "Don't be in the least anxious. Even if my relation with you is severed, and it comes about that we cannot live together, I shall not be redeemed by Tahei. If we are thwarted by his money, and my master delivers me [to him], I'll show them a magnificent suicide." But look at this. Before I've been out of the way ten days, she is to be redeemed by Tahei. For that rotten woman, that four-legged [beast], I have no love left at all. But that Tahei will be bragging. He will spread the word throughout Osaka that Jihei's business has reached an impasse and he is pinched for money. Those with whom I have dealings in all the wholesale houses will stare at my face, and I shall be disgraced. My breast will be rent, my body will burn. How regrettable, how mortifying! My tears are more than hot tears, blood tears, gummy tears. I pour out tears of molten iron, *and throwing himself down, he weeps.*

Osan suddenly looks troubled:

Osan. Oh, oh, if that is the situation, it is pitiable. Koharu will indeed die.

Jihei. There! However intelligent you may be, you're still a typical townsman's wife. Why would that unfaithful woman die? She cauterizes herself with moxa and takes medicine to preserve her health.

Osan. No, that's not right. I had thought that I certainly would not say this as long as I live, but, if I keep this hidden and nonchalantly let her die, it would be a dreadful crime. I shall reveal this matter so important to me. There is not even a speck of unfaithfulness in Koharu-dono. The relation between you two was severed by my manipulations. When I saw indications that you were drifting toward suicide, I was too sad and [wrote] a letter [to Koharu] pleading with her: "Between women there is a mutual sympathy. Do what must seem the impossible and sever [your relations with him]. I beg you for my husband's life." Moved by this she replied: "He is my precious man, worth more to me than my life itself, but being caught in an inescapable obligation, I shall give him up." I have kept this as [if it were] a charm, not to be separated from my body. Would a woman as virtuous as this break her pledge with you and shamelessly go with Tahei? All we women are constant and do not change our minds. She will surely kill herself. Oh, this is disastrous. Please save her, *she says agitatedly.*

The husband is also in consternation.

Jihei. Among the vows which I had her return was an unknown woman's letter, which went into my elder brother's hands. This then was the letter from you. If that's the case, Koharu will kill herself.

Osan. Oh, this is sad. If I let this woman die, I shall not be meeting my obligations to a fellow woman. Now go quickly, and please see that she doesn't kill herself, *and clinging to her husband, she sinks into weeping.*

Jihei. But how can this be done? We would have to advance half of the money just to save her life. Unless we can pour in 750 *me* of "New Silver," [134] we cannot keep Koharu in this world. At present even if I were pounded and crushed, how could I produce this sum of 3000 *me* in "Four [Treasure Silver]"? [135]

Osan. You exaggerate. If it can be settled for that, it will be very easy, *and rising, she opens a small drawer of the dresser and, without any reluctance, flings open a bag [held shut by] a mixture of entwined cords, and tosses out a packet. Jihei picks it up.*

Jihei. What, money? Four hundred *me* of "New Silver" at that! Where is this from? *and his eyes widen at [the sight of] this money which he had not put there.*

Osan. You'll know the source of this money when I tell you about it later.[136] This is the sum I prepared to settle the account [payable] the seventeenth of this month for the Iwakuni [137] paper. But that matter can be discussed with your elder brother. [We'll make arrangements with him so that] the weakness of our business will not be revealed.[138] The matter of Koharu is more urgent. Here we have four [hundred *me* in "New Silver" or] 1600 *me* in "Four [Treasure Silver]." [139] [We need] 1400 *me* more.

She opens the lock of a large drawer; like birds from the dresser fly [a garment of] (greyish-brown) Hachijō [silk] and [a garment] of capital crepe with a pale brown lining. [She] (*does not know that when today is gone*), *there will be no tomorrow in her husband's life.[140] Her daughter Osue's padded garment with its exterior and lining of red silk makes her being burn.[141] She adds a padded sleeveless coat of Kantarō's. When this is pawned [142] he will have no padded garment left and will be in difficult straits.[143] She also takes a garment of Gunnai [144] striped silk with a pale yellow lining which she* (*has been saving*), *and [her] one holiday garment of black habutai [145] bearing the family crest of an ivy leaf in a circle. In the inseparable relationship [146] [of man and wife] one can go naked at home, but outside [one must wear] fine clothes.[147] [However, Osan has to] take even her husband's padded garment, [which is so important] for appearances. This makes fifteen items.* Surely there will be no question about being advanced 350 *me* of "New Silver"[148] at the very least, *she says. With an expression of having even what* (*she does not have*)*, she wraps together into one bundle [149] her husband's shame and her obliga-*

tion and includes in it her devotion.[150] Even if I and the children have nothing to wear, what is important is my husband's [reputation in] society. Redeem Koharu and save her life, and please maintain your honor in front of this Tahei fellow, *she says, but the entire time Jihei's face remains cast down, and he is sobbing.*

Jihei. After we save her by making a deposit and [later complete] redeeming her, is she to be set up as my concubine, or is she to be brought into this house? What is to become of you? *These words bring Osan up short.*

Osan. Why, that's right. What shall I do? I can be a nurse for the children or a cook, or I can even go into retirement,[151] *she cries out, and sinks down, weeping.*

Jihei. The divine punishment [awaiting] me is too fearful. Even if I should escape punishment [for my offenses against my] parents, heaven, and the Buddhist and Shintō deities, just the punishment [for my offenses against my] wife alone means that my future will not be good. Forgive me, I beg you, *and with hands together in supplication he pleads and laments.*

Osan. That is too much. This is nothing to pray to me about. Even to having my fingernails and toenails pulled out,[152] it would all be [a wife's] service to her husband. To pay the bills at the paper wholesalers, I have been pawning my clothes for some time to tide us over.[153] My dresser is completely empty, but why should I regret that? Whatever one may say, if we are too late [in redeeming Koharu], it will be irreparable. Come, change your padded robe quickly and go off with a smile. *[He puts on] an undergarment of Gunnai [silk],*[154] *a [padded] garment of black habutai,*[155] *a striped coat, and a satin* [156] *sash, and he wears a medium-length sword* [157] *with gold ornamentation. Probably none but the Buddhas know that tonight [this sword] will be stained with Koharu's blood.*

Jihei. Sangorō, come here, and *[Jihei]* [158] *raises the bundle onto [Sangorō's] back and has him go along. [He] places the money safely next to his body, and they are about to step out the door, when:*

Gozaemon. Is Jihei at home? *and doffing his fur cap, in steps— good heavens!—it is his father-in-law, Gozaemon.*

Jihei and Osan. Well, well. This is opportune indeed. Welcome back,[159] *say the husband and wife in utter confusion.*

[Gozaemon] wrenches away from Sangorō the bundle he is bearing, sits down with a thud and says in a harsh voice:

Gozaemon. Woman, sit down! Mr. Son-in-law,[160] that is an extraordinary [costume]. You are gaily dressed indeed, [even to] a sword and coat. [This looks like] the free spending of a wondrously wealthy man. You don't look like a paper dealer. You're starting off for the [Sonezaki] Quarter? How much energy you expend! You don't need a wife at home. Why not divorce Osan? I have come to take her back, *and he says these rancorous words with a sour expression.*[161]

Jihei is unable to utter a word.

Osan. Father, how good of you to walk over on such a cold day as today. First, a cup of tea? *and using the teacup as her opportunity to come close to him, [she continues]:* About my husband's visits to the [Sonezaki] Quarter, Mother and Magoemon were just here, and after their thorough admonitions, he was in such a spirit of conversion that he shed hot tears and signed a vow. This was given to Mother. Haven't you seen it yet?

Gozaemon. Is this what you mean by a vow? *and he draws it from his breast.* Vows of a man who goes in for such foolish dissipation are dashed off and scattered here and there and everywhere like [a merchant's] bills. I thought it suspicious and I came over here, and it was just what I expected. With this costume on, [do you still swear by] Brahma and Indra? [162] In the time it took [to write] this, you can sign a divorce paper, *and tearing [the vow] to shreds, he throws it away.*

The startled couple exchange glances and are too astonished to speak. Jihei claps his hands [in supplication] and bows his head.

Jihei. You have good reason to be angry, and I beg your pardon for what has happened heretofore. From this present moment today I shall accept everything you do as benevolent. Please [only] allow me to remain with Osan. Even if I should become a beggar outcast [163] and have to sustain life on leavings from others' tables, I shall be certain to place Osan in the seat of honor, spare her sorrows, and subject her to no hardships. I have a great debt of gratitude [which obligates me] to remain with her. You will understand the circumstances of this when you see, as the days and months pass, my application [to business] and the recovery of my finances. Until then cover your eyes and please let me remain with Osan, *and with tears of blood falling rapidly, he presses against the floor mats, pleading forgiveness.*

Gozaemon. Even less will she be the wife of an outcast. Sign the divorce paper, sign the divorce paper. [We shall] verify the number of furnishings and clothes Osan brought with her [as dowry] and affix [your] seal, *and as he approaches [the dresser], Osan is flustered.*

Osan. The number of clothes is complete. It is not necessary to verify it, *and she rushes to block his way, but he thrusts her aside and draws open (a drawer).*

Gozaemon. Here, what's happened! *He pulls open another and it is empty. He opens them all, but there is not even a foot of cloth for patching.* [Learning that] *the wicker trunk, the long chest, and the clothes chest are all equally empty, the father-in-law's eyeballs are fixed in his rage. The couple now feel as mortified at the opening as had Urashima (when he opened)* [his box].[164] *They edge toward the covered brazier and quilt* [165] *and look as though they would even like to crawl into the fire.*

Gozaemon. I'm also concerned about this bundle, *and untying it, he pulls out and scatters the contents.* So that's it. So you were going to squander these also at a pawn shop? Yes, Jihei, you would peel the skin off your wife and children to acquire the means to chase a harlot.[166] You pickpocket! [167] My wife is an aunt to you, but to me, Gozaemon, you are completely unrelated. I have no such intimacy [with you] that I am willing to suffer losses [because of you]. I'll negotiate with Magoemon, and have him, your elder brother, repay me. Now, the divorce paper, the divorce paper.

Even if he could escape from the sevenfold doors, the eightfold chains, and the hundredfold enclosures,[168] *this is a pressing situation from which it is impossible to escape.*

Jihei. I shall not sign a divorce paper with a brush. See this; farewell Osan, *and he places his hand on his sword. Osan clings to him.*

Osan. This is so sad. Father, [Jihei] has done wrong, and he has apologized for it all. You are pressing your advantage too far. Jihei-dono indeed is not a relative of yours, but the children are your grandchildren, and have you no pity for them? I shall not accept a divorce paper, *and, embracing her husband, it is only natural that she raises her voice and wails.*

Gozaemon. All right, all right. You don't need a divorce paper. Come along, woman, *and he pulls her along.*

Osan. No, I shall not go. What hatred makes you sever our relation of enduring love and expose in broad daylight [169] the shame of a husband and wife? *she pleads in tears, but he pays no attention.*

Gozaemon. What further shame could you have? I'll shout it to the whole street as we go. *He pulls her along, she shakes herself free, but he catches her frail arm, and as she totters, with faltering feet, the tips of her toes pathetically strike against the two [sleeping] children. They open their eyes.*

Kantarō and Osue. Why are you taking our dear mother, you Grandpa? [170] Who will sleep with us from now on? *they yearn for her.*

Osan. Oh, how pathetic. Since you were born, you haven't spent a single night away from your mother's side. From tonight, sleep with your daddy. Don't forget that, before the two children have their snack before breakfast, you must be sure to give them their Kuwayama [pills].[171] Oh, this is sad, *she says as she leaves, and, abandoning [her husband] and abandoning her children, the couple [who were like a] two-forked bamboo in a grove* [172] *are parted forever.*

Act 3

The shoals of love and affection are here at the Shijimi River [Quarter].[173] *Its flowing waters make no sound, nor does the passing of people at three in the morning.*[174] *In the sky, the moon of the fifteenth night*[175] *is clear, while the lights have burned low in the gate lanterns, [one of which bears the name] "Yamatoya Dembei"*[176] *written with one [unbroken] stroke. The wooden clappers of the night patrolman*[177] *[beat] drowsily in time with his staggering walk.*[178] *"Be careful [of fire],*[179] *be careful [of fire]," and his voice also makes it [seem] late.*

Maid. Palanquin bearers, it has become very late, *says a maid from an upper street*[180] *to the palanquin [bearers] who have also come along to call for someone. She slides open the side door*[181] *of Yamatoya with a clatter and steps in.* I wish to "take"[182] Koharu-san of Kiinokuniya. I have come to accompany her. *Only these words can be faintly heard, and then three or four civilities, and in a moment she steps out of the side door.*

Koharu-sama is staying here overnight. Palanquin bearers, you should go straight to bed. Oh, I forgot to say something. Say, proprietress, please be careful of Koharu. [The arrangements for] redeeming her by Tahei-sama have been completed. The money has been received and so forth, [so she is now] on loan. Please do not let her have too much sake, *and from the doorway, sowing and scattering the seed which will make Jihei and Koharu dirt before day comes, she returns home.*[183]

Even the teakettle of a chaya rests for a two-hour period at night between two and four.[184] *The only thing moving is the flame of the short lamp*[185] *grown thin in the late night. The river wind [blows] coldly, and the frost grows thick.*

Proprietor. It is still the dead of night. I'll have someone accompany you home. Jihei-sama is leaving. Waken Koharu-sama. Here, call her, *the proprietor says. Jihei opens the side door with a clatter.*

Jihei. Here, here, Dembei. Not a word to Koharu. If she hears, I shall be detained until dawn. So I'll let her sleep well and slip out to return home. After the day dawns, waken her and send her back. After I get home, I must immediately go up to the capital to do some purchasing. As I have a great amount of business, it is not certain that I shall return in time for the "interim payment." [186] With the money I just [entrusted to you],[187] settle my account with you. [Pay] Kawa-shō 150 *me* of "Four Treasure Silver" for the Latter Moonviewing [party] [188] and please get a receipt. And the Saietsu priest [189] of Fukushima [190] has bought a Buddhist altar. Please give him a contribution of one silver coin [191] and have him say memorial masses [for my family].[192] Isn't there some other [expense] in which I am involved? Oh, that's it, that's it! A tip for Isoichi [193] of five silver pieces.[194] That's all. Close up and go to sleep. Goodbye, goodbye, I'll see you when I return, *and he takes two or three steps and comes back quickly.* I forgot my sword. Hurry, hurry. Eh, Dembei, townsmen are easygoing about this. A samurai would probably commit harakiri on the spot, wouldn't he? [195]

Proprietor. I had completely forgotten that I was keeping it for you.[196] And it is equipped with a knife.[197] *He hands it [to Jihei, who] takes it and slips it securely [in his sash].*

Jihei. When I just have this, I have the strength of a thousand men.[198] Sleep well, *and he leaves.*

Proprietor. Come down [from the capital] soon. It was good to have you come, *and he promptly [fastens] the cross bar with a bang, and it becomes so quiet that there is not a sound.*

Jihei looks as though he is going straight home, but he turns back again with stealthy steps. He clings to the door of Yamatoya, and is peering in when the forms of people close at hand startle him. He conceals himself in the shadow of the building across the street to wait until they have passed.

Koya Magoemon appears first, greatly worried about his younger brother, and after him the apprentice Sangorō, bearing on his back (the nephew) Kantarō. They come running up with the lantern as their objective, and pound on the door of Yamatoya.

Magoemon. I should like to make an inquiry. Isn't Kamiya Jihei here? Would you please let me see him a moment? *he calls. Jihei, [realizing that] this is his elder brother, does not move his body and conceals himself the more. From within comes a man's drowsy voice:*

Proprietor. Jihei-sama left for home just a short while ago, saying that he was going up to the capital. He is not here, *and once again there is no sound. Magoemon's tears fall freely [as he says to himself]:*

Magoemon. If he left for home, it seems to me we should have met him on the way. It doesn't sound plausible that he is going to the capital. My body is trembling from anxiety. [I wonder] if he didn't take Koharu with him. *[The thought] pierces his breast, and his anxiety is unbearable. Again he pounds on the door.*

Proprietor. Who is that so late at night? We've gone to bed.

Magoemon. This is an imposition, but I should like to make another inquiry. Has Koharu-dono of Kiinokuniya left? Didn't she perhaps go with Jihei?

Proprietor. Say, what are you talking about? Koharu-dono *is* asleep on the second floor.

Magoemon. Ah, I am relieved. He is not planning a love suicide. Where is he concealing himself [199] while he causes us this worry? He surely does not know that the entire family, parents and brothers, are intensely anxious and sick from worry. We are afraid that in his resentment against his father-in-law he may forget himself and even commit suicide. We have come looking for him, bringing along Kantarō to give him cause for reconsideration, but that was needless. What does it mean that we haven't met him by this time? *he says to himself through his tears. When Jihei, who is hiding not far from him, hears this, he has to hold his breath and swallow his tears.*

Magoemon. Sangorō, don't you know any other places the fool goes at night? *says [Magoemon], but Sangorō taking himself to be the fool [referred to], says:*

Sangorō. Yes, I do know [a place], but I am too embarrassed to tell you here.

Magoemon. If you know, tell me where it is.

Sangorō. After you hear, don't scold me. The place [I] go every night on the sly is below the storage sheds [200] at Ichi-no-kawa.[201]

Magoemon. You big fool, who would inquire into that? Come, let us look for him on the back street.[202] Don't let Kantarō catch cold. He has a good-for-nothing father—oh, the pity of it—and he is subjected to this cold. It would be all right if this cold were all there is to it, but what if by some chance he is caused to suffer grief? How detestable! *But these inmost thoughts have behind them pity [for Jihei].*

Come, let us go and look on the (back) street, *and they go by.*
When their forms have moved away, [Jihei] *runs out, and on
tiptoe looks longingly after them.*[203] *He says in his heart:*

Jihei. Jihei, you greatest of sinners. [204] Even if you die, they cannot abandon and forget you. You will continue and continue to
be trouble for them. You are unworthy of this, *and, placing his
hands together, he kneels in supplication.* In addition to this kindness, [would you look after] the children? *and saying only this, he
remains for a time choked with tears.*

In any case, since we have made our resolution [of suicide],
Koharu is probably waiting. *As he peers through a crack in the
side door of Yamatoya* [he sees] *the figure of a person flitting
within.* Isn't that Koharu? [he says to himself]. *To inform her that
he is waiting, he gives the signal—a cough—ehen, ehen. But there
is mingled with the cough the "katchi, katchi" of the wooden clappers of the night patrolman who comes from an upper street* [205]
coughing (over) *and over with a cold on this* (windy) *night, and
coughing and coughing as* (he hurries) *on his rounds to caution
against fire.*[206] *"Be careful* [of fire], *be careful* [of fire], *be careful*
[of fire]," *and* [Jihei], *who is avoiding people, for it would be trying* [to be discovered], *hides himself like the god of Kazuraki,*[207]
and lets [the night patrolman] *pass.*

*Then when Jihei comes again to watch through the crack, the
side door is opened slightly from within.*

Jihei. Is that Koharu?

Koharu. Are you waiting? Jihei, I want to go out quickly, *she
says impatiently, but the quicker* [the door] *is opened, the more
people will hear the wheels of the door. If it is lifted when opened,
it will sound only of the lifting. It thunders in their ears and
through their breasts. Jihei lends a hand from the outside. Their
hearts flutter and their fingers tremble. Three tenths* [of an inch],
*four tenths, five tenths, one inch. More than the suffering of hell
but* (one inch) *ahead,*[208] [they fear detection, but] *before the demon appears,*[209] *they finally open it. As joyous as on* (the dawning
of) *New Year's morn, Koharu slips out. They take each other's
hands. Should they go north? Should they go south? West, or east,*
[they know not] *their destination/* (destiny) . *The swift rapids in
their hearts subside, and* [turning] *their feet against the declining
moon* (flowing) *on the* (Shijimi) *River,*[210] *they hasten along.*

Farewell Memories Along All the Bridges [211]

*As a rule the (running) writing [212] of nō texts is in the Konoe style,[213] the caps of boy actors are pale purple,[214] and the fate of a man who is infatuated with the evil quarter ends like this. Is this also in the teachings of Buddha? [215] [They] would like to see today the karma of [their] wretched lives [according to] the (Karma) (Sūtra).[216] Tomorrow in popular gossip his reputation as a lover will be strewn about, and [it will be known] that Kamiya Jihei [committed a] love suicide. The fullest particulars will be carved on [blocks of] cherry wood, and appear on the blockprint paper of an illustrated leaflet.[217] The god of death (if there is one among the gods,) entices him along, and he resigns himself to this retribution for neglecting his business; and yet it is natural that he should feel some reluctance as he walks along in torment. Now even by the [full] moon of the fifteenth night of the tenth month, he cannot discern his future. Isn't this a sign that his heart is in the darkness [of worldly desire]? The frost which is forming now will vanish tomorrow. It is a metaphor for transiency, and yet sooner than that [their lives] will fade away. In the bedroom they had slept, bound together [thinking] how sad, how pitiable [is their fate], and what is to become of the fragrance they were exchanging. (The flowing) Shijimi River he sees toward the west morning and evening when he crosses this bridge called Tenjin Bridge.[218] Long ago when [the deity] (Tenjin) was known as Sugawara no Michizane,[219] on his way to exile at Tsukushi, [220] [he stopped here]. One hears to this day the story of his plum tree * which longed for his master, and in only one leap (flew) to Dazaifu.[222] [He was also] followed by his (old) pine tree.[223] † His cherry tree ‡ lamented, and sorrowing over the separation, withered away. [Such is] the efficacy of single poems.*

Jihei. Although I am born a parishioner of such an exalted deified man [i.e., Michizane], I shall kill you and die myself. This is because I do not have enough discretion to fill one of those tiny shells of the Shijimi [River].[226] The (Shijimi) Bridge [227] is short.[228] Things that (are short) are our stay in this life and an autumn day. (We are tired of living.) [Although] we are [only] nineteen and twenty-eight,[229] this very night is the end, the moment to throw away our two lives. We vowed to live devotedly to-

* (Plum) -field Bridge.[221]   † (Green) Bridge.[224]   ‡ (Cherry) Bridge.[225]

gether until our end as an aged man and woman, but before we have had three full years of intimacy, we have met * with calamity. Look there. [We have come] past the Naniwa Small Bridge ²³¹ to the bank by Funairi Bridge.²³² We've come this far, and the farther we go the closer we get to the road to Hades, *he laments, and she clings to him.*

Koharu. Is this road already Hades? *and they look at each other, but their tears are falling so [fast] that they can hardly see each other's faces, and they seem to flood the bridges over the Horikawa.*²³³

*Jihei.*²³⁴ If I should walk toward the north, I could have another glimpse of my home, but I do not look that way. I suppress in my breast [thoughts of] my children's futures and my wife's pitiable lot. Toward the south stretches the bridge ²³⁵ (which we cross) with its innumerable piles. [The other shore has] (innumerable) houses, so why should it be named "Eight Houses"? ²³⁶ We must hurry along the road before the boat from Fushimi lands there.²³⁷ [I wonder] who are (sleeping) together on it. To us, who are abandoning this world, it is frightening even to hear of the demon.† The two rivers, the Yodo and the Yamato, flow into one stream, the Ōkawa.²³⁹ The water and fish go along together [inseparably], [just as] the two, Koharu and I, go together, [and cross] the River Styx by the blade of one sword.²⁴⁰ I should like to receive [this river water] as an offering of water [from the living].²⁴¹

Koharu. What is there to lament? Although indeed we cannot go together through this life, in the future one, needless to say, and in the next and next, and through all future worlds we shall be man and wife. As a request [that we be reborn on] one lotus [calyx],²⁴² I have performed the "summer writing" ²⁴³ of one copy each summer ²⁴⁴ of the most merciful, most compassionate *Fumombon* of the *Lotus Sūtra.*²⁴⁵ When we cross (Kyō) Bridge,²⁴⁶ we reach the other bank (Nirvana).²⁴⁷ We will mount the lotus calyx, (attain the Law),²⁴⁸ and achieve‡ the form of Buddha. If I may save mankind as I wish, I should like to protect prostitutes so that hereafter they will never commit love suicides. *This unattainable wish is a worldly complaint. It makes us sympathize with her and pity her. In the inlet toward Noda,*²⁵⁰ *the mist rises from the water, and [beyond one sees], faint and white, the edge of the hills.*

---

* (Ōe) Bridge.²³⁰   † (Temma) Bridge.²³⁸   ‡ (Onari) Bridge.²⁴⁹

Jihei. There, the bells of the temples are resounding. We cannot remain like this.[251] We cannot live out our lives, so let us hurry our end. Come this way, *and holding in their hands the rosaries of 108 beads* [252] *which become intermingled with beads of tears as they tell them* [253] *and with "Praise Ami[da Buddha]" [on their lips], [they reach] (Ami)jima.*[254] *On the outer side of the grove at Daichō Temple,*[255] *above the overflowing sluice gate of a small stream, they arrive at their place of death.*

Jihei. No matter how long we wander on, there will never be a place which [we will feel] is definitely *the* place for us to die. Come, this will be our death place, *and, taking her hand, he sits on the ground.*

Koharu. Yes; but while you may say that it does not matter where we die, I have been thinking along the way that if it is reported that Koharu and Kamiya Jihei committed a love suicide and our two dead faces were side by side, I shall be making wastepaper of my letter in which I vowed, when Osan-sama begged me not to let you die, that I certainly would not, and that I would cut off my relations with you. If I entice her beloved husband to a love suicide, she will consider me a typically deceitful prostitute, a treacherous person who has no sense of obligation. I should certainly rather have a thousand, a myriad people [think this], than to have the contempt and hatred of Osan alone. That she will surely resent me and hate me is the only concern I have about [entering] the future life. Kill me here, and you choose a place for yourself somewhere else, (a little) to one side, *she asks, leaning against him, and he too entreats, weeping:*

Jihei. You keep [worrying] about unreasonable things. Osan was taken back by my father-in-law. Since he has brought about the divorce, she is no relation of mine. What obligation do you have to my divorced wife? As [you] said on our way here, the two of us have vowed to be husband and wife in the next and next and through all future worlds, and so who would criticize us, who would despise us for dying side by side?

Koharu. Well, whose work was that divorce? It is you rather than I who are the more unreasonable. Do our bodies accompany us to that world? Even if we die in different places and these bodies are pecked at by kites and crows, I ask only that our two souls be bound together and go together to hell or to Paradise, *and again she sinks into weeping.*

Jihei. That's right, that's right. These bodies are of earth, water, fire, and wind,[256] and when we die they revert to the void. [Our souls] will not decay through future rebirths, (through five reincarnations), through seven reincarnations. Let us show that the souls of this husband and wife shall not be separated. I agree [with you]. *He draws his sword with a flourish and cuts his own black hair off cleanly along the edge of the topknot cord.* See this, Koharu. While I had this hair, I was Kamiya Jihei, husband of Osan. When I cut my hair, I became a monk. I have left the turbulent world,[257] and I am now a Buddhist monk unencumbered by wife and children and by valuables.[258] Since I do not have a wife, Osan, you have no obligations to uphold toward her, *and, weeping, he throws aside [his hair].*

Koharu. Ah, I am happy, *and Koharu also raises the sword.* [*Her hair, which*] *she has so often washed and combed and smoothed down,* [*now dressed*] *in the hanging Shimada [style],*[259] *(without) any regret she cruelly cuts off and casts away. How tragic it is to see it scatter and tangle in the pampas grass on the withered moor, covered with midnight frost.*

Jihei. As a nun and monk who have escaped this transient world/ (miserable life), our obligations [to each other] as man and wife [to die side by side] are of our secular past. It would be better to have completely differing places of death, such as a mountain and a river. [This spot] above this sluice gate we shall liken to a mountain and it will be your death place. I shall hang myself in this stream. Although our deaths will be at the same time, we shall have differing methods and places of suicide and shall be upholding the obligations toward Osan. Hand me your lower sash,[260] *and* [*he takes this sash*] *of pale purple silk crepe,* [*which was long enough to go*] *twice around her. (The pale purple)* [*suggests her*] *(youthful beauty) and fragrance, which is (to be scattered) in this wind of transiency, and which* [*now touches*] *(both) this world and the next. He ties* [*the lower sash*] *securely to the top beam of the sluice gate, and the other end he knots into a noose which will strangle him, as on the hunting ground a pheasant (is snared) because of his mate.*[261]

[*As Koharu*] *watches him make the preparations for his own death, her eyes grow dizzy, her heart anguished.*

Koharu. Is that how you are going to die! Since you are going to die at a place apart, you will be by my side only a short time. Come here, come here, *and they take each other's hands.* [I shall] die by the sword in an instant, but I believe you are certain to suffer.[262]

It is pitiable, it is pitiable, *and she is unable to stop her quiet sobbing.*

Jihei. In dying there is no difference between strangling and being stabbed through the throat. Don't disturb your last thoughts by distracting your mind with such trivial things. Worship the moon which moves ever toward the west as [if it were] Amida, and do not take your eyes from it. Do not forget the Western [Paradise].²⁶³ If you have anything on your mind, state it and then die.

Koharu. I have nothing at all, I have nothing at all. But you are probably concerned about your two children.

Jihei. There, you've spoken of something unfortunate, and will cause me to weep again. Although their father is to die now, they are sleeping peacefully in their innocence. I see their darling [sleeping] faces, and this is the only thing I cannot get out of my mind, *and slumping forward, he sinks into weeping.*

Competing with his voice is the cawing of flocks of crows leaving their roosts. [It is as though] they are mourning this tragedy,²⁶⁴ and their tears flow the faster.

Jihei. There, listen to that. Those crows are welcoming the two of us to Hades. It has been said since ancient times that every time a vow is written on the back of a [Kumano] charm, three of the Kumano crows die at the mountain [shrines].²⁶⁵ You and I have signed vows as our first-writing at the beginning of the new year,²⁶⁶ and have written vows at the beginning of every month. Killing three crows each time, how many we must [have felled]! Usually it sounds as though they cry: "Pitiful, pitiful," ²⁶⁷ but to my ears tonight it sounds as though, resenting those crimes of destroying life, [they cry] "Retribution, retribution." ²⁶⁸ Who is to blame for this retribution? It is because of me that you will suffer a cruel suicide. Please forgive me, *and he embraces her and draws her close.*

Koharu. No, it is my fault, *and they hold each other close, their faces pressed together. The side locks of their hair, drenched with tears, freeze in the stormy wind off the moor.*

Behind them resounds the [dawn] bell of Daichō Temple.

Jihei[?]. Good heavens! This has been a long [winter] night, and yet it has been a short night for our life as man and wife, [*he laments*] *as the dawn breaks early at the "morning period."* ²⁶⁹ (*Bravely*) [*he says*]:

Jihei. This is our last moment, *and he draws her close.* Don't let the face you leave behind in death be tearful.

Koharu. I won't, *and she smiles. As Jihei sees her (smiling) face shimmering whitely, benumbed by frost, his hands quiver. It is Jihei who first grows dizzy. Through his tears he can(not) see where to plunge his sword. [He exhorts himself:]*

Jihei. Don't be jittery, don't be jittery.

Koharu. Hurry! hurry! *and it is the woman who has the strength to spur him on. The prayer which the wind carries to them [seems] a "Praise Amida Buddha" offered to them.*[270] *[As if his] were the sharp sword of Amida,*[271] *he plunges it into her. He tries to pull her forward, but she bends backwards, writhing and twisting. How can this be, when the sword point has severed her windpipe? She may not die until she has suffered in retribution at her moment of death. Jihei is also in agony. He rallies his tormented spirit, and pulling her forward, plunges the whole sword into her up to the guard. He twists it and in agony [her life] fades away like an unfinished dream at dawn. He arranges her corpse, her head toward the north, her face toward the west, lying on her right side,*[272] *and covers her with [his] coat.*[273] *Unable to cry himself out at this sad farewell, he turns away.*

He draws toward himself her lower sash and slips the noose around his neck. The voices at the Temple [chanting] the prayers [have reached] the closing sentence of the mass for the dead: "Believers, unbelievers, and all the universe [will receive divine favor]." [274] *With that as his last moment, from above the sluice gate [he cries]:*

Jihei. Rebirth on the same lotus calyx. Praise Amida Buddha, *and leaps off. For a time he is in agony, like a gourd tossing in the wind. Gradually his passage of breath is choked off, and, at the dammed-up opening in the sluice gate, his breath (is stopped up), and his connection with this world is cut.*

Fishermen out in the morning discover them in the meshes of their nets.[275]

Fishermen. Suicides! here are suicides! Come here, come here, *they call, and it spreads from mouth to mouth until the story soon becomes [a play], the Amijima Love Suicide, [and they probably] (directly attain) Buddhahood and deliverance [from reincarnation], [in accordance with] the vow of [the Buddha's] net. In the eyes of all [who see it] there are tears.*[276]

Notes to the Translation

Notes to the
Translation

1. In the title the word *shinjū* is introduced as it is in all of Chikamatsu's love-suicide plays in which the lovers carry through their suicides. *Ten no ami*, "heaven's net," contains a Taoist and a Buddhist allusion, which are discussed in the Introduction, p. 41. *Ami* is also part of the place name, Amijima. The word *ami* carries an additional overtone, when in the final line of the play the audience is told that the bodies of the dead lovers are discovered by fishermen in their nets (*ami*).

As in the case of certain other plays, there is a fuller title in which are prefixed the names of the principal characters. The original edition of this play was known as *Kamiya Jihei Kiinokuniya Koharu Shinjū Ten no Amijima*. The name of the *okiya*, Kiinokuniya, to which Koharu was indentured, was derived from the name of Kii Province (Kiinokuni). The alternate reading, Kinokuniya, also appears several times in the play.

2. These opening lines of jargon set a lively mood, as the play begins in the Sonezaki Gay Quarter. Several theories have been advanced concerning what meaning might be contained in this passage. Fujii (*Chikamatsu zenshū* 12.273) selected certain initial syllables which he pieced together to form what sounds like a few lines from a popular song. Ueda and Higuchi (*Chikamatsu goi*, p. 512ab) found in it words which they suggested were drawn from the *Lotus Sūtra*. Tanaka Minoru wrote an article in which he attempted to reconstruct from it a Tibetan song, "Shinjū Ten no Amijima bōtō no kayō ni tsuite," "On the song in the opening lines of *Shinjū Ten no Amijima*" in *Kokugakuin zasshi* 36 (October, 1930), pp. 76–86.

3. The Shijimi River at this time flowed between the Sonezaki Quarter on the north and the Dōjima Quarter on the south. The gay quarter meant here is Sonezaki, which was laid out in 1708; by the date of this play, Dōjima had already lost its character as a quarter for prostitutes. (See Introduction, p. 22, and map, p. 2.)

4. This figure of speech contains the idea basic to the entire play, that love is an emotion which cannot be measured or controlled. The text reads: (*Kore ka ya koi no*) *daikai o kae mo hosarenu Shijimi-gawa*. This involves a play on the word *shijimi*, "corbicula," and combines two popular sayings: *daikai o kaigara de kaehosu yo*, "like ladling dry the ocean with a shell," and *shijimi-gai de umi o sukuu/hakaru*, "to ladle/measure the sea with a corbicula." These sayings are probably derived from a passage in the *Han Shu, Tung-fang So chuan* (*Wu-chou t'ung-wên shu-chü* ed., Shanghai, 1894) 65 (*ts'ê* 48). 1927, reading *i li ts'ê hai*, lit., "to measure out the sea with a gourd ladle." *Li* is generally glossed as "gourd ladle," but a second tradition

exists, in Japan as well as in China, that here it is read *lo* (J. *rei*) "scallop shell," and it is probably from this interpretation that the Japanese sayings are drawn. As a possible source for Chikamatsu, I would suggest the *yōkyoku Kiso* (*Yōkyoku taikan* 2.821–822), where there appears the phrase, *rei o motte kyokai o hakari*, lit., "measuring out the vast sea with a scallop shell/gourd ladle," followed immediately by another saying contained in *Amijima*, discussed in note 48.

5. *Moji ga seki*, lit., "a barrier of characters." The word *seki*, 關, "barrier" is introduced into the text merely to form a play on words with *moji*, 文字, "characters," the latter being a homonym with the name of the city, Moji 門司. Through association, *seki* would stand for Shimonoseki 下關, which faces Moji across the channel between Honshu and Kyushu. Of course the names of the cities have no meaning in this context.

6. *Naya hauta*. *Naya*, "sheds, warehouses," in Osaka referred particularly to *hama-naya*, the commercial warehouses along the river banks, called *hama* (lit., "beach") in Osaka. The word *naya* was borrowed to refer to the annexes at the rear of *chaya* and facing on the river bank. *Hauta*, a term used in contrast to *nagauta*, were popular songs, largely concerned with the gay quarter. These songs, often quoted by Chikamatsu, were contained in anthologies of the period, such as *Matsu no ha*, *kan* 3 (1703, 5 *kan*, in *Shin gunsho ruijū* 6.62–87, in *Kokusho kankōkai* Series 1, 1907), compiled by an author known only by his pen name, Shūshōken; and *Wakamidori*, *kan* 3–4 (*ca.* 1706, 5 *kan*, *ibid.* 6.131–153), compiled by Seiunkaku-shujin (pen name).

7. *Mombi*, probably from *monohi*, were festival days in the gay quarter when the guests were obliged to pay high rates and give special tips. The date of the action in Act 1, the 6th day of the 10th month, is listed as a *mombi* by two guidebooks to the Shimmachi Quarter in Osaka (*Ōsaka Shimmachi saiken no zu*) *Miotsukushi* (publ. 1783 and 1798, 1 *kan*, in *Kinsei bungei sōsho* 10.458, in *Kokusho kankōkai*, Series 2, 1911–1912), and (*Uso to makoto*) *Sato namari, kan* 2, 1794, 3 *kan, ibid.* 10.477–483). In addition to the regular festival days, many special *mombi* were designated for certain gay quarters and even for individual establishments by the shrewd proprietors. *Chikamatsu goi*, p. 353, quotes a standard list of Osaka *mombi* from an *ukiyo-zōshi* by Nishizawa Ippū (1665–1731) entitled *Chakei hizorigao* (1708, 3 *kan*; I have not seen this work), which lists 33 *mombi* augmented by the cyclical days *kōshin*, which would add a maximum of 6 *mombi*. In some of the gay quarters, however, there were many more, for *Miotsukushi* lists about 140 for Shimmachi, *Sato namari* lists over 200 for the same quarter, and there are 120 listed for the Shimabara Quarter in Kyoto by an historical account of that district, entitled *Hitome sengen* (1801, 1 *kan*, *Kinsei bungei sōsho* 10.404–405). The fact that this was not a late development can be seen from a comic, exaggerated account quoted below from an anonymous *ukiyo-zōshi*, entitled *Kōshoku mankintan*, *kan* 1, pt. 3 (1694, 5 *kan*, *Ukiyo-zōshi shū* 9.14–15, in *Nihon meichō zenshū*, 1928): "*Mombi* which are set and on which [the prostitutes] must work, unlike the situation in other provinces, are very numerous in Naniwa (Osaka). If one were to spread out the calendar and place a *go*-stone on each *mombi* from New Year's day to the last day of the year, out of 360 stones there would be only 25 remaining. . . *Mombi* are set and the prostitutes are importuned to work until they send a petition to the group of five town elders (*gonin-gumi*)." Moreover, in the *Shikidō ōkagami*, by Hatakeyama Kizan (1628–1704), *kan* 1 (in *Zoku enseki jisshu* 2.415, in *Kokusho kankōkai*, Series 1), *mombi* are defined as "the days of work for prostitutes in each month." The last two quotations might be interpreted either as satire, or as meaning that *mombi* were increased so recklessly in certain quarters that they became synonymous with days of business.

8. *Nakai*, "maid." The maids welcomed and sometimes solicited the visitors, were attendants to the prostitutes, and served as waitresses, but they were not prostitutes. Here, the man is not her lover, but the lover of one of the prostitutes of her house.

9. The words and actions are a parody on a passage in the *yōkyoku Kagekiyo* describing the personal combat at the battle of Yashima (1185) between Taira no (Akushichibyōe) Kagekiyo and the Genji warrior Mionoya Jūrō. This martial recitation in the *nō* style is a sudden change of tempo and intonation from the preceding part. The play opened with lively *jōruri* rhythm, which was followed by the poetic cadence of the narrative in alternating phrases of seven and five syllables, ending with "Kiyo, the maid, recognizes him." The following *yōkyoku* passage is quoted with only several minor changes which make clever plays on words. The passage in *Kagekiyo* reads: *Mionoya ga kitarikeru kabuto no shikoro torihazushi torihazushi, ni san do nigenobitaredomo, omou kataki nareba nogasaji to tobikakari* . . . "[Kagekiyo] clutches again and again at the neck-flap of the helmet which Mionoya is wearing, and although he slips away from him two or three times, he is determined not to let this chosen adversary escape, and throwing himself upon him. . ." Chikamatsu changes the opening phrases to read: *Mi o nogare ga kitarikeru[.] zukin no shikoro. . .* "One who is trying to evade her has come. (She clutches again and again at) the neck-flap of his cap. . ." *Omou kataki,* "chosen adversary," is changed to read *omou oteki,* "expected lover." *Kataki* and *teki,* written with the same character, are cognate words, both meaning "enemy, adversary; match, mate." *Oteki* (also *teki* and *teki-sama*) has a special usage in gay society as the word a prostitute and her lover use in referring to each other. (See *Shikidō ōkagami, kan* 1, *Zoku enseki jisshu* 2.413.) For the passage in *Kagekiyo,* see *Yōkyoku taikan* 1.645–646. A freer translation of this passage appears on pp. 132–133 of Arthur Waley, *The Nō Plays of Japan* (London, 1921), p. 319.

10. This action clears the stage for the appearance of the heroine.

11. *Ume sakura,* "plum [and] cherry," refer to the bridges Umeda-bashi and Sakura-bashi which span the Shijimi River (see map).

12. *Hana,* "flower," is a play on words, and here means "beautiful woman," as in the phrase *kaigo no hana,* lit., "flower which understands words."

13. *Yukata* is an unlined cotton garment for summer undress, which is also used as a bathrobe. It is used here figuratively for a "bath girl" (*yuna*) of a "bathhouse" (*furoya*). These girls were employed originally to scrub the patrons' backs and wash their hair, but in time their function as prostitutes became institutionalized. Despite the attempts after 1651 of the Tokugawa Shogunate to suppress them, the nominal "bathhouses" continued to flourish, and some offered all the diversions of a *chaya,* including drink, song, music, and dancing, as illustrated in Niimi Masatomo (1651–1742), *Yaso no okina mukashi banashi* (*ca.* 1731, 1 *kan,* publ. 1837, in *Nihon zuihitsu taisei,* Series 2, 1928, 2.590–591). For an illustration of a *yukata*-clad bath girl scrubbing a patron, see Kitagawa Morisada, (*Ruijū*) *Kinsei fūzoku shi,* pt. 2, p. 44, (original title, *Morisada mankō,* compiled 1837–1853, publ. 1908 and 1913, modern ed., 33 secs., 2 pts. pp. 586 + 621).

14. Minami, "South," refers to a specific part of Osaka, the Shimanouchi Gay Quarter, as opposed to the North district (Kita no shinchi), which by this time meant only the Sonezaki Quarter. Hamamatsu Utakuni (1776–1827), *Setsuyō kikan, kan* 5 (posthumously completed in 1833, 60 *kan,* in *Naniwa sōsho,* 16 vols., 1926–1930, 1.254), explains this usage. Under the heading "Other names for the Shimanouchi Gay Quarter" he writes: "When one says merely 'South,' for this to refer only to Shimanouchi, is, to take some respectable analogies, like saying 'the Mountain' to mean Hieizan, 'the Temple' to mean Miidera, or 'the Festival' to mean the Kamo [Shrine]'s Aoimatsuri, and this is because [Shimanouchi] is the premier gay quarter of south [Osaka]."

15. Koharu, the professional name of the heroine, is a poetic name for the 10th month, and literally means "small spring," that is, Indian summer.

16. The audience sees the action which the reader can only guess at. Koharu, accompanied by a maid, appears on her way from Kiinokuniya, the *okiya* to which

she is indentured, to a *chaya*, to which she has been summoned at the request of a visitor.

17. The first part of the sentence is contracted by the use of double meanings, and it contains an allusion to a classical poem:

Koyoi wa tareka	Tonight who
yobu-kodori	calls/cuckoo
obotsukanaku mo	faintly
ando no kage. . .	lantern's light. . .

Obotsukanaku, "faintly," refers both to "calls" and to "lantern's light," and the word is also associated with "cuckoo." *Yobu* is used to mean "call" and is extended into *yobu-kodori,* "cuckoo," which has no meaning in the sentence, except that it is followed by *obotsukanaku mo,* which is intended to recall to the listener the juxtaposition of these two words in poem 29 (*kan* 1) of the first Imperial anthology of poetry, the *Kokinshū* (905, 20 *kan*):

Ochikochi no	Deep in the mountains
tazuki mo shiranu	where I have lost my bearings
yama naka ni	
Obotsukanaku mo	A cuckoo calls
yobu-kodori kana	faintly.

Chikamatsu's immediate source for this association of words was probably a contemporary one, however, for there is a cleverer application of this allusion in Ibara Saikaku (1642–1693), *Kōshoku ichidai onna, kan* 5, pt. 2 (1686, 6 *kan,* in *Kindai Nihon bungaku taikei,* 1928, 24 vols., 3.301): *Ichiya o gin rokumomme nite yobukodori, kore denju-onna nari. Obotsukanakute tazunekuru ni, furoya-mono o saru to iu narubeshi.* "Those who are called for six *momme* of silver a night are called *yobukodori*(?) ; these are *denju-onna.* If this is *not clear,* and you ask for an explanation, you will be told it is like calling a bath girl a monkey." Considerable explanation is necessary to unravel Saikaku's joke. *Yobukodori,* traditionally glossed as "cuckoo," is one of the "three birds of the secret tradition (of the *Kokinshū*) (*Kokin*) *denju sanchō,* which was transmitted orally from master to pupil. Here Saikaku, after introducing *yobukodori* in reference to a prostitute, says that she is a *denju-onna,* "a woman who has a secret tradition," "a woman who is an initiate." He says this is analogous to calling a bath girl a monkey (*saru*), which was a common synonym in this period, derived from the girls' initial function of scrubbing the patrons' backs.

18. Kamiji, a contraction of the name Kamiya Jihei, Koharu's lover and the hero of the play. It is bad for business for a prostitute to fall in love, and Koharu's proprietor is attempting to prevent Jihei from summoning her to a *chaya.*

19. Tahei, the rival suitor from the town of Itami, in Settsu Province, which consisted of parts of the present Osaka and Hyogo Prefectures. He wishes to buy Koharu out to be his concubine or wife.

20. *Itami iru wai na,* a pun on the place name, Itami.

21. *Itoshibonage* is an instance of metathesis of *itōshinage,* but is based on a transposition of its *kana* spelling (*itohoshinage*) rather than of its modern pronunciation. Metathesis appears frequently in Chikamatsu in cognate words, as *itoshiboi* for *itōshii* and *itoshiboge* for *itōshige.* There are other examples in Chikamatsu, such as *kien* for *engi* and *gurihama* for *hamaguri.*

22. Kawashō is the contraction of the name of the proprietor of the *chaya* called Kawachiya. His personal name would begin with Shō-, and might be Shōhei or Shōzaemon, etc.

23. *Namaida bōzu,* a begging street entertainer, who impersonates a monk and, to the accompaniment of a bell, recites selections from *jōruri* and popular songs, burlesqued with an admixture of the flavor of Buddhist invocations (*nembutsu*). *Namaida* is a popular contraction of *namu Amida[Butsu],* "Praise Amida[Bud-

dha]," as explained by Motoori Norinaga (1730–1801) : *"Namu Amida butsu* is popularly pronounced *nammamida butsu,* and when this is said rapidly in reciting *nembutsu* in unison, it is pronounced *namaida."* See *Kakaika, kan* 2 (1787–1790, 2 *kan, Ueda Akinari zenshū* 1.443, *Kokusho kankōkai,* Series 6, 1923) , a compilation of discussions between Motoori Norinaga and Ueda Akinari (1734–1809), in the section dealing with phonetic change of the syllable *mu* into *n, bu,* etc.

24. *Tengō nembutsu. Tengō* is defined as meaning "joke" in Edo in an anonymous wordbook of the Osaka dialect, *Naniwa kikigaki* (or *Naniwa hōgen*), p. 19 (1819, in *Katakoto, Butsurui shōko, Naniwa kikigaki, Tamba tsūji* in *Nihon koten zenshū,* Series 4, 1931) .

25. *Nonko,* abbreviation of *nonko-mage,* a specific style of coiffure, the sides narrow and flat, and the knot high.

26. *Hōroku zukin,* "parching-pan cap," a round, flat cap, resembling a large beret, originally worn by monks, physicians, and old men but by the Genroku period also popular among younger men. See *Wakan sansai zue* by Terajima Ryōan, *kan* 29 (1712, 105 *kan,* 2 vols., *Nihon zuihitsu taisei,* 1929, 1.376) . It is probably introduced here because a *hōroku zukin* was worn by Wankyū (cf. note 31) .

27. *Gongon hodeten hodetengo nembutsu.* Three elements are woven into this phrase: (1) the sound of the bell, *ten-ten gon-gon,* (2) *tengō nembutsu* (see note 24) , and (3) *hodetengō,* "mischief, waggishness," a Kyoto word, as defined in the leading colloquial dictionary of the Tokugawa period, the *Rigen shūran* (26 *kan*) , attributed to Murata Ryōa (1772–Feb. 2, 1844) , but perhaps merely his revision of the work of Ōta Hō (*gō, Zensai*) (1759–1829). First published as (*Zōho*) *Rigen shūran* (1900 and 1905, 3 vols.) , edited by Inoue Yorikuni (1839–1914) and Kondō Heijō, 3.313.

28. *Dōguya* is an abbreviation of *Dōguya-bushi,* a heroic, martial style of recitation, originated by Dōguya Kichizaemon (*fl. ca.* 1673–1710) and later incorporated into *Gidayū-bushi.*

29. This passage is a quotation from Chikamatsu's own play and greatest success, *The Battles of Coxinga* (*Kokusen'ya kassen,* 1715) , Act 4. In this action, Coxinga (J: Kokusen'ya; Ch: Kuo-hsing-yeh, Cheng Ch'eng-kung; Dutch: Koxinga, etc.; see Arthur W. Hummel, ed., *Eminent Chinese of the Ch'ing Period* [Washington, 1943] 1.108–109) (1624–1662) is seeking to pass through Ummon barrier (Ummonkan) at Nanking.

Han Kai is Fan K'uai (d. 189 B.C.) , and the reference is to his gate-crashing technique on the occasion when he fought his way into the camp of Hsiang Chi (T. Yü) (232–202 B.C.) at Hung-men, to save his general, Liu Pang (247–195 B.C.) , the future Han Kao-tsu, from assassination. See *Shih chi, Hsiang Yu pen-chi* (Wuchou t'ung-wen shu-chü ed.) 7 (*ts'e* 30) . 15a3, translated by Edouard Chavannes, *Les Memoires Historiques de Se-ma Ts'ien* (Paris, 1897) 2.279. Also see the biography of Fan K'uai, *Shih chi* 95 (*ts'e* 20) . 2b10.

Asahina is Asahina Yoshihide who in the Wada revolt against the Hōjō in 1213 distinguished himself by crashing through the south gate of the Kamakura palace.

Uryōko and Saryōko are fictitious traitors against the Ming dynasty.

The passage ends with the phrase *tsuki hi no seki ya,* derived from the saying *tsuki hi no sekimori nashi,* lit., "there is no barrier guard to stop the sun and moon," a metaphor for the relentless passing of time. This saying appears in the *yōkyoku Matsuyama kagami, Yōkyoku taikan* 5.2871.

The quotation from *The Battles of Coxinga,* as recited by the chanting monk, is only slightly modified from the original (cf. *Chikamatsu zenshū.* 10.932) : "Han Kai's style is not unique. For crashing down gates, watch the style of Japan's Asahina! Then hauling down the gate's crossbeam and the entanglement of felled trees, he strikes down those who oppose him, seizes and hurls those who flee, slays Saryōko and Uryōko, and without difficulty passes through the barrier, as [irresistible as] the sun and moon." Miyamori Asatarō's synoptic translation of *Kokusen'ya kassen* in *Tales from Old Japanese Dramas* (New York, 1915, pp. 359–403), completely omits this act.

30. *Bun'ya-bushi*, a lamenting style of *jōruri* recitation, originated in Osaka by Okamoto Bun'ya (*fl.* 1681–1687), popularly called *naki-bushi*, "weeping style."

31. This is an excerpt from the *jōruri Wankyū sue no Matsuyama*, Act 3, "Journey," as it is preserved in the version of the *jōruri* school of Miyako Itchū (d. 1724), published in 1707. In this scene, Wankyū, the profligate and disinherited son of a wealthy merchant, half crazed by his frustrated love for the prostitute Matsuyama, is wandering in search of her, wearing a *hōroku zukin*, "parching-pan cap" (see note 26). The story is based on the life of a merchant named Wan'ya Kyūemon (d. 1677), and is part of a large corpus of *jōruri, kabuki*, and prose stories known as *Wankyū-mono*, which relate the vicissitudes of his romance with Matsuyama. By this time it represented a theme which had been worked over repeatedly for half a century. In this particular version Wankyū's complete name is Wan'ya Kyūhei, and his father is called Wan'ya Kyūemon. The Itchū text is sometimes attributed, partly on the basis of this citation in *Amijima*, to Chikamatsu or to his follower, Sadoshima Saburōzaemon (*fl.* 1708–1721). It is strikingly similar to a play of the same title of the *jōruri* school of Toyotake Wakadayū (1681–1764), written by Ki no Kaion (1663–1742) and first performed in 1708. It has not been established which version was written first. For a discussion of these problems, see the Introduction by Kuroki Kanzō in *Jōruri meisaku shū*, 1.19–23, of *Nihon meichō zenshū*, and his *Chikamatsu igo* (1942, 272 pp.), pp. 32–36. I have not seen the Itchū text, but the citation in *Chikamatsu goi*, p. 517, suggests that the version in *Amijima* is an exact quotation except for the introduction of *ē ē wā wā wā*.

32. *Uta* 歌 is the style of recitation for a song (*uta* 唄) which is quoted in Gidayū *jōruri*. In this case it is a song consisting of seven-syllable lines which originally accompanied a dance (see note 33).

33. This passage is a quotation from a major success of Chikamatsu's, *Tamba Yosaku matsuyo no komuro-bushi* (1708), which was revived as *Tamba Yosaku* (1712) (*Chikamatsu zenshū* 8.602). These are the opening lines of the "epilogue" of this play, "Yosaku odori," a congratulatory dance and recitation, which is itself a "summary" of the story of an earlier love-suicide play of Chikamatsu's, *Shinjū Kasane-izutsu* (probably late in 1707) (*Chikamatsu zenshū* 8.349–397). However, this "epilogue" has no direct connection with the plot of *Tamba Yosaku*, nor is the subject matter in itself congratulatory, except in the sense that it celebrates the fact that a love suicide has just been happily prevented in *Tamba Yosaku*.

The story of *Shinjū Kasane-izutsu*, a knowledge of which is essential to unraveling the quotation, must be given here. Tokubei, through a fortunate marriage, has become the proprietor of a dyeing establishment, but he is still in love with a prostitute named Fusa. As suggested in this passage, this involves him in financial and love difficulties, and, unable to achieve any solution, Tokubei and Fusa commit suicide.

Chikamatsu's purpose in introducing this allusion to another love suicide was probably carefully calculated. The audience of his day, their memories pricked by this allusion, would undoubtedly be quick to see the close parallel between *Kasane-izutsu* and *Amijima*: love for a prostitute leading to financial troubles, and ultimately to a love suicide; we also find in both plays the arbitrary father-in-law, the admonishing elder brother, and the submissive wife. The similarity in personality between Jihei and Osan, and Tokubei and Otatsu of *Kasane-izutsu* has already been remarked (see Introduction, notes 67–69).

The awareness of the approaching tragedy in *Amijima* is heightened by the speeches of Sugi which follow this passage.

The passage from "Yosaku odori" is quoted with only minor modifications, and it is a good example of the use of associated words, puns, and fluid grammar. It is translated on three levels in an attempt to show the use of these stylistic devices:

Kon'ya no Tokubei	Fusa ni motoyori		koi somekomi no
(1) The dyer Tokubei	with Fusa originally		love-dyed
(2) dyer	tassel		dark-dyed
uchi no shindai	aku	demo	hagezu
(1) personal fortune	dissipate.		
(2)	lye	even though	does not fade.
(3)	satiate	even though	does not fade.

The associated words on the second line are "dyer," "-dyed," "lye," "does not fade," and probably, "tassel." This entire quotation, and practically all of "Yosaku odori," is seven-syllable phrases because it is a dance rhythm.

For namamida, a less contracted form of namaida, see note 23.

34. There is a question whether this "speech," consisting of the word nanzo, is made by the monk or Sugi. In the former case it could be translated "What is it?" and in the latter, "What's the idea?" Only Itō (p. 94) advocates the latter interpretation.

35. It may be that Chikamatsu is reminding the audience by this remark that he has written no love-suicide plays about prostitutes in the Northern Quarter (including Dōjima) for a decade. Three of his first five love suicides were associated with this Quarter: Sonezaki shinjū (1703), Shinjū nimai ezōshi (1706), and Shinjū yaiba wa kōri no tsuitachi (1709).

36. Edo is an abbreviation of Edo-bushi, a style of jōruri recitation originated by Edo Handayū (fl. 1688–1719).

37. This passage of jōruri, which is given as an improvisation by the monk, contains some clever plays on words: Tatta is-sen ni-sen de san-zen yō ri o hedatetaru Daiminkoku e no nagatabi wa awanuda butsu, awanuda, awanuda, butsu-butsu iute yukisuguru. There is the play of is-sen ni-sen "one sen two sen" with san-zen "three thousand," or "three sen." Also, awanuda butsu is of course similar in sound to namaida Butsu; awanuda means "doesn't pay," and is followed by butsu-butsu, "grumbling." Itō (p. 96) soberly points out that 3000 ri is not the actual distance to China, and that it is used only for the play on words. He cites the Wakan sansai zue (1712), kan 62, 2.680, as saying that the distance from Nanking to westernmost Kyushu is 340 ri. However, Chikamatsu did not invent the number 3000 here to make a pun, but rather drew it from another source for that purpose. The use of that number is really an allusion to his Battles of Coxinga, in which he says that the distance between China and Japan is san-zen yō ri, "over 3000 ri" (Chikamatsu zenshū, 10.901), and san-zen ri "3000 ri" (10.913). In actuality it might be described as a pseudo-number, for it is occasionally used in Chinese poetry to mean "a great distance." It appears in Japanese literature also, as in the "Suma" chapter of Murasaki Shikibu's Genji monogatari (ca. 1021, 54 kan), Nihon bungaku taikei (1927–1928, 25 vols.) 6.317; and in Bashō's Oku no hosomichi (1689). For a discussion of the expression in Chinese and Japanese literature, see Higuchi Isao, Oku no hosomichi hyōshaku (1930, 526 pp.) pp. 18–19.

The four snatches of jōruri recited by the monk must have been of great interest to contemporary audiences, the first three being taken from famous plays of recent years, and the last simply a clever, comic improvisation. Also, four different jōruri styles were used; imitation of the styles of other schools inserted in a Gidayū play gave added interest. However, the excerpt about a love suicide is in the Gidayū style probably because it is of real importance for the atmosphere of Act 1. As pointed out in note 9, the play opens with jōruri rhythm, followed by poetic measures, with a sentence of yōkyoku in close sequence. Then comes a second section of narrative in poetic phrases of seven and five syllables alternately, followed by conversational passages. After this Chikamatsu has inserted these four jōruri sections of sharply contrasting types, making sudden changes of pace. The comic improvised passage of the monk completes the cycle of recitation styles that begins with the jargon *jōruri* at the opening of the play, which is itself the type of gibberish that could be expected of the monk.

Another calculated feature of this section is Chikamatsu's self-advertisement in the citation of two of his famous successes, *Kokusen'ya* and *Tamba Yosaku*, and also, perhaps, the suggestion that this is an occasion of importance when he again writes a love-suicide play about the Northern Quarter.

38. *Harubaru de Koharu-sama. Harubaru* is a poetic word meaning "from afar," "distant," and as Itō suggests (p. 101), it may be used here by extension to mean "long absent." This is undoubtedly an example of forcing a word into the text for its phonetic quality, in this instance for euphony. Its use here is given a further overtone by another meaning of *harubaru* in poetry, "many springs," "every spring."

39. *Aruji no kasha*, "the proprietor's wife." Kasha is usually used by Chikamatsu in this meaning. In the Kamigata area it less frequently had the meaning of *yarite* "female manager," which was its usual meaning in Edo. This is explained in the *Kinsei fūzoku shi (Morisada mankō*, compiled 1837–1853 in Edo), pt. 2, p. 126: "Morisada says that long ago *yarite* was called *kasha* 香車. Now it is called only *yarite*, and the name *kasha* has fallen into disuse. In Kyoto and Osaka the wife of the proprietor of an *ageya* or *chaya* is still called *kasha* 花車." (For an explanation of *yarite* see J. E. DeBecker, *The Nightless City, or the "History of the Yoshiwara Yūkwaku,"* 5th edition revised, Yokohama, ca. 1905–1906.)

40. Ri Tōten, the fictional archvillain of *Kokusen'ya kassen.*

41. *Eshirenu hito no adana o tate.* I have followed Itō (p. 104) in translating "to give without knowledge a scandalous reputation to people." Some commentaries, however, interpret *eshirenu* as modifying *hito* rather than *adana*, which would mean "to give a scandalous reputation to people (or someone) you (or I) don't even know."

42. *Koban*, an oblong gold coin, weighing at this time about 17 grams, which was worth one (gold) *ryō* equal to 60 (silver) *momme.* (See note 47.)

Such boasting of wealth and making of public advances toward a woman, even though a prostitute, were considered even more offensive in Japanese culture than in Western.

43. For a discussion of *inga*, "karma," see Introduction, pp. 28–29.

44. *Temma Ozaka sangō.* Ōsaka, in this period, was popularly called Osaka or Ozaka. Hamamatsu Utakuni, in his *Setsuyō ochiboshū, kan* 1 (1808, 10 *kan,* in *Shin enseki jisshu* 5.345, *Kokusho kankōkai,* Series 3, 1913), states under the heading "Concerning the three districts of Osaka": "That which is spoken of as the three districts consists of Kita-gumi, Minami-gumi, and Temma-gumi. However Osaka [strictly speaking] has two districts, and Temma is in Minami-nakajima." In the play Temma is probably mentioned specifically, since it was the residence of Kamiya Jihei (see map).

45. For chart of family relationships, see Introduction, p. 32.

46. The payment of amounts due *(shikiri [-gin/gane])* in the settlement of accounts was frequently carried out, not at the end of each month, but five or six times a year on certain festival days, known as the *sekki.* This practice is explained in *Naniwa kikigaki* (1819), p. 28: "*Sekki:* before the 3rd month festival [3rd month, 3rd day], before the 5th month festival [5th month, 5th day], before the *Bon* [7th month, 15th day], before the 9th month festival [9th month, 9th day], the last day of the 10th month, and the last day of the year. These are called the *sekki.* The last day of the 10th month is called *nakabarai* ("the interim payment"). On each of these the various accounts are settled. The interval between *sekki* is called *hitoae,* or also just *ai.*"

47. Ten *kamme* meant 10,000 *me* of silver; one *me (momme)* was equal to 3.75

grams. Later in the play we learn that the price of redeeming Koharu was 6000 *me* (see note 135) of *Shihōgin*, the coinage of 1711. Tahei is probably including tips and for effect is making the cost sound more formidable. A rough idea of the amount involved can be obtained by calculating on the basis of the price of rice at the time of the play, when it was about 200 *me* a *koku* (about 5 bushels) ; 10,000 *me* was equal to 50 *koku*, or roughly the annual income of an average peasant after paying taxes.

48. *Tōrō ga ono de gozaru*, translated "a preposterous undertaking," is lit. "to be a case of front legs of the mantis." This is derived from an expression current in this period, *tōrō no ono o motte ryūsha ni mukau*, lit., "the mantis with his front legs opposes a high carriage," used as a metaphor for not knowing one's own limitations, and hence engaging in an impracticable undertaking. See Kaibara Kōko (1664–1700), *Kotowaza gusa, kan* 2 (publ. 1700, 7 *kan*, in *Ekken zenshū* 3.839), a dictionary of sayings and figures of speech. This figure appears a number of times in *yōkyoku* (e.g., *Kiso;* cf. note 4) and in such works as the *Gempei seisuiki* and *Taiheiki*. Its origin is Chinese, and the form of the Japanese expression suggests that it was introduced either in *Hou Han shu, Yüan Shao chuan* 104 (*ts'e* 82)20b8 or *Wen hsüan* (in *Liu ch'en chu Wen hsüan* ed., *Ssu-pu-ts'ung-k'an*) 44(*ts'e* 23)11b9. The saying appeared earlier in somewhat different form: *Chuang-tzu* (in *Chuang-tzu chi-shih* ed., annotated by Kuo Ch'ing-fan, *Ssu-hsien-shu-chü*, 1895) 4(*ts'e* 2)18b6 and 12(*ts'e* 4)13b9; *Han-shih wai-chuan* (*Ssu-pu-ts'ung-k'an* ed.) 8.18b5; and in other works.

49. *Morau*, lit., "to receive," had a specific usage in the language of the gay quarters, meaning to get a prostitute away from another guest who had summoned her or who had reserved her.

50. *Katana wakizashi*, also called *daishō*, were the long and the short sword, approximately 4 feet and 1½ feet long respectively (*cf.* note 81), which samurai were required to wear during most of the Tokugawa period. The section on weapons in the *Wakan sansai zue* (1712), *kan* 21, 1.325, contains the statement: "Nowadays a long one is called a *katana* and a short one is called a *wakizashi*. In general, in the *katana* the tip of the scabbard is flat and untapered, and in the *wakizashi* it is round and tapered. These are the differences between the long and short ones. First, one girds on the *katana*, and then one girds on the *tantō* (i.e., *wakizashi*), and therefore it is called *wakizashi* [lit., 'gird on beside']. In the 2nd year of Tenna [1682] for the first time there was a law that samurai wear a long and a short one, and farmers, artisans, merchants, and the like, may carry a *tantō*."

51. This improvised recitation is a parody on the passage from "Yosaku odori" in *Tamba Yosaku*, quoted on p. 65 (see note 33), and similarly consists entirely of phrases of seven syllables. It is alive with puns, mostly concerning paper, and in order to indicate them I shall translate the puns on three levels. Six types of paper are mentioned, but some of them, like the coins mentioned, convey no essential meaning. This passage is called a *kami-zukushi* (see Introduction, p. 46) :

	Kamiya no Jihei		*Koharu gurui*		
	Paper dealer Jihei		infatuated with Koharu		
	ga sugi-hara-gami de		*ichibu*	*koban*	*-shi*
(1)	to excess		1 *bu*[coins]	*koban*[coins]	
(2)	Sugihara paper			small writing	paper
(3)			prestige		
	chiri-chiri-gami de		*uchi no shindai*	*suki*	*yare*
(1)	scatters		personal fortune	cracks	form
(2)	toilet paper				
(3)	scatters			holey-	
	-gami no	*hana mo*	*kamarenu*	*kami*	*-kuzu Jihei*
(1)	Kami[ya]'s	nose even	cannot blow	Kami[ya]	Jihei.
(2)	paper	nose[paper]		wastepaper	

Sugihara-gami is a thin, soft paper, originally produced at Sugihara-mura, Harima Province (the present Hyogo Prefecture). (See *Wakan sansai zue, kan* 15, 2.252.) *Ko-hanshi* is small-size *hanshi*, or ordinary writing paper. *Sukiyare-gami* is paper marred in the making, and containing fissures.

52. *Amigasa* were large, mushroom-shaped hats woven of rush or straw which were worn usually to conceal the identity of the wearer. They could be rented at the entrances to the gay quarters.

53. *Tahei ga nembutsu kowakuba Namu-amigasa mo morōta.* In this passage, *Namu-amigasa* starts out to be *Namu Amida Butsu,* but instead of being completed the expression pivots on *ami* and turns into the word *amigasa,* which starts a new thought. The translation, then, reads: "If you're afraid of Tahei's incantation, [say] *Namu Ami[da Butsu* and worship me]. Let's have the *(ami)gasa.*"

54. Tahei, who has just been so glib, is now unable to utter *nen* or *butsu,* i.e., *nembutsu,* "Buddhist invocation."

55. *Shingin,* "New Silver," refers to the good-quality coinage of the beginning of the Kyōhō period (1716–1736), which contained 80 per cent of silver to 20 per cent of copper. It was four times the value of the *Shihōgin* of 1711, which, although nominally a silver coin, was 80 per cent copper and only 20 per cent silver. See Kusama Naokata (1753–1831), *Sanka zui, kan* 18 (1815, 20 *kan*) (Hakutōsha edition, 1932, 1246 pp.), pp. 572, 579–580. As illustrated there these "coins" were oblong lumps of metal of irregular shape rather than coins of conventional shape. Although there were copper and gold coins at this time in Japan, the minting of real silver coins did not begin until later in the eighteenth century.

The spirit of a wealthy *chōnin* is depicted in Tahei's reiteration that money can do anything: *koban no hibiki,* "the clink of my gold coins" (p. 66), *kane no chikara,* "the power of my money" (p. 66), and *shingin no hikari,* "the glitter of 'New Silver'" (p. 67).

56. Nakamachi is the central street in Dōjima (see map).

57. The samurai could not afford to be involved in a brawl in the gay quarter, for it would result in dishonorable publicity and disciplinary action by his lord. The gay quarter, as the social playground of the *chōnin,* was granted a liberal amount of self-rule through the group responsibility of the elders of the quarter. In the houses, business came first, and the samurai and *chōnin* were treated alike. In this extralegal area, where the pressure of class discrimination was considerably relieved, it is probable that such acts of discourtesy by *chōnin* toward samurai were not uncommon.

58. This speech of the flippant maid contains a series of rather farfetched plays on words, which result in a sort of humorous double-talk:

ato-zumete	*shippori to Koharu-sama*	
engage whole night	intimately Koharu	
shitataru	*taru no kijōyu*	*Kasha-sama* . . .
captivatingly.		Proprietress
dripping	keg of pure soy.	
nochi ni aona	*no hitashimono.*	
later probably meet		
green vegetables	steeped [in soy].	

The first line of literal translation gives the primary meaning of the passage. The second line shows that two words are being used also as puns, and this second meaning leads to the insertion of words associated with them (*engo*): *shitataru* suggesting *taru no kijōyu,* and *aona* suggesting *hitashimono.* Thus, the second line of translation is connected through the association of ideas, which, although not directly related to the primary meaning, contains a shred of meaning, in addition to the obvious sensual suggestions. If Koharu pleases and detains her guest, it will result in his ordering more food from the proprietress.

The association of ideas in *shitataru taru no kijōyu* did not seem so farfetched to Chikamatsu's audience as it might to us, because they were probably intended to recognize in it an allusion to Chikamatsu's first and hitherto most popular love suicide, *Sonezaki shinjū* (1703), which contains the passage (*Chikamatsu zenshū* 6.587):

Ima wa tedai to	*umoregi no*	*kijōyu no*
Now as a clerk	living in obscurity	soy [tradesman Tokubyōe]
sode *shitataruki*	*koi* *no yakko*	*ni ninawasete,*
captivating	love's slave	
sleeve dripping	dark by his servant	have carry,

The primary meaning of this passage is: "Now the soy tradesman Tokubyōe is living in obscurity as a clerk, but he soon will become notorious as the slave of a captivating, intimate love." The secondary meaning is contained in the latter part of the passage: "Tokubyōe has the servant carry the keg of pure soy, and his sleeve is darkly stained with its drops."

59. *Katade*, "uprightness (of character)," is primarily a term used for the hardness of pottery, and in this passage it is an *engo* with *chaire chawan*, "a tea caddy or a teacup," following, and the *hitashimono*, "[dish of] steeped vegetables," preceding. The word *katade* appeared also in his *Ikutama shinjū*, Act 3 (1715) (*Chikamatsu zenshū* 10.834): *oya wa katade no chawan to chawan,* [*Kaheiji*:] "My father [and I collided] like two hard teacups."

60. *Mi o chawan chaire ni suru ka*, "do you take me for a tea caddy or teacup?" phrased in this form calls to mind the expression *cha ni suru*, "to make a fool of (someone)," and in this sentence, followed by *ka*, would be translated, "Is it to make a fool of me?"

61. (*Naburare ni wa*) *ki-mōsanu. Mōsu* here functions as an auxiliary verb suffixed to the verb the speaker uses to express his action and is an indication of respect to the listener. Other words used by the samurai also indicate an overuse of the honorific as *ojorō* in addressing Koharu, and *kasha-dono* in addressing the proprietress. This betrays the overformalized and unsophisticated speech of a gentlemanly samurai or someone unfamiliar with the gay quarter.

62. *Yashiki*, "residency," here means *kura-yashiki*, "storehouse residency," which term appears in the text on p. 74. It is the branch office of a fief (*han*), which is maintained in Osaka to market the fief's rice and other produce through the merchants (see Introduction, p. 6). The "chief official" of this office is known as the *rusui*.

63. *Yado* here has the special meaning of *chaya* or *ageya*, rather than the usual "inn." *Shikidō ōkagami, kan* 1, in *Zoku enseki jisshu* 2.414 has the entry: "*Yadoya*—similarly means *ageya*. It is an odd name, but it is also an alternate word used for *ageya.*"

64. *Futokoro de zeni yomu yō*, "like counting pennies in one's bosom." Japanese keep their purse in their bosom where the left side of the kimono crosses the right. This has become a stock expression for hanging one's head, which Itō (p. 131) believes may have originated with Chikamatsu.

65. *Jūya*, "the Ten Nights," the 6th to the 15th of the 10th month, when special Buddhist services were conducted in the temples of the Jōdo (Pure Land) Sect. There is a popular saying: *Jūya no uchi ni shinda mono wa hotoke ni naru*, "Those who die during the Ten Nights will become Buddhas" (i.e., will attain salvation).

66. The exit of the proprietress and the quickly sketched description of the hour, the sky, and the street shift the scene from the interior to the exterior of the house, and prepare the way for the appearance of the hero, Kamiya Jihei.

67. These lines introduce the hero, Jihei, as he appears on the stage, stating his occupation, place of residence, and immediate problem. This follows the convention of the *nō* and *kyōgen* of supplying such details to the audience immediately upon

the arrival of a character on the stage, but here it is done more subtly by a punning third-person narrative. The type of introduction used in the *nō* can be illustrated by the *yōkyoku Atsumori* (*Yōkyoku taikan* 1.125) : "I am a resident of Musashi Province, called Jirō Naozane of Kumagae, but I have taken orders and am a priest called Rensei. I killed Atsumori in battle and this has caused me such grief that I have come to this condition. Now I am going down to Ichinotani to pray for Atsumori's salvation." The *kyōgen Koyakuneri* ("The Ointment Maker") (*Nihon bungaku taikei* 22.344) : "I am an ointment maker of Kamakura. I have thought that there is no ointment maker as renowned as I in the realm, but I hear that in the capital there is also a renowned ointment maker. Therefore, I am now on the way up to the capital where I plan to vie with him in making ointment."

This passage in *Amijima* is remarkable for its nimble use of associated words and puns. Because of double layers of meaning, the translation is much longer than the Japanese. These levels cannot be diagrammed satisfactorily to show the trains of meaning, but the following will indicate alternate and overlapping translations:

Temma ni toshifuru	*chihayafuru kami ni wa aranu*	
In Temma pass many years	efficacious deity	is not
		virile
Kami-sama to yo no waniguchi	*ni norubakari.*	
Kamiya in society wide reputation	spread.	
deity prayer bell		
Koharu ni fukaku au/ō -nusa no kusariaitaru		
With Koharu deeply in love	unlucky liaison	
paper wand	linked together	
mishimenawa, ima wa musubu no Kanna -zuki		
now marriage- god not.		
sacred rope tying tenth month.		

This passage, a *kami-zukushi*, contains a maze of *engo*, words associated with *kami* (deity) : *Temma, chihayafuru, kami-sama, waniguchi, ōnusa, mishimenawa* (hence *kusariaitaru* and *musubu*), *musubu no kam[i]*, and *Kannazuki* (see Introduction, p. 46).

Temma was one of the three districts (*gō*) of Osaka (see note 44), and was named for Temma-gu, one of the most flourishing shrines in the city. The shrine was named for its chief deity, Temma Tenjin, the deified name of Sugawara no Michizane (845–903). (See note 219 and map.)

Waniguchi, "crocodile mouth," is a circular, flat, metal bell, hung under the front eaves of the worship hall of a temple or shrine, which worshipers ring by swinging against its side a hanging rope. Its name comes from its wide, slit mouth, according to *Wakan sansai zue, kan* 19, 1.303, which also contains an illustration of *waniguchi*. The word also means "a scandalous reputation."

Ōnusa, or *nusa*, known also as *gohei*, is a wand which has strips of cut paper attached, used by Shintō priests in religious ceremonies. See illustration, *ibid.* 1.303.

(*Mi*)*shimenawa* is a sacred Shintō straw rope from which hang tufts of straw or paper. See illustration, *ibid.* 1.303.

68. The entire passage introducing Jihei to this point has been in slow rhythm of alternating seven- and five-syllable phrases. In the next line, when he hears the news he has waited so long to hear, this rhythm is dropped and the phrases move in a quick, uneven tempo.

69. *Niuriya*, "eating house," was a small restaurant or stand in the gay quarter which served sake with boiled fish and vegetables. In 1708, when Sonezaki shinchi was opened, permission was given to establish 98 *chaya* and 56 *niuriya*. See *Ōsaka-shi shi* (6 vols., 1913–1915), 1.472.

70. *Kōshi* is the lattice grillwork of wood which protects the sliding windows. *Kōshi* made up a large part of the front of the *chaya*, facing on the street.

71. *Zukin*, "hood," unlike the *hōroku zukin*, "parching-pan cap," mentioned in note 26, is a tight-fitting, masklike hood which fits under the chin. The samurai is wearing it under his *amigasa*.

72. Umeda and Kitano, north and east of Sonezaki respectively, were both rather secluded areas where temples with cemeteries were located and which would be suitable for suicides. The words *fuku*, "to blow" (here used in the phrase *fukikomu*, "to inform secretly"), *tobu*, "to fly," Umeda and Kitano, are all *engo* of Temma (Sugawara no Michizane), as explained in notes 221–223.

73. *Namu sambō*, a Buddhist expression, meaning to devote oneself to the three precious ones, i.e., the Buddha, the Law, and the Order. Here it is an ejaculation of alarm, the equivalent of "good heavens" or "hope to God."

74. The text does not specify whether the samurai cannot stand by and see Koharu die (1) because it is a samurai's duty to help people, or (2) despite the fact that he is a samurai, supposedly hardened to bloodshed. Wakatsuki (p. 198) favors the former interpretation, but Itō's (p. 156) latter explanation seems preferable.

75. Hachiman, a deity in both the Shintō and the Buddhist pantheons, who is popularly considered to be the apotheosized Emperor Ōjin (the 15th Emperor). He is the deity of arms and the protector of warriors.

76. *Iro hoka ni arawaru*, "it is revealed in one's face," is the second part of the saying *omoi uchi ni areba, iro hoka ni arawaru*, "since it is in one's thoughts, it is revealed in one's face." The full saying appears earlier in Chikamatsu's *Meido no hikyaku* (1711), *Chikamatsu zenshū* 9.370. It is found in two *yōkyoku* of the fifteenth century, *Yuya* (*Yōkyoku taikan* 5.3250) and *Matsukaze* (*ibid.* 5.2832) and is derived from a similar figure in the Chinese classics, *Ta hsüeh, Meng-tzu*, and in the *Shih chi*.

77. *Nen* means *nenki*, "term of service." Koharu still has five years to serve of the term for which she was indentured.

78. *Sodegoi hinin*. *Sodegoi* is a beggar. *Hinin*, a category of the pariah class (*semmin*) in the Tokugawa period, was second in size to the *eta*. The *hinin* could be roughly described as those outcasts who were engaged in nonproductive occupations such as entertainment, fortunetelling, begging, and jail and execution duties. This class was entered not only by birth, but by committing a crime, by an unsuccessful love suicide, or by one's choice of occupation. The *eta*, on the other hand, were engaged in productive occupations, such as working with leather, making sandals of bamboo sheath, and making lamp wicks. There was less mobility in and out of the *eta* category. The pariahs, being below the four recognized classes of society, had inferior legal status. Takigawa Masajirō, *Nihon shakai shi* (1929, 377 pp.), pp. 337–338. The word *hinin* is used later in the play with reference to Jihei (see note 163).

79. *Ki kara ochitaru gotoku*, "as if he had fallen from a tree." The phrase is based on a popular saying, *ki kara ochitaru saru*, "a monkey which has fallen from a tree." It is used not to indicate surprise so much as the feeling of being at a loss, of losing that on which one has depended. This is illustrated by the use earlier of the complete figure in Chikamatsu's *Ikutama shinjū*, Act 3 (1715), *Chikamatsu zenshū* 10.837. A similar phrase, *ki o hanaretaru saru*, "a monkey which is away from a tree," appears in such works as the *Akazome Emon shū* of the late Heian period and the thirteenth-century *Gempei seisuiki*, and all are based on figures appearing in Chinese works such as the *Chan kuo ts'é, Shuo yüan*, and *Wên hsüan*.

80. *Kinchaku-kiri me*, "thieving whore," really contains two words: *kinchaku*, originally "purse," which came to mean "prostitute," and *kinchaku-kiri*, lit., "cutpurse," i.e., "pickpocket." The latter is an *engo* to the preceding *ubau*, "stole," and *kiri* alone to the following *kirōka*, "shall I cut her down?"

81. *Isshaku nana sun*, "one *shaku* seven *sun*," or roughly 1.7 feet, refers to the length of Jihei's *wakizashi* (cf. note 50).

82. Seki no Magoroku, "Magoroku of Seki," was a renowned swordsmith, Magoroku Kanemoto of Seki, in Mino Province. He worked in the opening years of the sixteenth century, and several of his successors were called by his name. That swords bearing this name were well known during the early eighteenth century is indicated by the fact that there is another reference to Seki no Magoroku in Nishizawa Ippū's *Onna daimyō Tanzen nō, kan* 7 (1702, 8 *kan,* in *Ukiyo zōshi shū, Kindai Nihon bungaku taikei* 4.327).

83. The text uses the word *shōji,* "sliding window," rather than *kōshi,* "lattice grillwork," which protects the window (see note 70). The text a few lines previously shows that the meaning here is the "lattice grillwork."

84. *Ikihaji o kaku*(go) 生恥を搔く/覺(悟) "to bring living shame on oneself," that is, the disgrace of bringing upon oneself great shame while still alive, as in the saying *ikihaji kaku yori shinu ga mashi,* "it is better to die than to bring living shame on yourself." *Kaku,* lit., "to scratch," is an *engo* to *inu,* "dog." *Kaku* here serves a double usage, as it is also the first element in the compound *kakugo,* "realize."

85. *Bonnō ni tsunagaruru inu,* "a dog tied to worldly desires," is a corruption of sayings containing the figure *bonnō no inu,* "worldly desire is like a dog," such as *bonnō no inu wa uttemo mon o sarazu,* "worldly desire is like a [devoted] dog, which you may strike but which will not leave your gate." This figure comes from the *Daihatsu nehangyō* (Skt. *Mahāpari-nirvāna-sūtra*) *kan* 14 (36 *kan*) (*Daizōkyō* 12.696a); it appears in Japanese literature as in the *yōkyoku Kayoi Gomachi* (*Yōkyoku taikan* 2.768). The phrase *bonnō no inu* appeared earlier in Chikamatsu's *Sagami nyūdō sembiki inu,* Act 2 (*Chikamatsu zenshū* 10.362).

86. Tahei returns without his companions.

87. *Iki-zuri-me, dō-zuri-me* as expressions of abuse are not adequately rendered by "Pickpocket! Pickpocket!" *Zuri* is a "pickpocket," and *iki* and *dō* are prefixes of abuse, *me* a suffix of abuse.

88. *Gandō:* a robber who intimidates his victims by force. *Gandō* was a contemporary popular pronunciation of the modern *gōtō.* (See *Wakan sansai zue, kan* 10, 1.144.) *Gandō* is here followed by the pejorative nominal suffix *me.*

89. *Gokumon,* lit., "prison gate," in the Edo period became the name of the punishment of decapitation and exposure of the head on the prison gate. It was the penalty for such crimes as plotting against the shogunate, murder of one's master or parents, illegal passage of a barrier, and *gōtō* (see preceding note). *Gokumon* is also suffixed by *me,* so that it means, "you who should be executed and have your head exposed on the prison gate."

90. In Japan it is a much more serious form of insult than in the West to kick or trample on a person. There is hardly a domestic play by Chikamatsu in which this form of abuse is not introduced, usually to the humiliation of the hero. In this act there is a distressing inclination of the characters to trample those who do not have a fair chance of retaliating. According to Western ideas of sportsmanship, it would be improper for the hero, at least, to act in this way. However, later in this act, Jihei in a fit of rage kicks even his love, Koharu.

91. *Fumarete mo ano otogai,* "even after he has been trampled, how he jaws." This usage of *otogai,* "chin" as a pejorative for talking, is employed by Chikamatsu in an almost identical passage in *Nebiki no kadomatsu* (1718), Act 1 (*Chikamatsu zenshū* 11.270): *fumarete sae ano otogai,* "even after he has been trampled, how he still jaws."

92. *Munagura,* "bodice," is the point where the left and right "lapels" of the kimono cross high on the chest.

93. Jihei's age is given as 28 (*sai*) in the text on p. 91.

94. *Rokuken guchi* means a house with a frontage (*maguchi*) of 6 *ken.* One *ken* is approximately 6 feet.

95. *Enja oyako naka,* "relationships of marriage and blood." *Enja* here has the

special meaning of "relatives by marriage," as opposed to *shinrui*, "relative by blood," as defined in *Wakan sansai zue, kan* 8, 1.119. *Oyako,* lit., "parent(s) and child(ren) ," is here used in a special meaning, found in certain dialects, of *shinrui*, "relatives by blood," as defined in *Rigen shūran* 1.457. This usage also appears later in this play (see note 101) , and in Chikamatsu's *Yūgiri Awa no Naruto* (1712) , *Chikamatsu zenshū* 9.626.

96. *Yukusaki ni mato ga tatsu,* "wherever you go, you will be a target [for the arrow of divine punishment]," that is, you can never escape punishment for your crime. This expression appeared in several *ukiyo-zōshi* of the preceding decade. (See Higuchi, p. 459, and *Chikamatsu goi,* pp. 502–503.)

97. Koya no Magoemon. *Koya,* or, in the modern reading, *konaya,* "flour dealer," indicates Jihei's elder brother's trade. Jihei succeeded to the family paper business, while Magoemon entered a new business, in which he was successful and became the model of a prudent tradesman. For a note and illustration on *koya,* see *Jinrin kimmō zui, kan* 4, p. 162 (1690, 7 *kan,* in *Nihon koten zenshū,* Series 3, 1929) .

98. *Matsuri no nerishu,* "fancy-dress participants in a festival procession." It was the custom of some of the shrines in Osaka during their summer festivals to have processions of townsmen dressed as samurai, wearing helmets and long and short swords, called *musha gyōretsu,* "warrior processions." An illustration of one of these processions appears in *Naniwa kagami, kan* 3 (1680, 6 *kan, Naniwa sōsho* 12.272) , by Ichimuken Dōji(?) (pen name) .

99. *Kozume yakusha,* lit., "actors packed into a small room [backstage]," hence "bit actors."

100. *Kura-yashiki,* "storehouse residency" (see note 62) .

101. *Oyako ichimon,* "relatives and family" (see note 95) .

102. *Yajiri-kiri,* "housebreaker," literally, "house-rump cutter," often abbreviated in Chikamatsu to *yajiri,* is a burglar who cuts his way through the rear wall of a house or godown. *Wakan sansai zue, kan* 10, 1.144b.

103. *Mamori bukuro,* "amulet bag," in which paper or wooden religious charms are kept.

104. *Kishō,* "written vows," are made before the Buddhist and Shintō deities on special forms issued by temples and shrines. For the text of such a vow, see note 130. The custom of exchanging such written pledges of love is described in detail in *Shikidō ōkagami, kan* 6, *Zoku enseki jisshu* 2.511–513.

105. *Bushinjū ka, shinjū ka,* "is she unfaithful or faithful?" Since a special meaning of the word *shinjū* is "love suicide," this also suggests the question, "will she not or will she commit a love suicide?"

106. These last two "sentences" carry a double and at points a triple meaning:

Ta ga	*fumi*	*mo minu*	*koi no michi*
(1) Someone	the letter	has not seen	love's course.
(2)		has not appraised	Koharu's love
(3)		has not been trampled	love's road
wakarete		*koso*	*wa kaerikere*
(2) not known,			
(3) separate		and indeed return home.	

The phrase *fumi mo minu,* "has not been trampled," is an allusion to a similar phrase, *mada fumi mo mizu,* "has never been trampled/trodden," in the famous poem of the Heian poetess Koshikibu no Naishi in the *Kin'yōshū,* 10 *kan* (*ca.* 1127) , in *Hachidaishū* 2.88, in (*Kōchū*) *Kokka taikei* (1928) , vol. 4:

Ōeyama	As the road by Mount Ōe
Ikuno no michi no	and Ikuno
tōkereba	is so long,
Mada fumi mo mizu	I have not had a letter/
	(I have never trod on)
Amanohashidate.	Amanohashidate.

This poem, one of the *Hyakunin isshū*, is discussed in Miyamori Asatarō, *Masterpieces of Japanese Poetry Ancient and Modern* (2 vols., 1936) 1.326–329. Undoubtedly Chikamatsu has this poem in mind in this passage, as most of it is reworked into five-seven-five phrases in his *Kako no Kyōshin nanapaka meguri* (1702): *Fumi mo minu, Ikuno no michi ya, Ōeyama.*

Act 2

107. Amamitsu-kami is the *kun* reading of Temma-no-kami, the deity to whom Temma Shrine is dedicated. This *kun* reading, considered more euphonic, is sometimes used in poetry and prose, as in the *yōkyoku Dōmyōji* (*Yōkyoku taikan* 3.1827).

108. For the place names, Tenjin Bridge (Tenjin-bashi) and Deity's Front Street (Miya no Maemachi), lit., "the street in front of the shrine," see map. Tenjin here means Temma Tenjin (see note 67).

109. These opening lines of Act 2 set the action at Kamiya Jihei's shop near Temma Shrine. They contain many of the stylistic characteristics which usually appear at the beginning of an act; a narrative in poetic form of alternating phrases of five and seven syllables, the repetition of wordplays, the use of certain syllables, and the insertion of a popular saying. For wordplays, *kami*, a homonym meaning "god" 神 and "paper" 紙, is introduced five times, and there are at least four *engo* of "god," as well as other double meanings.

Another device used here is the repetition of a single or double syllable in consecutive lines to produce a varied rhythm:

> (*Itonamu waza mo*)
> kami *mise ni*
> Kamiya *Jihei to*
> *na o tsukete*
> *chihaya*-furu *hodo*
> kai *ni* kuru
> kami *wa shōjiki*
> shō*bai wa*
> *tokoro gara* nari
> *shinise* nari.

The phrase *kami wa shōjiki* has a double meaning, "the paper is genuine" and "gods [reside in] honest [heads]." The latter meaning is understood because the phrase is part of a popular saying, *kami wa shōjiki no kōbe ni yadoru* "gods reside in honest heads," i.e., "honesty brings good fortune." The saying in this form is found in the *yōkyoku Shironushi* (*Yōkyoku taikan* 3.1486) and in *Yoshino Shizuka* (*ibid.* 5.3285). The more common form of this saying is *shōjiki no kōbe ni kami yadoru*.

110. *Kotatsu*, "covered brazier," is a charcoal-burning brazier, protected by a wooden frame and covered with a large quilt. It is generally located in the middle of the room. On wintry days, the members of the family sit or nap with their legs under the quilt.

111. *Makura byōbu*, "pillow screen," is a low, two-panel screen placed around the pillow to protect the sleeper from drafts.

112. Many worshipers are passing the shop on their way to the special religious services, because this is the last night of the Ten Nights, that is, the 15th day of the 10th month (cf. note 65).

113. The entire opening narrative of Act 2 to this point where Osan speaks is in alternating phrases of five and seven syllables. The front of the building facing the street is the shop, and the rear is the residence. That the business is conducted vigor-

ously and is reputable is due to the attentiveness of Osan. Her husband, Jihei, is dozing during business hours in a manner most unbecoming a merchant.

114. Ichi-no-kawa was a popular name for the vegetable market located at the southern edge of the Temma district on the north end of Tenjin Bridge. The phrase came to be used as a designation for the strip along the north bank of the river in Temma (see map). In a work which describes this market in detail, it is stated that about 150 middlemen had shops located there. See *Settsu meisho zue* (*Illustrated Guide to Famous Places in Settsu*), *kan* 4 (1796–1798, 9 *kan*), by Akisato Ritō, in *Dainihon meisho zue* (20 vols., 1919) 5.445. For an illustration of this market, see pp. 446–447. For a description also see *Setsuyō gundan*, *kan* 9 (1701, 17 *kan*) by Okada Keishi, in *Dainihon chishi taikei* (40 vols., 1929–1933) 28.146.

115. *Miya*, "the Shrine," refers to Temma Shrine (Temma-gu).

116. Osue's age was given as 4 (*sai*) on p. 73 of the translation. Converted to the Western method of reckoning age (see note 56 to Introduction), during this month Osue would be between 34 and 46 months of age. It was not unusual for Japanese children to be nursing at the age of 3.

117. The pun involves two meanings of the verb *kurawasu:* (1) to beat, and (2) to have (someone) eat. Sangorō pretends that he understands that Osan means he is to be fed, not beaten.

118. *Ojisama*, "uncle." Osan speaks of Magoemon as "uncle," meaning uncle to her children. He is, of course, her cousin and brother-in-law.

119. In this comical jumble of mock computations and instructions, the two are made to overlap by pivoting on two of the names:

. . . *ni fun no kan   -tarō Osue.* . .
. . . two *fun*   short.
                    Kantarō, Osue. . .
and:
. . . *ichi san ga san.   Sore Osan, ocha agemashiya.*
. . . 1 [times] 3 is 3.   Here Osan, serve some tea.

120. *Niwa* here probably does not have the usual meaning of "yard," as Miyamori translates it (p. 241), but is a special usage of the Kyoto-Osaka (Kamigata) area to designate the earthen- or tile-floored part of the house—either the vestibule where the customers stand or the kitchen.

121. Imabashi here refers to Imabashi Street (*suji*) which ran east and west between the Imabashi (Bridge) over Higashi-yokobori to Nishi-yokobori (see map).

122. *Hakujin* 白人 "prostitute," is derived from the *on* reading of the word for amateur, *shirōto* 白人 (now written 素人). Originally the term meant a young woman who plied her trade without being associated with a house, but by this period it was used to designate one of the higher classes of institutionalized prostitutes, ranking next to the *tayū* and *tenjin* (see Introduction, pp. 21–22). For a discussion of this term, cf. *Chikamatsu goi*, p. 279, and Itō, pp. 217–220.

123. *Chaya* is here used in a broad sense, rather than in the specific usage of *chaya*, as a house of entertainment to which prostitutes are called by the guests, as opposed to *okiya*, the house to which the prostitutes are indentured. Kinokuniya is strictly speaking an *okiya*. (See Introduction, p. 21.)

124. *Daijin*, "great spender," is a man who spends lavishly, specifically in the gay quarter.

125. That is, before Jihei pawns or sells Osan's clothes, which had been her dowry, in this way breaking the sets of kimono and obi (sashes).

126. *Kōyodōsei* is the posthumous Buddhist name of Jihei's father, used here to emphasize the extent of his failure in not observing his ancestral as well as his filial duties.

127. *Warifu*, "tally." A tally was made of bamboo or some other wood, bore certain identifying characters, and was divided between the two contracting parties. It

was used to prove the identity of the two individuals who had made an agreement concerning business or some other obligation.

128. *Kumano goō*, "charm of the Kumano Shrines." Certain Shintō shrines and Buddhist temples issued paper charms, bearing a sacred seal (*hōin*), and these were believed to be efficacious for protection against calamities such as fire and epidemic. The reverse side of the charms came to be used for writing vows, probably to indicate that the gods were witnesses of the vow. The charms of the three Kumano Shrines in Kii Province were especially popular for this purpose, perhaps because of the belief that their deities had the authority to inflict punishment for falsehoods. Such charms were used for vows between warriors as early as the middle of the twelfth century, and the Kumano charms are mentioned in this connection in the *Gempei seisuiki, kan* 26 (48 *kan*), in *Nihon bungaku taikei* 16.56. In the Tokugawa period, these charms were peddled throughout Japan by nuns from the Shrine called *Kumano bikuni*, and were also available in shops. On the face of the Kumano charms were six characters, *Kumano goō hōin*, written in a style which resembled Sanskrit script, formed by clusters of crows, totaling 75 in all, according to the *Wakan sansai zue, kan* 19, 1.302–303. Crows were believed by popular tradition to be the messengers of the Kumano deities and had other special associations with the Kumano Shrines which will be discussed in note 265. On the reverse of the Kumano charm was a form entitled "Divine Punishment Vow" (*Tembatsu kishōmon no koto*), which was filled out when making a pledge. For the text of such a vow, see note 130.

129. *Muragarasu hiyoku no seishi*, "vows of eternal love, [suggested by] the clusters of crows [on the charm]." The word *hiyoku*, literally, "to match wings" (of birds in flight), is a common poetic figure, derived originally from the Chinese, used to symbolize the lasting harmonious relationship of man and wife. *Hiyoku no seishi*, then, means "vows of eternal love." Jihei now fills out a Kumano charm, identical to the ones on which Koharu and he had pledged eternal love. The clusters of crows (*muragarasu*), which form the characters, suggest an *engo* with hiyoku, literally, "to match wings." Miyamori, in a note on p. 244, erroneously states that *muragarasu* means "the Village crows," being misled by the *ateji*, mura 牝 "village," used for mura 群 "group, or cluster." Also, the charms are not known as *Kumano Goō no Muragarasu*, as he states, but merely as *Kumano goō*.

130. The text of the vow Chikamatsu had in mind is very similar, if not identical, to an oath used in swearing loyalty in feudal relation which appears in a guide to officials, *Jikata ochiboshū, kan* 7 (14 *kan*, 1763), by an unidentified author, in *Nihon keizai taiten* (55 vols., 1928–1930), ed. by Takimoto Seiichi, 24.136–137. First are listed the articles of the oath, followed by this text: "The preceding items will be observed without fail. If they are violated: I should incur the punishment of the gods (*kami*) and the punishment of divine fate by Brahma, Indra, the Four Great Devas, all the greater and lesser gods of heaven and earth of the sixty-odd provinces of all Japan, and especially the deities of both Izu and Hakone, the deity of Mishima, the Bodhisattva Hachiman, the deity Temma Tenjin, and deities of this category. I make a vow according to the above articles." This text is followed by the date, name, and seal in blood of the individual making the vow. The formal statement translated above, from "I should incur" to "articles," is written with exactly sixty-six characters, representing the deities of heaven and earth of the sixty-six provinces of Japan.

In Chikamatsu's text, *Bonten* means *Brahmadeva*, i.e., Brahmā, the ruler of the world. *Taishaku[ten]* is *Sakra devānām Indra*, i.e., the sovereign Sakra; Indra. *Shidai* is an abbreviation of *Shidai tennō, Catur-mahārājās*, the four Deva kings. Miyamori (p. 244) and Wakatsuki (p. 218) did not realize that *Shidai* is an abbreviation of *Shidai tennō* and interpreted *Shidai* as meaning *Mahābhūta*, the four elements of which the world is made (see note 256). The text translated above from the *Jikata ochiboshū* shows the error of this interpretation.

Chikamatsu has utilized the names of the witnessing deities in a way which is strikingly similar to passages in two *yōkyoku* involving the same deities in oaths; cf. *Enoshima* (*Yōkyoku taikan* 1.495) and *Shōzon* (*ibid.* 2.1363).

131. *Kōshi-jima,* "grill-striped," is introduced as the pattern of the quilt cover to form an *engo* with Sonezaki. Houses of prostitution, as in the Sonezaki Quarter, had large surfaces of grillwork to cover the windows facing the street (see note 70). Note the repetition of the syllable *ko* in this sentence:

Kado okuri sae
soko soko ni
shikii mo kosu ya
kosanu uchi
*ko*tatsu *ni Jihei*
mata korori
kaburu futon no
kōshi-jima.

132. The day of the zodiacal sign of the Boar (*inoko*) in the middle of the 10th month was considered by the townsmen to be the most auspicious date to conduct a warming ceremony for the covered brazier (*kotatsu*) as the winter season set in. See *Rigen shūran* 3.741a.

133. This passage bears some similarity to a children's song still current in Osaka.

Inoko no ban ni   "On the night of the day of the Boar
oni ume, ja ume;   demons are born, serpents are born;
tsuno no haeta   nonchinkorome
nonchinkorome.   which has grown horns."

According to Itō (p. 240), this song has been suggested by Fujii Otoo in an article in the periodical *Kamigata* (No. 2) as a source for this passage in Chikamatsu.

134. On *Shingin,* "New Silver," see note 55.

135. *Yotsu sankamme. Yotsu* is an abbreviation of *Yotsuhō[gin],* a variant reading of *Shihō[gin],* or "Four Treasure [Silver]." This name was derived from the fact that the character *hō,* "treasure," appeared four times on the face of the coin. It was one-fourth the value of the *Shingin* (see note 55), and therefore the sum *sankamme,* or "3000 *me,*" was equal to 750 *me* of *Shingin.* This was merely the down payment, or one-half of the necessary total for redeeming Koharu.

136. The source of the money is explained on p. 83. See note 153.

137. Iwakuni in Suō Province was well known for its ordinary writing paper (*hanshi*), known as *Iwakuni-gami.* The *Wakan sansai zue, kan* 15 (1.252b), has the note: "Hanshi: Superior [*hanshi*] is a product of Yanagawa in Chikugo Province. [That of] Iwakuni in Bōshū [i.e., Suō Province] is also good." Iwakuni is the present Iwakuni-machi in Kuga-gun in Yamaguchi Prefecture.

138. *Shōbai no o wa misenu,* lit., "the tail of the business must not be revealed." The figure here is that the tail reveals the true nature, betraying a fox or badger which has been transformed to bewitch people.

139. *Shi shi no ikkan roppyaku me* means 400 *me* (*momme*) of Shingin multiplied by four, or 1600 *me* of *Shihōgin* (see note 55).

140. This passage contains a number of wordplays which form two levels of meaning:

tansu o   *hirari to tobi*   *Hachijō.*
from the dresser   kite-[colored] Hachijō [silk].
from the dresser nimbly   flies   eighty feet.
kyō   *chirimen*   *no asu wa nai*
Capital   crepe
[When] today is dissipated there will be no tomorrow,
otto no inochi   *shira*   *cha*   *ura.*
                          pale   brown lining.
in [her] husband's life [she] does not know.

Tobi, "kite" (the bird) , is an *engo* with "nimbly," its own homonym, "flies," and is used here to mean not the bird, but its color, "greyish brown," a shade popular during the Genroku period. Hachijō means *Hachijō-ginu*, a type of striped or plaid silk which was a product of Hachijō Island, the southernmost of the seven Izu Islands. For a description and illustration of Hachijō silk, see *Wakan sansai zue, kan* 27, 1.358.

141. *Koyasu*, "to burn," is an *engo* of *momi*, "red silk."

142. *Mageru*, lit. "to bend," but here meaning "to pawn," is an interesting example of a secret word. The common word for "pawn" is *shichi* 質, which is sometimes written, to soften the harshness of its meaning, with the character of a homonym *shichi* 七, meaning "seven." The character "seven" 七 resembles a bent "ten" 十, hence the word *mageru*, "to bend," became a secret word for "to pawn."

143. *Te mo wata mo nai*, lit., "to have neither hands nor cotton," is meaningless unless we reconstruct the two expressions which have been compressed here. The first is part of the idiom *te mo ashi mo dasenu*, lit., "to be unable to put out one's hands and feet," that is, "to be unable to take any action," or "to be in a difficult position." This is combined with a second phrase, *wata[ire] mo nai*, "[he] has no padded garment."

144. Gunnai in Tsuru-gun of Kai Province, in the modern Yamanashi Prefecture, produced a famous striped and plaid silk. For a description and illustration of this silk see *Wakan sansai zue, kan* 27, 1.358.

145. *Habutae*, "habutai," is a soft, plain-woven silk.

146. "Inseparable relationship" is expressed by the phrase *noki mo nokare mo senu naka, lit.*, "a relationship which cannot be removed if one wished to remove it." *Noki* 退 "remove" is a homonym of *noki* 軒 "eaves," the latter being an *engo* of *tsuta no ha*, "ivy leaf" just preceding. The quality of ivy as clinging and difficult to remove suggests the relationship of husband and wife. These double associations of *noki* and *tsuta no ha* may well have been suggested by their use in a popular song contained in the collection *Zōho matsu no ochiba, kan* 5 (1710, 6 *kan*, in *Shin gunsho ruijū* 6.236) by Seiunkaku-shujin (pen name) :

Ochiyo ochiyo to	"Let's fall, let's fall," [say the ivy leaves to the others,]
otoshite oite	but they leave the others fallen,
kabe ni tsuta no ha	the ivy leaves on the wall,
noki kokoro. . . .	[and become] distant-/(eaves) hearted.

The implied meaning of this fragment of the song is that one person has pleaded urgently for the other's love, but when the second meets that demand with sincere love, it is coldly ignored by the first. Chikamatsu has carried over none of the meaning of the original song, but has utilized only the wordplay.

147. *Uchi hadaka demo, soto nishiki*, lit., "at home even if naked, outside brocade." The *Rigen daijiten* by Nakano Yoshihira (1933, 1083 + 424 pp.) , p. 117b, and the *Gengo daijiten* by Fujii Otoo (1910, 1159 + 254 pp.) , p. 135c, both recognize this as a saying (*kotowaza*) , giving *Amijima* as the only source, but they misquote it as saying *kazari*, "ornament," instead of *nishiki*, "brocade."

148. 350 *me* (*momme*) of *Shingin* is equal to 1400 *momme* of *Shihōgin*.

149. The word here translated "bundle" is *furoshiki*, a piece of cotton or silk cloth, a yard or more square, used to wrap bundles of all types.

150. This entire narrative passage from "and opening the lock of the large drawer," except for the short "speech" of Osan's, is in alternating phrases of five and seven syllables.

151. According to the ideal ethic of the Tokugawa period, jealousy is considered one of the more serious offenses a woman could be guilty of. Osan's attitude of willingness to sacrifice blindly her own status for her husband's prestige in society is a model of how women should behave.

152. The pulling out of fingernails and toenails is one of the methods by which

prostitutes and other lovers were said to have demonstrated the sincerity of their love. See *Shikidō ōkagami, kan* 6, in *Zoku enseki jisshu* 2.510–511, in *Kokusho kankōkai,* Series 1.

153. This explains the source of the money referred to on p. 82.

154. See note 144.

155. See note 145.

156. *Saya,* a figured silk damask, usually with a swastika or lightning figure. The method of weaving this cloth was introduced into Japan from China at the end of the sixteenth century, and seems to have come originally from Europe. The name itself is derived from the Portuguese *Saia,* or Spanish *Saya.*

157. This is a medium-length *wakizashi,* which itself is a relatively short sword. See note 50.

158. It is not made clear in the text whether the speaker is Jihei or Osan. Wakatsuki (p. 228) interprets it to be Jihei, whereas Itō (p. 275) argues in favor of Osan. On the stage, of course, the intended speaker would have been apparent in the action of the puppets.

159. There is also controversy over the meaning of the expression used here, *yō okaerinasareta.* I have followed the interpretation of Itō (p. 276) and Higuchi (p. 473) , that it carries the usual meaning of "welcome back," and that it is used here because Jihei and Osan are so flustered by the untimely appearance of Gozaemon that they say "welcome back" instead of "welcome" (*yō oidenasareta*) . Wakatsuki (p. 226) says that *okaeri,* "welcome back," can be used in place of *oide,* "welcome," in addressing an intimate.

160. Gozaemon speaks to his daughter in abusive, vulgar language, *merō, shita ni kekkarō,* which is stronger than the translation of "woman, sit down." He then addresses his son-in-law with sarcastic formality, calling him *muko-dono,* "Mr. Son-in-law," and he uses other honorifics in mockery.

161. *Kuchi ni hari aru nigai kao,* lit., "a bitter face [as if he] had needles in his mouth." This colorful expression seems to have been original with Chikamatsu. The inspiration for it may have come from a classical saying of quite a different meaning: *kuchi ni mitsu ari, hara ni ken ari,* "in his mouth there is honey, but in his belly there is a two-edged sword." This metaphor of the bee is used to describe a man whose words are honeyed but in whose heart is treachery. The saying stems from the Chinese, a description of Li Lin-fu (d. 752) (Giles 1170) , in *Tzu-chih t'ung-chien* (1084) 215.3a. by Ssu-ma Kuang (1019–1086) (Giles 1756) : "People said, as for Lin-fu, in his mouth there was honey, but in his belly there was a two-edged sword."

162. The mention of these gods recalls Jihei's vow, p. 79. See note 130.

163. *Kojjiki hinin,* "beggar outcast," is the same in meaning as *sodegoi hinin* which appeared on p. 71. See note 78. *Kojjiki* is read *kojiki* in modern Japanese.

164. This allusion is to the famous legend of Urashima Tarō, a fisherman of Tango Province (now part of Kyoto Prefecture). One day when he was fishing from his boat, he caught a large five-colored turtle. The turtle transformed itself into a princess, and persuaded Urashima to accompany her to a palace in the middle of the sea. There he married the princess, but after three years asked to return to his native village for a visit. When he left, the princess gave him a box, warning him never to open it if he wished to return to her. When Urashima reached his village, he found none of his friends and discovered that three hundred years had passed since his disappearance from the village. Ignoring the warning of the princess, he opened the box, and out rose a cloud of vapor which turned him into a white-haired old man. This is perhaps the best known of the early versions of this universal legend which have been preserved in Japan. It is from the *Tango fudoki,* which is dated about 730–750 by Karl Florenz, who translated this legend in his *Japanische Mythologie, Nihongi, "Zeitalter der Götter,"* Supplement to the *Mittheilungen der*

Deutschen Gesellschaft für Natur- und Völkerkunde Ostasiens (Tokyo, 1901), p. 341; see pp. 293–299. The Urashima legend has been reworked in countless stories and plays, including two *jōruri* by Chikamatsu: *Urashima nendaiki (ca.* 1700), in *Chikamatsu zenshū* 5.717–814, and a more chaotic account in *Matsukaze Murasame sokutai kagami* (1694), *ibid.* 4.245–340.

165. Chikamatsu uses two puns as he weaves in a popular saying about Urashima Tarō, who is here referred to by a more classical name, Urashima-no-ko:

Fufu   ga kokoro imasara ni akete   kuyashiki
The couple's hearts   now   [at the] opening   were mortified.
              Opening [the box], was mortified
Urashima no   kotatsu-   buton ni mi o yosete. . .
   To the striped covered-brazier quilt   they edged. . .
Urashima-no-   ko.

The phrase *akete kuyashiki Urashima,* "Urashima, opening the box, was mortified" has become a popular saying in the form *akete kuyashiki tamatebako,* "the box, when opened, mortified [Urashima]." This phraseology is used in two *yōkyoku: Ama,* in *Yōkyoku taikan* 1.182 as *akete kuyashiki Urashima ga;* in the *yōkyoku* entitled *Urashima,* in *Yōkyoku sōsho* (3 vols., 1914, compiled by Haga Yaichi and Sasaki Nobutsuna) 1.269 as *akete kuyashiki Urashima ga hako,* and again in the same play, 1.268, as . . . *tamatebako, akete kuyashiki kokoro kana.* In Chikamatsu's *Matsukaze Murasame sokutai kagami* (1694), *Chikamatsu zenshū* 4.293, appears the phrase *akete kuyashiki tamatebako* in precisely the form of the modern saying. These all presumably stem from similar phraseology used in a poem in the *Man'yōshū, kan* 11 (759, 20 *kan*), in *(Shinshaku) Nihon bungaku sōsho* (1922–1923, 12 vols.) 6.295, line 15.

166. *Oyama,* "harlot," is a word used in the Kamigata area for a low-class prostitute. It is a more pejorative word than *hakujin,* used on p. 78; see note 122. For a discussion of the word *oyama,* see *Kinsei fūzoku shi, kan* 19, 2.97–98, and *Chikamatsu goi,* p. 65.

167. *Ike-dō-zuri-me.* Both *ike* (i.e., *iki*) and *dō* are prefixes of abuse, and *me* is a suffix of abuse. This expression, then, has the same meaning as the words Tahei used to abuse Jihei, *iki-zuri-me, dō-zuri-me,* pp. 72–73, see note 87.

168. *Nanae no tobira, yae no kusari, momoe no kakomi,* "the sevenfold doors, the eightfold chains, and the hundredfold enclosures." This is perhaps based on a popular Buddhist tradition about the palace of one of the rulers of purgatory, Emma-ō (Skt. Yama-rāja). It bears some resemblance to the description of Emma's palace in the *Jō a gon gyō* (Skt. *Dīrghâgama-sūtra*): "Its walls are sevenfold, its balustrades are sevenfold, its nets are sevenfold, its rows of trees are sevenfold." See *(Taishō shinshū) Daizōkyō* (Tokyō, 1924–1934, 97 vols.) 1.126b.

169. *Hiruhinaka,* "broad daylight." Itō (pp. 290–291) goes to some pains to point out that the time is actually evening, and that this is an instance of "an oversight by a wise man." It is, nonetheless, effective as a figure for emphasis.

170. The children use a mild pejorative in addressing their grandfather, *jiisama-me,* by suffixing the abusive *me.*

171. *Kuwayama* pills were said to be efficacious in curing children of congenital syphilis and stomach-aches, according to the *Chikamatsu goi,* p. 110. The method of making them was said to have been introduced into Japan by Kuwayama, a retainer of Toyotomi Hideyoshi (1536–1598), after he participated in the Korean campaign. In the chapter on the famous products of Osaka in *Setsuyō gundan, kan* 16 (28.341b), is the following: "Kuwayama pills. They are to be obtained at Sango-ji (temple), Teramachi, Tennōji, in Higashinari-gun. They were transmitted by the priest, Kuwayama, and are a good medicine for the myriad diseases of children." Itō (p. 292) believes this priest to have been Kuwayama Shigeharu (1524–1606).

172. *To iisutsuru, ato ni mi-sutsuru, ko o sutsuru (yabu),* "she says as she leaves,

and abandoning her husband and abandoning her children (grove) . . ." The word *yabu*, "grove," is not essential to the meaning, but its presence is not obtrusive because it forms an *engo* to "bamboo." The reason for introducing it, however, was evidently to suggest a popular saying, *ko o sutsuru yabu wa aredo, mi sutsuru yabu wa nashi*, lit., "although there is a grove in which to abandon your child(ren) , there is no grove in which to abandon yourself." That is, in case of extremity, you will put yourself before your child. This saying appeared earlier in an *ukiyo zōshi* by Nishizawa Ippū, *Gozen Gikeiki, kan* 7 (1700, 8 *kan*) in *Kindai Nihon bungaku taikei* 4.181. It probably stemmed from a poem in the *Kin'yō shū* (*ca.* 1127) in (*Kōchū*) *Kokka taikei* 4.100.

In the case of this saying, as in many previously mentioned, Chikamatsu does not intend to inject any of the meaning of the saying into his text. He is merely using a succession of words from the saying in his text in another meaning as a stylistic device. This usage here involves a pun on *mi*. In the saying, *mi sutsuru*, "to abandon oneself," also means "to abandon while seeing," that is, an intensive of "to abandon."

Chikamatsu also used part of the saying in *Shinjū Kasane-izutsu* (*ca.* 1708) , *Chikamatsu zenshū* 8.393, when the couple are seeking their place of suicide: *Daibutsuden no kanjinjo, mi o sutsuru yabu to narinikeri*, "the subscription office at the Great Buddha Hall becomes the grove in which to abandon their lives."

The above passage in *Amijima* is directly followed by the words which conclude the act: *yabu ni fūfu no futamata-dake, nagaki wakare to*. The figure is that a husband and wife are inseparable, like a bifurcated bamboo, which has sent up two trunks from one set of roots. They are to be separated, literally "for long," and "long" is an *engo* to bamboo. Notice the repetition of the syllable *fu* (*bu*) .

Act 3

173. This echoes the opening sentences of the play: "The prostitutes of the Shijimi River [Quarter] have deep affections. It is like an ocean of love. . ." *Se*, "shoals," is an *engo* to "Shijimi River" and "flowing waters," and here it carries the meaning of "the important place" or "*the* place." The phrase *koko o se ni sen*, "here is the shoals (place) ," is a line from a poem by the famous poet Saigyō (1118–1190) in the eighth Imperial anthology, the *Shin kokinshū, kan* 3 (1206, 20 *kan*) :

Kikazu tomo	Although I do not hear [one]
koko o se ni sen	here is *the* place [for]
hototogisu	cuckoos,
Yamada no hara no	On the field at Yamada
sugi no muradachi	by this group of cryptomerias.

174. *Ushi mitsu* was the time between 3:00 and 3:30 A.M. In the Tokugawa period the day was divided into 12 periods of 2 hours (*toki*) , beginning from midnight. *Ushi*, the second zodiacal sign, was the period from 2 to 4 A.M., and *mitsu* meant the third quarter of it.

175. The 15th night of the month in the lunar calendar was the full moon, and the last of the Ten Nights.

176. The first part of Act 3 takes place at the *chaya* Yamatoya, and the proprietor's personal name is Dembei.

177. *Banta* is an abbreviation of *bantarō*, "night patrolman." He was a menial, often a *hinin* outcast, hired by the individual block (*machi*) to patrol the streets from late at night through the early morning hours, beating wooden clappers or a drum. See sketch of a *bantarō* in *Chikamatsu goi*, p. 294c.

178. *Ashidori chidori-ashi*, "staggering walk," is a good example of the euphonic

repetition of syllables. *Chidori-ashi,* lit., "plover feet," is usually a figure for a drunken walk, as resembling the zigzag course of a plover, but here the *banta* is probably staggering from weariness.

179. *Goyoza* is an abbreviation of *(hi no) goyōjin (Itō,* p. 301), or *(hi no) go-yōjin sōrō/saburau,* "be careful (of fire)." This cry of a neighborhood watchman is still to be heard at night in some cities.

180. *Ue no machi* probably means "an upper street" in the Sonezaki Quarter. The maid, then, has come from the direction of Sonezaki 1-chōme. To balance the word "upper," the word "lower" is introduced: *ue no machi kara shimo-onago,* "from an upper street [comes] a lower woman" (i.e., a maid).

181. *Kuguri,* "side door," is a small door cut in one side of the main gate or door which is used late at night when the larger one is barred shut.

182. *Karu,* "to take," lit., "to borrow, to hire," has a special usage in the gay quarter, meaning one visitor's taking a prostitute away from another visitor who had engaged her. Its meaning is essentially the same as *morau* (usually "to receive") discussed in note 49, except that *karu* is a milder term, its original meaning of "to borrow" suggesting a temporary loan. Here it does not mean that Koharu is being called by another visitor, but merely that her proprietor wishes to have her return to Kiinokuniya.

183. That is, Koharu and Jihei overhear in their upstairs room in Yamatoya that Koharu has been bought out by Tahei, and the two of them resolve on suicide that night.

184. This sentence is rich in its repetition of the syllable *ya,* alone and in *cha* (spelled in *kana, chiya*):

> chaya *no* cha-*gama mo*
> *yo hitotoki*
> *yasumu wa* yatsu *to*
> *nanatsu to no.*

Sassa (p. 125) believes the first part of the sentence to be a contemporary saying to be found in Saikaku, but he admits his inability to recall the reference. Even the gay quarter, the so-called "nightless city" *(fuyajō),* has its two-hour period of inactivity.

Yatsu to nanatsu, "2 A.M. and 4 A.M." The periods of two hours which were known by zodiacal signs (see note 174) were also designated by the number of times the temple bell was rung at the beginning of each period. *Yatsu,* "eight," when the bell was struck eight times, was 2 A.M., and *nanatsu,* "seven," was 4 A.M. See Itō, pp. 49–51.

185. *Tankei,* "short lamp," as contrasted to a *chōkei,* "tall lamp," stood about 2 feet high.

186. *Nakabarai,* "the interim payment," the last day of the 10th month. See note 46.

187. This money is presumably the 400 *me (momme)* of *Shingin* which Osan had prepared originally to pay for the Iwakuni paper, and which Jihei had on his person that evening.

188. *Nochi no tsukimi,* "the Latter Moonviewing," was a customary night for enjoying the beauty of the moon. It fell on the 13th night of the 9th month, in contrast to *tsukimi,* "Moonviewing," which was the 15th night of the 8th month. Higuchi's statement (p. 479) that *nochi no tsukimi* is the 15th night of the 9th month is not to be followed.

189. Saietsubō, the popular name of a certain priest, might mean that he served at a temple, either real or fictional, called Saietsu[ji]. In Chikamatsu's *Shinjū yoigōshin* (1722), Act 3, *Chikamatsu zenshū* 12.679, there appears a Sainembō who is supposed to be a priest of Sainenji (Temple) in Kōzunomiya, Osaka, but who serves as a messenger and go-between for merchants. Higuchi (p. 479) and Itō (p.

310) suggest that the Saietsubō may be one of the rather worldly priests of this period who frequented parties in the gay quarter, helped to arrange the entertainment, and enlivened the occasion with witticisms and recitations. This was the function of the male entertainers of the gay quarter, known as *taiko-mochi* or *hōkan* or *otoko-geisha*, "male geisha." These men, like the physicians of the Tokugawa period, frequently imitated the practice of monks of shaving their heads and suffixing *-bō* to their professional names.

190. Fukushima was the district neighboring Sonezaki on the west.

191. *Gin-ichimai* meant *chōgin ichimai*, or one *chōgin* silver coin, which weighed 43 *momme*. The text does not specify whether the currency was *Shingin* or *Shihōgin*, but it was presumably the latter (see note 55).

192. The proprietor would assume that these memorial services were for the ancestors of Jihei's household, but Jihei had in mind that they would also be for himself after his suicide.

193. Isoichi is evidently the name of a male entertainer. Itō (p. 311) argues that the second part of the name, *ichi*, means that he is probably a special type of *hōkan*, called a *za-gashira*, a blind entertainer who plays the samisen and sings. He cites a *za-gashira* called Yokuichi who plays the samisen for the prostitutes in Chikamatsu's *Hakata Kojorō namimakura*, Act 1 (1718), *Chikamatsu zenshū* 11.580–581, translated by Miyamori as "Adventures of the Hakata Damsel," pp. 265–309; see pp. 274–275.

194. *Gin-itsutsu* meant *mameita-gin itsutsu*, or 5 *mameita* silver pieces. A *mameita* piece varied in weight from 1 to 5 *momme* (1 *momme* was 3.75 grams).

195. In making this ironic joke, Jihei, who is soon to commit suicide, probably intends to mislead Dembei by feigned high spirits. The sword of a samurai was said to be his soul, and to forget his sword was an extremely serious dishonor. In the best-known *jōruri* version of the story of the 47 *rōnin*, the fact that Yuranosuke has forgotten his sword in a *chaya* and has let it become rusty is taken as strong evidence by those spying on him that he has abandoned the samurai's code of conduct, and that it need not be feared that he is plotting to avenge his lord's death. *Kanadehon chūshingura*, Act 7 (11 acts, 1741), by Takeda Izumo (1691–1756), Miyoshi Shōraku (ca. 1696–?), and Namiki Sōsuke/Senryū (1695–1751), in Higuchi, 2.284:

[*Sagisaka Bannai:*] Say, he left his sword here.

[*Ono Kudayū:*] Indeed, that is really the proof of a great fool. See the soul of his accomplishment. [Unsheathes sword.] Well, it is a tarnished, rusty sword (*akaiwashi*, "red [salted] sardine").

[*Bannai:*] Aha!

[*Kudayū:*] His true character is being revealed more and more. You [should] be relieved, you [should] be relieved. . .

196. In the *chaya* the visitors were required to entrust their swords to the proprietor before they went up to the second floor, to prevent any disputes which might arise during the evening from becoming too serious.

197. *Kogatana*, "knife," of about 6 inches in length, was slipped into a slot in the side of the sword sheath.

198. This statement, ostensibly made in reference to his trip home and to the capital (the present Kyoto), carried the hint that he is putting his complete reliance in the sword, and that the purpose is suicide. The attention directed to the sword in these lines impresses on the minds of the audience the part it is to play at the end of the play.

199. *Kagande*, from *kagamu*, here means "to hide, to conceal oneself," as well as the usual meaning, "to bend, to crouch." The audience, of course, sees Jihei crouched in the shadows near Magoemon.

200. *Naya* here has the original meaning of "sheds"; cf. note 6. The cheapest type of prostitutes, such as the streetwalkers, frequented that area.

201. On Ichi-no-kawa, see note 114.

202. *Uramachi*, "back street," is the street one block north of the main street through the Sonezaki Quarter.

203. In Chikamatsu's second *sewamono*, *Shinjū nimai ezōshi* (1706), there is a similar scene. Late at night when Ichiroemon is hiding by Temmaya, the house from which his love Shima is about to escape, his brother comes searching for him in the hope of saving him from suicide. He bangs on the door, inquires if Ichiroemon is there, and then walks away ignorant of the fact that his brother is hiding nearby. (*Chikamatsu zenshū* 7.661; 694.)

204. *Jūakunin*, literally "ten-evils person." The ten evils according to Buddhist teachings are: "killing, stealing, adultery, lying, double-tongue, coarse language, filthy language, covetousness, anger, and perverted views." (See Soothill and Hodous, *Dictionary of Chinese Buddhist Terms*, p. 50a.)

205. On *ue no machi*, see note 180.

206. The original contains a close parallelism in two pairs of lines of seven and five syllables, matching an onomatopoetic word, verb, and two nouns:

kuru-kuru taguru   kaze no yo wa
seki-seki mawaru   hi yōjin

These lines contain three puns: *kuru*, "to come," and representing onomatopoetically the sound of a cough; *kaze*, "a cold" and "wind"; *seki*, "hurrying" and "coughing." There is also assonance in the first line, with *kuru* repeated in its *nigori* form of *guru*.

207. The god of Kazuraki, usually read Katsuragi, was the deity Hitokotonushino-kami of Mount Katsuragi (Katsuragi-yama) in Yamato Province (the present Nara Prefecture). According to an old myth, he was ordered by the recluse hermit En no Shōkaku (also read En no Ozuna) to build a stone bridge from Mount Katsuragi to Mount Kimpu (Kimpusan) in the Yoshino mountains. He was so ashamed of his ugly face that he avoided people and appeared only at night, and consequently never finished his work. This story appears in the *Nihonkoku gempō zen'aku ryōiki/reiiki* (contracted to *Nihon ryōiki/reiiki*), *kan* 1 (ca. 810–823, 3 *kan*), by the monk Keikai in *Gunsho ruijū*, *kan* 447 (1904 edition, 19 vols.) 16.42–43. For a German translation, see Hermann Bohner, "Legenden aus der Frühzeit des japanischen Buddhismus, Nippon-koku-gembō-zenaku-ryō-i-ki," *Mittheilungen der Deutschen Gesellschaft für Natur- und Völkerkunde Ostasiens* 27 (1934–1935), 245, 91; see Textband, pp. 95–96 and Band Anmerkungen, pp. 21–27.

The use of the word *tsuraki*, "trying," makes a repetition of syllables in *tsuraki Kazuraki*. This reading of Katsuragi as Kazuraki is used as a title for a nō play, and this may be the source of Chikamatsu's reading, as he uses in this passage a phrase found in that play, *kami-gakure*, "god-hiding." See *Yōkyoku taikan* 1.698.

208. The phrase *issun no saki ni jigoku*, "hell one inch ahead," is formed by combining parts of two common sayings: *issun saki wa yami*, "an inch ahead is darkness," that is, it is impossible to see into one's future; and *issun (shita) no jigoku*, "hell an inch below," an expression for the dangers of sailing in a ship, that hell is just below one inch of board.

209. *Oni no minu ma*, "before the demon appears," is the first part of the popular saying *oni no konu ma ni sentaku*, "[do] the laundry before the demon comes." It seems probable that *sentaku* is a corruption of *shintaku*, in which case the expression originally meant "[move to] a new house before the demon comes" so that you can rid yourself of him. Here, of course, the demon means some member of Yamatoya. There is an interesting chain of *engo* here: "hell" suggests "demon," which in turn is associated with "New Year's morn," because that is when the demons are exorcised, and "New Year's morn" suggests *haru*, "spring" (in Koharu's name), as in the old Japanese calendar New Year's day was the beginning of spring.

210. The moon and the Shijimi River are both moving west, while the couple start along the river toward the east. This part of Act 3 ends with some of the same words with which it began. Compare the following two lines which appear near the beginning and end respectively of this part of the act:

se ni sen Shijimi-gawa nagaruru mizu
haya-se Shijimi-gawa nagaruru tsuki

Se, "shoals," becomes haya-se, "swift rapids"; nagaruru mizu, "flowing waters," becomes nagaruru tsuki, "flowing (and declining) moon." The first line creates a calm mood, the second is agitated and leading to violent action. There are, of course, no swift rapids in the Shijimi River. In this passage, "swift rapids" has a double function:

kokoro no haya-se	Shijimi-gawa
swift rapids	Shijimi River
the heart's swift rapids	subside.

211. The title of the michiyuki is Nagori no hashi-zukushi. Nagori carries the overtones of several meanings: "the sad feeling of parting," "last memories," and "the image of something past." Hashi-zukushi, as explained in the Introduction, p. 46, means that the bridges will be "used up" or "exhausted," that is, all the bridges along the route will be mentioned. A hashi-zukushi was included in an earlier love suicide play by Chikamatsu, Imamiya shinjū (1710), Chikamatsu zenshū 9.140–148.

212. Hashiri-gaki, "running writing," is a cursive, flowing style of writing. Hashiri, the opening word of the michiyuki, is a pivot word, serving as the concluding verb for the last line in the preceding section of Act 3, meaning "run, hasten." For a third meaning that is claimed for it, see the anecdote in Okina gusa, Introduction, pp. 48–49.

213. Konoe style is a school of calligraphy originated by Konoe (Sammyakuin) Nobutada (1565–1614).

214. Yarō bōshi, "the caps of boy actors," are the small caps of purple silk crepe which were worn over the shaved forelock to simulate the appearance of women's hair. Boy actors who played female roles in the kabuki were required after 1652 to shave their forelocks to conform to the masculine fashion; see Introduction, p. 10. These two rules which Chikamatsu mentions here appeared earlier in the ukiyo zōshi Imayō nijūshi kō, kan 3 (1709, 6 kan), by Getsujindō (pen name, fl. 1708–1712), in Ukiyo zōshi shū, in Kindai Nihon bungaku taikei 4.936; "Nō texts are in the Konoe-dono style, the caps of boy actors are purple. . ."

215. Shaka, Sākyamuni, the historical Buddha.

216. Ingakyō, Karma Sūtra, or Cause and Effect Sūtra, is a contraction of the title of a Hinayana text, the Kako genzai ingakyō. Chikamatsu evidently has in mind a passage from the Ingakyō (4 kan), Daizōkyō 3.620–652: "If you wish to know the past cause, look at the present effect; if you wish to know the future effect, look at the present cause." Chikamatsu utilized this passage in the jōruri Imagawa Ryōshun (ca. 1700), Chikamatsu zenshū 5.445 "Indeed, is it true that if you look at the present result, you will know the past and future." Also, in Tamba Yosaku (1708), ibid. 8.594: "Both the past and the future can be known from the present."

217. There is a series of engo based on sakuragi, "cherry tree/wood," including chiri-yuku, "strewn about [of falling petals]," ne-hori ha-hori, "fullest particulars," lit., "digging the roots, digging the leaves," hori, "carved," which appears as a pun imbedded in ne-hori ha-hori, and han(suru), "block (printing)." This entire progression of engo leads up through ezōshi, "illustrated leaflet" and "block printing" to kami, "paper," the symbol of Jihei's business.

Ezōshi, "illustrated leaflets," consisted of one or two pages of a crudely printed and illustrated account of some popular news, such as a natural calamity, uprising, vendetta, execution, or love suicide. They were generally printed from blocks of dried clay, but in this case the superior material of cherry wood was used. These "extras" were also known as *yomiuri* or *fureuri*. The earliest one extant bears news of the summer campaign against Osaka castle in 1615. They dealt more frequently in scandals, and were therefore periodically banned, as in 1684 and 1698, but they were quickly revived, and became the forerunners of the Japanese newspapers of the Restoration period. They were usually recited on the streets by strolling reciters, called *ezōshi-uri*. The *Jinrin kimmō zui* (1690), *kan* 4, pp. 161–162, says: "*Ezōshi-uri.* [They take] the news of something unusual which has happened, some scandal [affecting] a person's position, and without regard for the harm it does many people, make it into a song or a *jōruri* recitation, and hawk it with the aid of an accompanying reciter. Ignorant people, men and women, young and old, . . . buy these for their own enjoyment." No news created greater excitement than a love suicide, and the title of one of Chikamatsu's *sewamono* illustrates this. *Shinjū nimai ezōshi* (1706) has a double meaning: "A love suicide, two/a two-page illustrated leaflets." Why there were two leaflets is explained in the last lines of the play, *Chikamatsu zenshū* 7.700: "In the world there is the rumor that this man [Ichirōemon] died, and the report that he did not die. Two illustrated leaflets—the living and the dead— are memorials to the way of love." Another of his plays, *Uzuki no momiji* (1706), contains this sentence, *ibid.* 7.839: "The end of this life will be put by someone into prose in a *yomiuri* for reciting, and be circulated by chanting even in the back country." (It should be pointed out that the term *ezōshi* is also used for the larger illustrated booklets containing stories or a *jōruri* text.)

218. Toward the west is the Shijimi River and the Shijimi (Sonezaki) Quarter where Koharu lives. Tenjin-bashi is at the foot of the street on which Jihei lives (note 108), and as it has this close association with him, it is the first of the twelve bridges to be mentioned. The others are enumerated in the order in which Jihei and Koharu pass or cross them on their journey from Sonezaki to Amijima (notes 221–249; see map). The names of the bridges are either worked into the meaning of the narrative or else are mentioned through wordplays. In the latter cases, in the six instances where they do not contribute to the meaning of the narrative, the name of the bridge has been placed as a note at the foot of the page in this translation in order not to break the continuity of the sentences.

219. Sugawara no Michizane (845–903) is here referred to as Kan Shōjō. Kan is the *on* reading of the character *Suga*. *Shōjō* was originally a Chinese term meaning "prime minister" which was occasionally used in Japan to mean the highest minister. Michizane actually did not reach that position, but as Minister of the Right (*Udaijin*) he excited the jealousy of the Fujiwara family, which monopolized most of the higher court offices, and he was exiled to Dazaifu, Kyushu, in 901. He was later apotheosized as Temma Tenjin (often abbreviated to Tenjin), and, among his many other functions, was considered a guardian deity of Osaka.

220. Tsukushi was an old name for Kyushu or northern Kyushu.

221. *Hito-tobi-ume-da-bashi* is to be understood in three ways: *hitotobi*, "one leap"; *tobi-ume*, "flying plum tree"; and *Umeda-bashi*, "Plum-field Bridge." The bridge, of course, has no meaning in the sentence, but is worked in because it is the name of the first bridge the couple pass on their journey upstream along the Shijimi River (see map, and note 11).

222. According to legend, when Sugawara no Michizane left his residence in the capital for exile, he composed a poem about his favorite plum tree:

Kochi fukaba	When the east wind blows
nioi okose yo	send some fragrance [to me],
ume no hana	plum blossoms.
Aruji nashi to te	Not having your master,
haru na wasure so	do not forget Spring.

This poem appears in *Gempei seisuiki, kan* 32 (*Nihon bungaku taikei* 16.283) and elsewhere. For variations in the text of the poem, see *Meika jiten* (1936), by Nakamura Kaoru, p. 217b.

The plum tree was so moved by this poem that it is said to have flown to Dazaifu (in the present Fukuoka Prefecture), where it transplanted itself at the temple, Anrakuji, which stood on the grounds of the present shrine, Dazaifu Jinja. This poem also appears in Chikamatsu's play about Sugawara no Michizane, *Tenjinki*, Act 3 (1713), *Chikamatsu zenshū* 10.208. The details of the legend of Michizane and his trees mentioned in this note and the following can be found in *Gempei seisuiki, kan* 32 (*op. cit.* 16.283–284), in an anonymous Muromachi period miscellany, *Tōten gyōhitsu, kan* 19 (20 *kan*) (work quoted by Itō, pp. 344–345) and the *yōkyoku Oimatsu*, in *Yōkyoku taikan* 1.521–534.

223. The cherry tree should be discussed before the pine tree, but Chikamatsu reverses the order so that he can mention the bridges in the proper sequence. According to the legend, the cherry tree in Michizane's garden, dejected because it had not been honored with a poem, withered away in a single night. When Michizane at Dazaifu heard this he composed the following poem:

Ume wa tobi	The plum tree flew,
sakura wa karuru	the cherry tree withered
yo no naka ni	in this world
Matsu bakari koso	Only the pine tree
tsurenakarikere	has not accompanied [me].

This poem appears in *Tōten gyōhitsu, kan* 19 (quoted by Itō, p. 345). For variations in the text of the poem, see *Meika jiten*, p. 114a. When this poem was composed the pine also flew to Anrakuji and transplanted itself there. The name of the pine, *Oimatsu*, is used by Chikamatsu as a pivot word to be interpreted in two ways: 老松 "the old pine tree"; and 追松 "the pine tree which followed after."

224. Midori-bashi, "Green Bridge," the second bridge, serves as an *engo* of "pine tree."

225. Sakura-bashi, "Cherry Bridge," the third bridge. See note 11.

226. *Shijimi* itself means "corbicula" and is an *engo* of "shells."

227. Shijimi Bridge, the fourth bridge, was a popular name for the Dōjima Bridge (Dōjima-bashi). (See *Setsuyo gundan, kan* 7, *Dainihon chishi taikei* 28.113b). Early in the twentieth century, the Shijimi River was filled in and these four bridges were demolished. However, the names Sakura-bashi and Shijimi-bashi were preserved as the names of trolley stops (Itō, p. 346).

228. The series of descriptions: "not enough . . . to fill," "tiny," and "short" are *engo*.

229. This is an example of three levels of meaning through the use of pivot words:

Shijimi-bashi	*mijikaki*	*mono wa*
(1) Shijimi Bridge is	short.	
(2)	Short	things are
wareware ga kono yo no sumai	*aki*	*no hi yo*
(2) our this life's stay and an	autumn	day.
(3) We have of this life's stay	tired.	
(4) Our this life's stay [by this]	autumn	day [is]
jūkyū to nijūhachi nen no. . .		
(4) 19 and 28 years. . .		

230. Ōe-bashi, the fifth bridge.

231. Naniwa-ko-bashi, a short bridge compared to the nearby Naniwa Bridge.

232. Funairi-bashi was a small bridge over a canal which led to the storehouse residency of the Nabeshima family, lords of the Saga fief in Hizen Province (the present Saga Prefecture). This bridge does not appear on most of the maps, but it

is shown on a panorama entitled "Sketch of the Sixteen Bridges of Naniwa," in the Osaka guidebook, *Naniwa no nagame, kan* 1 (1778, 5 *kan*), by (Hakuensai) Baikō (pen name) (1737–?) in *Naniwa sōsho* 12.402–403.

233. *Horikawa no hashi*, "the bridges over the Horikawa." Horikawa "canal" means the Temma Horikawa, which was a blind canal leading north out of the Ōkawa. (See *Setsuyō gundan, kan* 7, *Dainihon chishi taikei* 28.114a.) The couple probably cross over it on the bridge which is closest to the Ōkawa, the Taihei Bridge, and from this they could presumably see several of the other five bridges crossing it toward the north (see map), which the author fancies might be flooded by their copious tears. It is possible that *Horikawa no hashi* means the bridge called Horikawa-bashi, the fifth bridge north of Ōkawa, but of course the couple do not cross that bridge.

234. This "speech" of Jihei's is an example of the manner in which dialogue (*kotoba*) and narrative (*ji*) sometimes shade into each other in the *michiyuki* (see Introduction, pp. 42–43). It is not really direct discourse, but rather expresses his thoughts and feelings and is not entirely satisfactory cast in the first person in translation. It consists largely of alternating phrases of five and seven syllables characteristic of the *ji*. It seems better, however, to handle the entire passage as discourse, because it is answered by Koharu's "speech," which is not intermingled with narrative and is largely in broken meter, although it does lapse into five-seven phrases toward the end.

235. The bridge referred to here is Tenjin Bridge, which has already been mentioned (see note 218; also note 108). It is unnecessary to repeat the name here as it has just been stated that to reach Jihei's home one turns north there. The large number of piles is mentioned because it was one of the three longest bridges in Osaka, the other two being its flanking bridges, Naniwa and Temma.

236. Hachiken'ya, "Eight Houses," was the name of the south bank of the Ōkawa between Tenjin Bridge and Temma Bridge. Why this area, which had so many buildings, bore this name is explained in *Rōka/Naniwa kidan*. This passage, as quoted in the *Settsu meisho zue taisei, kan* 2 (written *ca.* 1855, 15 *kan*), by Akatsuki no Kanenaru (commonly Kanenari) (1793–1860) in *Naniwa sōsho* 7.93: "The Hachiken'ya boat landing. The *Rōka kidan* says: 'Hachiken'ya [is a place which] in ancient times had eight houses in a row along the river. At that time there were no [other] houses along the river, and, because this was unique, it was named Hachiken'ya. It is merely a guess to say that it was named Hachiken'ya because there were eight inns there.'" It is probably because of this latter theory that for *ya*, instead of the character 家 "house," the suffix for an inn or shop, 屋, is used.

237. There were passenger boats which ran on the Yodo River (Yodo-gawa) between Fushimi, a southern suburb of the capital, and the Hachiken'ya landing at Osaka. The reference here is to the night boat which arrived at Hachiken'ya early in the morning. *Ibid.* 7.93–94.

238. This is a pun, taking *temma* in the meaning of 天魔 "demon" and 天満 "Temma [Tenjin]" as the deity. Temma Bridge, named for the deity, is the tenth in Chikamatsu's list.

239. Ōkawa, "Great River," is merely a popular name for a short stretch of what was properly called the Yodo River (see map). In modern times, however, the Yodo River has been directed around the north of the city into Osaka Bay, and the branch of the river which empties over the course mentioned here is called the Aji-gawa. The Yamato River (Yamato-gawa) mentioned here flowed from Kashiwara northwest to this confluence with the Yodo River, but, because of flooding, it was redirected in 1704 to flow directly west from Kashiwara around the south of Osaka into Osaka Bay. The old bed through Osaka served thereafter as drainage for irrigation. Although its course was changed sixteen years before the date of our play, the old name still survived. Today the old bed is known as the Neya-gawa.

240. Mitsuse-gawa, a rough equivalent of the River Styx, must be crossed on the way to Hades. Jihei and Koharu will cross it by using the sword on themselves. The name Mitsuse-gawa is substituted for Yamato-gawa, which the couple must cross to reach their place of suicide. In this passage there are *engo* of numbers: "two rivers," "one stream," "the two . . . together," "blade of one sword," and *Mitsuse-gawa*, lit., "three-fords river."

The Mitsuse-gawa is more commonly known as the Sanzu-no-kawa. According to Buddhist tradition it was a great river which had to be crossed after death to reach Hades. It had three fords of graduated depths, the deeper ones to be crossed by those whose sins during life had been more serious.

241. *Tamuke no mizu*, "offering of water," is the presentation of water as a gift before the Shintō and Buddhist deities. Jihei, seeing the river water, hopes that after his death with Koharu people will pray for them and make offerings of water.

242. Concerning rebirth on the same lotus calyx in the Western Paradise of Amida, see Introduction, p. 26.

243. *Gegaki*, "summer writing," was the copying of sūtras during the Buddhist "summer tranquil dwelling" (*ge-ango*). The "tranquil dwelling" (Skt. *varsās*, "the rains") was the retreat for meditation of Buddhist monks during the Indian rainy season, when it was said to be difficult to walk without injuring plant and insect life. This served as a time for the reading and copying of sūtras. In Japan the three-month summer period was usually from the 16th day of the 4th month to the 15th day of the 7th month inclusive, but it was sometimes practiced a month later. It was observed by some of the laity, and other instances of the practice by Japanese prostitutes are quoted in *Chikamatsu goi*, p. 122b, and Itō, p. 352.

244. The repetition of numbers as *engo*, pointed out in note 240, is continued here: "one lotus," "one copy," and "one summer" (translated "each summer.").

245. *Fumombon*, an abbreviation of *Kanzeon bosatsu fumombon* (Skt. *Samantamukhaparivarta-nāmāvalokiteśvara-vikurvana-nirdeśa*), is the 25th section (*hon*) of the *Lotus Sūtra*, the *Myōhō renge kyō* (Skt. *Saddharma-puṇḍarīka-sūtra*) (7 *kan*, 28 sections, in *Daizōkyō* 9.56–58), popularly called *Hōkekyō*. The *Fumombon* section was especially well known, as it told of the divine favor of the Kannon (Kanzeon), popularly "the Goddess of Mercy," and it was sometimes called the *Kannon-kyō* (*Kannon sūtra*).

246. Kyō-bashi crosses the Yamato-gawa.

247. *Ka no kishi*, "the other bank," suggests the other reading of these characters, *higan*, a Buddist term meaning "Nirvāna" or "rebirth into Paradise."

248. *Nori oete* 乗り終へて "complete mounting" is a word play, also to be read *nori o ete* 法を得て "attain the [Buddhist] Law."

249. Onari-bashi, the twelfth and last bridge in the enumeration, is a popular name for the Bizenjima-bashi, which crosses the Namazue River.

250. Noda refers to Noda-mura, the area northwest of Amijima (see map).

251. This passage contains a fine example of assonance in the repetition of the syllable *ko: tera tera no kane no koe kō-kō. Kō-shite . . .* "the tones of the bells of the temples [sound] *kō-kō*. Like this. . ." *Kō-kō* to represent the sound of a bell was used by Chikamatsu earlier in the same year in a *kabuki*, *Izutsu Narihira Kawachi gayoi* (1720). It stems from the *Li chi*.

252. *Hyakuhachi no tama no o* 百八の珠の緒 "a rosary of 108 beads," but the last phrase, *tama no o* 玉の緒, is used in poetry to mean "one's life." Hence, the suggestion is made that they take in their hands not only the rosaries, but also their own lives. The 108 beads are said to represent the 108 worldly passions of man which the worshiper attempts to subdue by telling his beads.

253. This figure of beads of tears mingling with the beads of the rosary appeared earlier in Chikamatsu's *Sonezaki shinjū* (1703), *Chikamatsu zenshū* 6.618–619. In the

michiyuki of that play, when the couple, Tokubyōe and Ohatsu, are approaching the place of their suicide: "The 108 [beads] of the rosaries which they are telling are increased in number by beads of tears, and they do not come to the end of them, but they end their misery (as they come to the end of their) road. Their hearts and the sky are shadowy and dark, and the wind pierces deeply as they arrive at the forest of Sonezaki."

254. Amijima, "Net Island." The *Settsu meisho zue taisei, kan* 12 (*ca.* 1855), in *Naniwa sōsho* 8.463, has the following note: "Amijima. It is east of Bizen Island. This [piece of] land is an embankment of the Yodo River and has row(s) of fishermen's houses, from which are sent a great many fresh fish to the markets. Because under every eave there are nets drying throughout the day, it came to be named this." In modern times, this area in Osaka City is called Amijima-chō.

255. Daichōji is a temple of the Jōdo (Pure Land) Sect, founded *ca.* 1605. Its central deity was Amida Buddha, as suggested indirectly in the text (*ibid.* 8.463). It is claimed that in the compound was located the double grave of Jihei and Koharu (*ibid.*, p. 464). At this time the temple stood at what in modern times is Higashinoda-chō, 2-chōme, but in 1907–1909 it was rebuilt several blocks to the northeast at Higashi-noda-cho 9-chōme. The grave was also moved at this time and was located in front of the main building of the temple. (Itō, pp. 12–13.)

256. *Chi sui ka fū*, "earth, water, fire, and wind," are the four elements (*shidai*, Skt. (*catvāri*) *mahābhūta*) of which all matter is made, according to the Buddhist doctrine. The *Daihōkō engaku shūtararyōgi kyō* (usually abbreviated to *Engakukyō*) (1 *kan*), *Daizōkyō* 17.914b, states that the body is made of the four elements and enumerates which parts revert to which of the elements.

257. *Sangai no ie*, "turbulent world," is literally "the three worlds, a house." It stems from the phrase *sangai no kataku*, "the three worlds, a fiery house," which is derived from the *Lotus Sūtra* (*Myōhō renge kyō*), *Daizōkyō* 9.14c. "The three worlds do not have tranquility; they are like a fiery house." The original meaning of the three worlds (Skt. *trailokya* or *triloka*) in the Buddhist doctrine is: the world of [sensuous] desire (*yokkai*); the world of form (*shikikai*); and the world without form (*mushikikai*). However, Jihei means merely that he has left the secular world.

258. *Saishi chimpō fuzuisha*, lit., "wife and children, valuables, unencumbered person." This expression appears in the *Daihōdō daishūkyō, kan* 16 (60 *kan*) (commonly abbreviated to *Daishūkyō*), *Daizōkyō* 13.109.

259. *Nage-shimada*, "hanging Shimada," is the Shimada style of coiffure, flattened and hanging down the back of the neck. For an illustration of the "hanging Shimada" coiffure see *Kinsei fūzoku shi, kan* 9, pt. 1, p. 311b. This "hanging Shimada" style was popular *ca.* 1695–1708, according to the *Kinsei onna fūzoku kō, kan* 1 (1893, 2 *kan*), by Ikkawa Shummei (1804–1890), in *Nihon zuihitsu taisei*, Series 1, 2.279. On the development and varieties of the Shimada styles, see *Rekisei josō kō, kan* 3 (1855, 4 *kan*), by Iwase Kyōzan (1769–1858), in *Nihon zuihitsu taisei*, Series 1, 3.641–642.

260. Kakae-obi, "lower sash," was worn below the main obi or sash, low around the hips to hold up the skirts of the kimono, and was tied either in the front or back. In the late seventeenth and early eighteenth century it was fashionable for prostitutes to wear such sashes of purple silk crepe. See *Kiyū shōran, kan* 2a (*ca.* 1830, 12 *kan*), by Kitamura Nobuyo (1784–1856), (Rikugōkan edition, 1926, 1932, 2 vols.) 1.173; and *Chikamatsu goi*, p. 71d. The illustrations of *kakae-obi* in the latter work are by one of the foremost illustrators of popular literature of the period, Yoshida Hambei (*fl. ca.* 1680–1692), and are taken from Saikaku's *Kōshoku gonin onna, kan* 3 (1686, 5 *kan*), in *Saikaku zenshū*, 6.53, in *Nihon koten zenshū*, Series 1 (1926). Better illustrations by the same artist of *kakae-obi* can be found in *Joyō kimmō zui, kan* 1.12b, *kan* 3.4a, 4b, 10a, 17ab (1685, 5 *kan*), by Okuda Shōhakuken, occupying vols. 13–17 in *Kisho fukuseikai sōsho*, Series 9 (1935).

261. It is because the pheasant calls to its mate that it is detected by hunters and

driven into a noose which has been laid as a snare. Similarly it is because of his mate, Koharu, that Jihei will lose his life in a noose. The fate of the pheasant was well known to the audience through sayings and poems, like the saying: *kiji mo nakazuba utare mai*, "If the pheasant did not call, it would not be shot," which was derived from the *Tso chuan*.

The image also appears in a *tanka* by Ōtomo no Yakamochi, (718–785) in the third Imperial anthology, the *Shūishū, kan* 1 (*ca.* 1005–1008, 20 *kan*):

Haru no no ni	In the Spring fields
asaru kijisu no	the foraging pheasant's
tsuma-goi ni	searching for its mate
Ono ga arika o	That he is there
hito ni shiraretsu	informs people.

This entire poem is quoted by Chikamatsu in his history play *Hyakunichi Soga* (1697), *Chikamatsu zenshū* 5.292. Chikamatsu's use of the parallel of the pheasant in *Amijima* is drawn from an earlier domestic play of his, *Satsuma uta*, Act 2 (1704), *ibid.* 6.755, in the scene of Oman's escape: "She leaps nimbly, but—good heavens!— her sash catches in a pine tree, and she is hanging in space. This is [like] the pheasant in the field, caught in a snare, suffering because of its mate."

262. This recalls the matter which concerned Koharu in Act 1 (p. 69), when she asked the samurai: "Then there is something else I should like to ask you. In committing suicide either by the sword or by hanging oneself, probably it would be much the more painful to cut one's throat, wouldn't it?"

263. *Saiho* [*jōdo*], "Western [Pure Land]" (or *Gokuraku jōdo*), the Western Paradise of Amida Buddha.

264. This refers to a popular superstition that crows are birds of ill omen which know in advance of the death of people. This same tradition exists in many parts of Asia and Europe. *Wakan sansai zue*, 43, 1.488b: "Crows are birds which are filial and loving, and they are long-lived. In mountains and forests, in villages and cities, they are numerous. When dawn is about to break, they fly in flocks, noisily calling, and assemble in the city or country and devour the various grains. Sometimes they wantonly eat chicken eggs and smelly dead flesh. Therefore people dislike them very much. . . From ancient times there is a tradition that crows are the messengers of the Kumano deities. When a sick person is about to die, the flocking and cawing [of crows] is a bad omen. This is greatly disliked."

265. This tradition perhaps originated to emphasize the gravity of making a vow. It is referred to in a *senryū*, a comic or satirical poem of seventeen syllables, of the 1760's, quoted in *Chikamatsu goi*, p. 489c:

Kumano de wa	At Kumano
kyō mo ochita to	today also [crows] fell.
umete yari	Bury them.

266. *Kakizome*, "first writing," was an ancient custom of writing propitious characters during the first days of the New Year to bring good fortune during the year.

267. *Kawai, kawai.*

268. *Mukui, mukui.*

269. *Jinjō*, "morning period," which begins at about 6 A.M. It was one of the six divisions of the day and night used in monasteries for designating the periods of duties for the monks. The bell which just sounded at the temple was known as the *jinjō/shō*, "morning bell." The word here has a double usage, as *jinjō*, "admirable; brave."

270. The couple hear chanting at the Ten Nights services at Daichō Temple, and it seems to them as though these prayers are being offered for them. There is a striking similarity between Chikamatsu's suicide scenes. Most of them mention the thin light of dawn, the voices of the birds at first light, and the religious invocations, all enhancing the sadness of the atmosphere.

271. *Mida no riken*, "the sharp sword of [A]mida," means that when the name of Amida is invoked, it is like a sharp sword which cuts away one's worldly desires and one's sins. It is derived from the *Hanjusan* (*Po-chou-tsan*) (662, 1 *kan*) by Shan-tao (613–681), *Daizōkyō* 47.448c: "The sharp sword, that is, [A]mida's name, when once praised aloud, removes all sin." This entire quotation appears in Chikamatsu's history play *Kaoyo uta-garuta* (1714), *Chikamatsu zenshū* 10.460. Miyamori, translation, "Fair Ladies at a Game of Poem-cards," pp. 107–178; see p. 135.

272. This is the position in which the dead were arranged by Buddhist tradition, because it was in this position that the historical Buddha, Shaka (Skt. Sākyamuni), died. The same sequence of characters was used by Chikamatsu earlier in his *Shaka nyorai tanjōe* (1695), *Chikamatsu zenshū* 4.638: "[Sakyamuni,] his head toward the north, his face toward the west, lying on his right side, at the age of 81 years (*sai*), on the 15th day of the 2nd month, was hidden by the cloud of Nirvāna."

273. This is presumably Jihei's coat (*haori*), because that garment was not worn by women until the practice was begun by the geisha of the Fukagawa Gay Quarter in Edo in the 1750's. They were sometimes called the *haori geisha*.

274. These are the closing phrases of a prayer used in memorial services in the Jōdo (Pure Land) Sect. For the text of the prayer, see *Chikamatsu goi*, p. 102b.

275. Chikamatsu's concern with making wordplays and associations led him to insert irrelevant words:

asade	no gyofu ga	ami no me ni	mitsukete
out in the morning fishermen		in [their] eyes	discovered
		net's meshes	discovered

The phrase *ami no me ni* is entirely unessential to the meaning and detracts from its clarity. Of course the bodies are not discovered in the nets, but this word serves as an *engo* to "fishermen" and *Amijima*. *Me* has the double meaning of "eyes" and "meshes," but is quite unessential in either sense.

276. *Chikai no ami*, "vow net," is a Buddhist phrase used in classical poetry and *yōkyoku* (Introduction, p. 4) which likens to a net the vows of the Buddha. The first of the four universal vows (*shiguzeigan*) of the Buddha and Bodhisattvas was "to save all living beings without limit." The vow referred to in this line is explained in the preceding phrase: *sugu ni jōbutsu tokudatsu no* (*chikai*), "directly to attain Buddhahood and deliverance [from reincarnation] (vow)." However, the phrase *chikai no ami* is a pivot, for it is followed by: *chikai no ami-jima shinjū* "the vow [to commit a] love suicide at Amijima." At the same time, Chikamatsu uses *Amijima shinjū* in this line to refer to the play he is just concluding. As the play ends, the audience is left with the comforting suggestion that despite the gravity of the offenses of Koharu and Jihei, they will attain Buddhahood and be freed from the sufferings of the wheel of transmigration.

Character List and Index

Ageya 揚屋
Aitaijini; see *Aitaishi*
Aitaishi 相對死
Aji-gawa 安治川
Aka-iwashi 赤鰯
Akane no iroage 茜の色揚
Akatsuki no Kanenaru (Kanenari) 曉鐘成
Akazome Emon shū 赤染衛門集
Akisato Ritō 秋里離島
Akusho 惡所
Ama 海士
Amamitsu-kami 天満神
Amayadori beni no hanagoza: see *(Oriku Jūbei) Amayadori beni
no hanagoza*
Amigasa 編笠
Amijima 網島
Ango 安居
Anrakuji 安樂寺
Arashi San'emon 嵐三右衛門
Aruji no kasha 主の花車
Asahina Yoshihide 朝比奈義秀
Ashidori chidori-ashi 足取千鳥足
Atsumori 敦盛
Ayatsuri nendaiki; see *Imamukashi ayatsuri nendaiki*
Bachi 罰
Baikō; see (Hakuensai) Baikō

Baishunfu imei shū 賣春婦異名集

Bantarō 番太郎

-Bashi; see *Hashi*

Bashō; see Matsuo Bashō

Biwa 琵琶

Bizenjima-bashi 備前島橋

-Bō 坊

Bon 盆

Bonnō ni tsunagaruru inu 煩惱に繫がるる犬

Bonten 梵天

Bōshū 防州

Bungaku 文學 (periodical)

Bunka sōsho 文化叢書

Bun'ya-bushi 文彌節

Bushi 武士

Bushinjū ka, shinjū ka 無心中か, 心中か

Butsu Mo Maya-san kaichō 佛母摩耶山開帳

Cha 茶

Chakei hizorigao 茶傾腹立顔

Chan kuo ts'ê 戰國策

Chaya 茶屋

Cheng Ch'eng-kung 鄭成功; see Kokusen'ya

Chikai no ami 誓の網

Chikamatsu gikyoku shin kenkyū 近松戲曲新研究

Chikamatsu goi 近松語彙

Chikamatsu Hanji 近松半二

(Chikamatsu hyōshaku) Ten no Amijima (近松評釋) 天の網島

Chikamatsu igo, 近松以後

"Chikamatsu jidai no Ōsaka no irozato oyobi yūjo" 近松時代の大阪の色里及び遊女

"Chikamatsu kenkyū bunken nempyō nōto" 近松研究文獻年表ノート

Chikamatsu kenkyū no johen 近松研究の序篇

Chikamatsu kessaku shū 近松傑作集

Chikamatsu kessaku zenshū; see *(Shinshaku sashizu) Chikamatsu kessaku zenshū*

Chikamatsu meisaku shū 近松名作集

Chikamatsu Monzaemon 近松門左衛門

Chikamatsu ningyō jōruri no kenkyū 近松人形淨瑠璃 の研究

Chikamatsu no kenkyū 近松之研究

"Chikamatsu sewa-jōruri kenkyū" 近松世話淨瑠璃研究

"Chikamatsu sewamono no ruikei" 近松世話物の類型

Chikamatsu sewamono zenshū 近松世話物全集

Chikamatsu to Shēkusupiya 近松とシェークスピヤ

Chikamatsu zenshū 近松全集

Chikugo 筑後

Chiri-yuku 散り行く

Chi sui ka fu 地水火風

Chō 町

Chōgin 丁銀

Chōkei 長繁

Chōnin 町人

Chōnin bungaku 町人文學

Chuang-tzu 莊子

Chuang-tzu chi-shih 莊子集釋

Chūgen uwasa no kake-dai 中元噂掛鯛

Dai Chikamatsu zenshū 大近松全集

"Dai Chikamatsu zenshū chūshaku jiten" 大近松全集註釋辭典

Daichōji 大長寺

Daihatsu nehangyō 大般涅槃經

Daijin 大盡

Daihōdō daishūkyō 大方等大集經

Daihōkō engaku shūtararyōgi kyō 大方廣圓覺修多羅了義經

Daikyōji mukashi goyomi 大經師昔曆

Dainihon chishi taikei 大日本地誌大系

Dainihon meisho zue 大日本名所圖會

Dai-on 大恩

Daishō 大小

Daishūkyō; see *Daihōdō daishūkyō*

Daizōkyō; see *(Taishō shinshū) Daizōkyō*

Danrin 談林

Dazaifu Jinja 太宰府神社

Denki sakusho 傳奇作書

Dō どう

Dōguya-bushi 道具屋節

Dōguya Kichizaemon 道具屋吉左衞門

Dōjima shinchi 堂島新地

Dōmyōji 道明寺

Dōtombori 道頓堀

Edo 江戸

Edo bungaku sōsho; see *(Hyōshaku) Edo bungaku sōsho*

Edo-bushi 江戸節

Edo Handayū 江戸半太夫

Edo jidai no danjo kankei 江戸時代ノ男女關係

Edo jidai shi 江戸時代史

Ekken zenshū 益軒全集

Emma-ō 閻魔王

Engakukyō; see *Daihōkō engaku shūtararyōgi kyō*

Engi 緣起

Engo 緣語

Enja oyako naka 緣者親子中

En no Ozuna; see En no Shōkaku

En no Shōkaku 役小角

Enoshima 江島

Eta 穢多

Ezōshi 繪草紙*; -uri* 賣

Fan K'uai; see Han Kai

Fuisanjin 不移山人

Fujii Otoo 藤井乙男

Fujimura Tsukuru 藤村作

Fujiwara 藤原

Fukagawa 深川

Fukushima 福島

Fumombon 普門品

Funairi-bashi 舟入橋

Furemai chaya 振舞茶屋

Fureuri 髑賣

Furoshiki 風呂敷

Furoya 風呂屋

Fushimi 伏見

Fushimi Sakamachi 伏見坂町

Futatsu ōgi Nagara no matsu 雙扇長柄松

Fuyajō 不夜城

Gandō 強盗

-Gawa; see Kawa

Ge-ango 夏安居

Gegaki 夏書

Geisha 藝者

Gempei seisuiki 源平盛衰記

Gendaigoyaku kokubungaku zenshū 現代語譯
國文學全集

Gengo daijiten 諺語大辭典

Gengo no kenkyū; see (Tokugawa jidai) Gengo no kenkyū

Genji monogatari 源氏物語

Genroku 元禄

Genroku bungaku jiten 元禄文學辭典

(Genroku jidai) Sesōhen (元禄時代) 世相篇

Getsujindō 月尋堂

Gidayū 義太夫

(Gikyoku shōsetsu) Kinsei sakka taikan (戯曲小説)
近世作家大觀

Gin-ichimai 銀一枚

Gin-itsutsu 銀五

Giri 義理

Gō 鄉 (district)

Gō 號 (pen name)

Gohei 御幣

Gojūnenki uta-nembutsu 五十年忌歌念佛

Gokumon 獄門

Gokuraku 極樂; *jōdo* 淨土

Gonin-gumi 五人組

Gōtō; see Gandō

Goyōjin; see (Hi no) goyōjin

Goyoza ごよざ

Gozaemon 五左衛門

Gozen Gikeiki 御前義經記

Gunki monogatari 軍記物語

Gunnai 郡內

Habutae 羽二重

Hachidaishū 八代集

Hachijō-ginu 八丈絹

Hachiken'ya 八軒屋

Hachiman 八幡

Haga Yaichi 芳賀矢一

Haikai renga 俳諧連歌

Haiku 俳句

Hakata Kojorō nami-makura 博多小女郎波枕

(Hakuensai) Baikō （白緣齋）梅好

Hakujin 白人

Hakutōsha 白東社

Hamaguri 蛤

Hamamatsu Utakuni 濱松歌國

Hama-naya 濱納屋

Han 藩

Hana 花

Hanjusan 般舟讃

Han Kai 樊噲

Han Kao-tsu 漢高祖

Hanshi 半紙

Hanshichi 半七

Han-shih wai-chuan 韓詩外傳

Han shu 漢書

Han(suru) 版 (摺る)

Haori 羽織 ; *geisha* 藝者

Harakiri 腹切

Harima 播磨

Haru 春

Hashi 橋

Hashijorō 端女郎

Hashiri-gaki 走り書き

Hashi-zukushi 橋盡し

Hatakeyama Kizan 畠山箕山

Hauta 端歌

Heiandō 平安堂

Heike monogatari 平家物語

Higan 彼岸

Higuchi Isao 樋口功

Higuchi Yoshichiyo 樋口慶千代

Hinin 非人

(Hi no) goyōjin (火の)御用心 ; *sōrō/saburau* 候

Hiruhinaka 晝日中

Hitoae 一間

Hitokotonushi-no-kami 一言主神

Hitome sengen 一目千軒

Hito-tobi-ume-da-bashi 一飛梅田橋

Hizen 肥前

Hō 寶

Hōin 寶印

Hōjō 北條
Hōjōgawa 放生川
Hōkan 幫間
Hōkekyō 法華經
Hokku 發句
Hori 彫り
Horie 堀江
Horikawa-bashi 堀川橋
Horikawa nami no tsuzumi 堀川波鼓
Horikawa no hashi 堀川の橋
Hōroku zukin 焙/炮烙頭巾
Hou Han shu 後漢書
Hōzō; see Takaragura
Hozumi Ikan 穗積以貫
Hsiang Chi 項籍
Hsiang Yü 項羽
Hsiang Yü pen-chi 項羽本紀
Hung-men 鴻門
Hyakunichi Soga 百日曾我
Hyakunin isshū 百人一集
(*Hyōshaku*) *Edo bungaku sōsho* (評釋)江戶文學叢書
Ibara Saikaku 井原西鶴
Ichi 都/市
Ichikawa Danjūrō 市川團十郎
Ichimuken Dōji 一無軒道治
Ichi-no-kawa 市の側
Iida Yutaka 飯田豐
Iikakekotoba 言掛詞
Ii Yōhō 伊井蓉峰
Ike; see Iki
Iken 意見
Iki 生
Ikkawa Shummei 生川春明

Ikutama shinjū 生玉心中

I li ts'ê hai 以蠡測海

Imabashi suji 今橋筋

Imagawa Ryōshun 今川了俊

Imamiya shinjū 今宮心中

(*Imamukashi*) *Ayatsuri nendaiki* (今昔) 操年代記

Imayō nijūshi kō 今様廿四孝

Inagaki Tatsurō 稲垣達郎

Inga 因果

Ingakyō 因果經

Inoko 亥子

Inoue Yorikuni 井上頼圀

Iro-otoko 色男

Irozato 色里

Isoichi 礒都

Isshaku nana sun 一尺七寸

Issun no saki ni jigoku 一寸の先に地獄

Issun saki wa yami 一寸先は闇

Issun (shita) no jigoku 一寸 (下) の地獄

Itami 伊丹

Itō Masao 伊藤正雄

Itoshibonage いとしぼなげ

Itōshinage いとほしなげ

Iwakuni 岩國

Iwanami kōza 岩波講座

Iwase Kyōzan 岩瀬京山

Izu 伊豆

Izutsu Narihira Kawachi gayoi 井筒業平河内通

Ji 地

Jidaimono 時代物

Jihei; see Kamiya Jihei

Jiisama-me 祖父様め

Jikata ochiboshū 地方落穂集

Jinjō 晨朝 (morning period)

Jinjō 尋常 (admirable, brave)

Jinjō/shō 晨鐘

Jinrin kimmō zui 人倫訓蒙圖彙

Jisei 辭世

Jiunsai 而慍齋

Jō a gon gyō 長阿含經

Jōdo 淨土

Jōruri jūnidan zōshi 淨瑠璃十二段草子

Jōruri meisaku shū 淨瑠璃名作集

Jōruri monogatari 淨瑠璃物語

Jōruri sakusha 淨瑠璃作者

Jōshi 情死

Jōshi no kenkyū 情死の研究

Joyō kimmō zui 女用訓蒙圖彙

Jūakunin 十惡人

Jūya 十夜

Kabuki 歌舞伎

Kabukigeki to sono haiyū 歌舞伎劇と其の俳優

Kagamu 屈む

Kagekiyo 景清

Kai 甲斐

Kaibara Kōko 貝原好古

Kaigo no hana 解語花

Kakae-obi 抱帶

Kakaika 呵刈葭

Kakekotoba 掛詞

Kakitsubata 杜若

Kakizome 書初

Kako genzai ingakyō 過去現在因果經

Kakoi 圍

Kako no Kyōshin nanapaka meguri 賀古教信七墓廻

Kamakura 鎌倉

Kami 神 (deity)

Kami 紙 (paper)

Kami-gakure 神隱れ

Kamigata 上方 (region)

Kamigata 上方 (periodical)

Kamijl 紙治

Kami wa shōjiki 紙／神は正直

Kamiya Jihei 紙屋治兵衛

Kamiya Jihei Kiinokuniya Koharu Shinjū Ten no Amijima
紙屋治兵衛きいの國ヤ小はる心中天の網島

Kami-zukushi 神盡し

Kami-zukushi 紙盡し

Kamme 貫目

Kanadehon chūshingura 假名手本忠臣藏

Kan hasshū tsunagi uma 關八州繫馬

Kanki 甘輝

Kannon 觀音

Kannon-kyō 觀音經

Ka no kishi 彼の岸

Kan *Shōjō* 菅丞相

Kantarō 勘太郎

Kanzawa Teikan 神澤貞幹 ; see Kanzawa Tokō

Kanzawa Tokō 神澤杜口

Kanze Motokiyo 觀世元清 ; see Zeami

Kanzeon bosatsu fumombon 觀世音菩薩普門品

Kaoyo uta-garuta 娥歌加留多

Karu 借る

Kasha 花車／香車

Kashiwara 伯原

Katade 堅手

Kataki 敵

Katakoto, Butsurui shōko, Naniwa kikigaki, Tamba tsūji
片言, 物類稱呼, 浪花聞書, 丹波通辭

Katana 刀

Katō Junzō 加藤順三

Katsuragi 葛城

Kawa 川／河

Kawachiya 河內屋

Kawai 可愛

Kawashō 河庄

Kawatake Shigetoshi 河竹繁俊

Kayoi Gomachi 通小町

Kazari 飾

Kazuraki; see Katsuragi

Keikai 景戒

Keisei Awa no Naruto 傾城阿波鳴門

Ken 間

Kessaku jōruri shū 傑作淨瑠璃集

Kieda Masuichi 木枝增一

Kiinokuniya 紀伊國屋

Ki-mōsanu 未申さぬ

Kimpusan 金峯山

Kinchaku-kiri me 巾着切め

Kindai Nihon bungaku taikei 近代日本文學大系

Ki no Kaion 紀海音

Kinokuniya 紀國屋; see Kiinokuniya

Kinsei bungaku sōsho 近世文學叢書

Kinsei bungei sōsho 近世文藝叢書

Kinsei fūzoku shi; see *(Ruijū) Kinsei fūzoku shi*

Kinsei Nihon kokuminshi 近世日本國民史

Kinsei onna fūzoku kō 近世女風俗考

Kinsei sakka taikan; see *(Gikyoku shōsetsu) Kinsei sakka taikan*

Kin'yōshū 金葉集

Kishō 起請

Kisho fukuseikai sōsho 稀書複製會叢書

Kiso 木曾

Kitagawa Morisada 喜田川守貞
Kita-gumi 北組
Kitamura Nobuyo 喜多村信節
Kitani Hōgin 木谷蓬吟
Kitano 北野
Kita no shinchi 北の新地
Kiyū shōran 嬉遊笑覽
Koban 小判
Kobayashi Zenhachi 小林善八
(*Kōchū*) *Kokka taikei* (校註)國歌大系
Kogasu 焦す
Kogatana 小刀
Ko-hanshi 小半紙
Koharu 小春
Kojiki; see *Kojjiki hinin*
Kojjiki hinin 乞食非人
Ko-jōruri 古淨瑠璃
(*Kokin*) *denju sanchō* (古今)傳授三鳥
Kokinshū 古今集
Kokka taikei; see (*Kōchū*) *Kokka taikei*
Kō-kō 鏗々
Koku 石
Kokugakuin zasshi 國學院雜誌
Kokusen'ya 國性／姓爺
Kokusen'ya kassen 國性爺合戰
Kokusho kankōkai 國書刊行會
Konaya; see *Koya*
Kondō Heijō 近藤瓶城
Konoe 近衞
Konoe (Sammyakuin) Nobutada 近衞(三藐院)信尹
Kōshi 格子
Kōshi-jima 格子縞
Koshikibu no Naishi 小式部内侍

Kōshin 庚申

Kōshoku gonin onna 好色五人女

Kōshoku ichidai onna 好色一代女

Kōshoku mankintan 好色萬金丹

Kōshokumono 好色物

Kotatsu 火燵

Kotoba 詞

Kotowaza 諺

Kotowaza gusa 諺草

Koya 粉屋

Kōyakuneri 膏藥煉

Koya no Magoemon 粉屋孫衞門

Kōyodōsei 光譽道清

Kozume yakusha 小詰役者

Kōzunomiya 高津宮

Kuga-gun 玖珂郡

Kuguri 潛

Kumano bikuni 熊野比丘尼

Kumano goō 熊野牛王; *hōin* 寶印

Kuo Ch'ing-fan 郭慶藩

Kuo-hsing-yeh; see Kokusen'ya

Kurawasu 食はす

Kura-yashiki 藏屋敷

Kurita Mototsugu 栗田元次

Kuroki Kanzō 黒木勘藏

Kusama Naokata 草間直方

Kuwayama 桑山

Kuwayama Shigeharu 桑山重晴

Kyakuhon 脚本

Kyō-bashi 京橋

Kyōgen 狂言

Kyōhō 享保

Lao-tzu tao-te-ching 老子道德經

Li chi 禮記

Li Lin-fu 李林甫

Liu ch'en chu Wen hsüan 六臣注文選

Liu Pang 劉邦

Lotus Sūtra; see *Myōhō renge kyō*

Machi 町

Machiai 待合

Machi bugyō 町奉行

Maejima Shunzō 前島春三

Mage 髻

Mageru 曲げる

Magoemon; see Koya no Magoemon

Magoroku Kanemoto 孫六兼元

Maguchi 間口

Makura byōbu 枕屏風

Makura-kotoba 枕詞

Mameita-gin 豆板銀

Mamori-bukuro 守袋

Man'yōshū 萬葉集

Masago-za 貞砂座

Matsukaze 松風

Matsukaze Murasame sokutai kagami 松風村雨束帯鑑

Matsunaga Teitoku 松永貞德

Matsu no ha 松の葉

Matsuo Bashō 松尾芭蕉

Matsuri no nerishu 祭の練衆

Matsuyama kagami 松山鏡

Me め

Me; see *Momme*

Meido no hikyaku 冥途の飛脚

Meika jiten 名歌辭典

Meng-tzu 孟子

Michiyuki 道行

Mida no riken 彌陀の利劔

Midori-bashi 緑橋

Minami 南

Minami-gumi 南組

Minami-nakajima 南中島

Minamoto no Yoshitsune 源義經

Mino 美濃

Mionoya Jūrō 三保の谷十郎

Miotsukushi; see (*Ōsaka Shimmachi saiken no zu*) *Miotsukushi*

Misejorō 見世女郎

(*Mi*) *shimenawa* （御）注連繩

Mi sutsuru 身/見捨つる

Mitamura Engyo 三田村鳶魚

Mitsuse-gawa 三瀬川

Miya 宮

Miyako Itchū 都一中

Miyamori Asatarō 宮森麻太郎

Miya no Maemachi 宮の前町

Miyatake Gaikotsu 宮武外骨

Miyoshi Shōraku 三好松洛

Mizutani Futō 水谷不倒 ; see Mizutani Yumihiko

Mizutani Yumihiko 水谷弓彦

Mombi 紋日

Momi 紅絹

Momme 匁

Monogatari 物語

Monohi 物日

Morau 貰ふ

Morisada mankō 守貞漫稿

Morita-za 森田座

Mōsu 申す
Motoori Norinaga 本居宣長
Mukui 報
Munagura 胸座／倉
Mura 村
Muragarasu hiyoku no seishi 群烏比翼の誓紙
Murasaki Shikibu 紫式部
Murata Ryōa 村田了阿
Muromachi 室町
Musha gyōretsu 武者行列
Mushikikai 無色界
Myōhō renge kyō 妙法蓮華經
Nabeshima 鍋島
Nagamachi onna harakiri 長町女腹切
Nagauta 長歌
Nage-shimada 投島田
Nagori no hashi-zukushi 名殘の橋盡し
Nagoya Sanzaburō 名古屋山三郎
Nagoya Sanzō; see Nagoya Sanzaburō
Nakabarai 中掃
Nakai 仲居
Nakamachi 中町
Nakamura Ganjirō 中村鴈治郎
Nakamura Kaoru 中村薫
Naka-no-shima 中之島
Nakano Yoshihira 中野吉平
Naki-bushi 泣節
Namaida bōzu なまいだ坊主
Namazue-gawa 鯰江川
Namiki Eisuke 並木永輔
Namiki Senryū 並木千柳; see Namiki Sōsuke
Namiki Sōsuke 並木宗輔

Namu Amida Butsu 南無阿彌陀佛

Namu sambō 南無三寶

Nanae no tobira, yae no kusari, momoe no kakomi
七重の扉，八重の鎖，百重の圍

Naniwa hōgen 浪華方言

Naniwa hyakuji dan 浪華百事談

Naniwa kagami 難波鑑

Naniwa kidan; see *Rōka kidan*

Naniwa kikigaki 浪花聞書

Naniwa-ko-bashi 難波小橋

Naniwa miyage 難波土産

Naniwa no nagame 浪花のながめ

Naniwa sōsho 浪速叢書

Nansui man'yū 南水漫遊

Naya 納屋

Nebiki no kadomatsu 壽の門松

Nehangyō; see *Daihatsu nehangyō*

Ne-hori ha-hori 根掘り葉掘り

Nembutsu 念佛

Nenki 年季

Neya-gawa 寢屋川

Nihon bungaku daijiten 日本文學大辭典

Nihon bungaku taikei 日本文學大系

Nihon engeki no kenkyū 日本演劇の研究

Nihon keizai taiten 日本經濟大典

Nihonkoku gempō zen'aku ryōiki/reiiki 日本國
現報善惡靈異記

Nihon koten tokuhon 日本古典讀本

Nihon koten zenshū 日本古典全集

Nihon meicho zenshū 日本名著全集

Nihon reiiki; see *Nihonkoku gempō zen'aku ryōiki*

Nihon rekishi 日本歷史

Nihon ryōiki; see *Nihonkoku gempō zen'aku ryōiki*

Nihon shakai shi 日本社會史

Nihon zuihitsu taisei 日本隨筆大成

Niimi Masatomo 新見正朝

Ningyō jōruri 人形淨瑠璃

Ningyō shibai to Chikamatsu no jōruri 人形芝居と
近松の淨瑠璃

Ninjō 人情

Nishiki 錦

Nishiyama Sōin 西山宗因

Nishizawa Ippō 西澤一鳳

Nishizawa Ippū 西澤一風

Niuriya 煮賣屋

Niwa 庭

Nō 能

Nochi no tsukimi 後の月見

Noda 野田

Nonko のんこ

Nusa; see *Ōnusa*

Ōe-bashi 大江橋

Ogino Yaegiri 荻野八重桐

Oimatsu 老松 (*yōkyoku*)

Oimatsu 老/追松

Ōjin 應神

Ojisama 伯父様

Okada Keishi 岡田後志

Okamoto Bun'ya 岡本文彌

Ōkawa 大川

Okina gusa 翁草

Okiya 置屋

Okuda Shōhakuken 奥田松柏軒

Okuni お國

Oku no hosomichi hyōshaku 奥の細道評釋

Ōmichi Waichi 大道和一

Omou kataki 思ふ敵

Omou oteki 思ふお敵

On 恩

Onari-bashi 御成橋

Oni no konu ma ni sentaku 鬼の来ぬ間に洗濯

Oni no minu ma 鬼の見ぬ間

Onna daimyō Tanzen nō 女大名丹前能

Onna kabuki 女歌舞伎

Onna koroshi abura no jigoku 女殺油地獄

Ōnusa 大幣

(Oriku Jūbei) Amayadori beni no hanagoza
(おりく重兵衞)雨防紅覚莚

Ōsaka 大阪/坂

(Ōsaka Shimmachi saiken no zu) Miotsukushi
(大坂新町細見之圖)澪標

Ōsaka-shi shi 大阪市史

Osan お三

Osue お末

Ōta Hō 太田方

Ōta Zensai 太田全齋 ; see Ōta Hō

Oteki お敵

Otogai 頤

Otoko-geisha 男藝者

Ōtomo no Yakamochi 大伴家持

Oyako 親子 ; *ichimon* 一門

Oyama 御山

Ozaka; see Ōsaka

Po-chou-tsan; see *Hanjusan*

Rekisei josō kō 歴世女装考

Ri 里

Ri Tōten 李踏天

Rigen daijiten 俚諺大辭典

Rigen shūran; see *(Zōho) Rigen shūran*

Rikugōkan 六合館
Rōka kidan 浪花奇談
Rokuken guchi 六間口
Rōnin 浪人
(Ruijū) Kinsei fūzoku shi (類聚) 近世風俗志
Rusui 留守居
Ryō 兩
Sadoshima Saburōzaemon 佐渡島三郎左衛門
Saga 佐賀
Sagami nyūdō sembiki inu 相摸入道千疋犬
Sai 歳
Saietsubō 西悦坊
Saigyō 西行
Saihō 西方
Saikaku; see Ibara Saikaku
Sainembō 西念坊
Saishi chimpō fuzuisha 妻子珍寶不隨者
Sakai 境
Sakamoto Kizan 坂本箕山
Sakata Tōjūrō 坂田藤十郎
Sakura-bashi 櫻橋
Sakuragi 櫻木
Samisen 三味線
San; see Osan
Sanari Kentarō 佐成謙太郎
Sanemori 實盛
Sangai no ie 三界の家
Sangai no kataku 三界の火宅
Sangorō 三五郎
Sanjinfuishi 散人不移子
Sankatsu 三勝
Sanka zui 三賛圖彙
San-zen ri 三千里

Sanzu-no-kawa 三途川

Saryōko 左龍虎

Sasaki Nobutsuna 佐佐木信綱

Sassa Masakazu 佐々政一

Sato namari; see *(Uso to makoto) Sato namari*

Satō Tsurukichi 佐藤鶴吉

Satsuma uta 薩摩歌

Saya 紗綾

Se 瀬

Seiunkaku-shujin 静雲閣主人

Seki 關

Sekine Mokuan 關根默庵

Seki no Magoroku 關の孫六

Sekki 節季

Semmin 賤民

Senryū 川柳

Sentaku 洗濯

Seppuku 切腹

Sesōhen; see *(Genroku jidai) Sesōhen*

Setsuyō gundan 攝陽群談

Setsuyō kikan 攝陽奇觀

Setsuyō ochiboshū 攝陽落穗集

Settsu 攝津

Settsu meisho zue 攝津名所圖會

Settsu meisho zue taisei 攝津名所圖會大成

Sewamono 世話物

Shaka 釋迦

Shaka nyorai tanjōe 釋迦如來誕生會

Shamisen; see *Samisen*

Shan-tao 善導

Shibai banashi 芝居ばなし

Shibai to shijitsu 芝居と史實

Shibasaki Rinzaemon 柴崎林左衛門
Shidai 四大
Shidai tennō 四大天王
Shigetomo Ki 重友毅
Shiguzeigan 四弘誓願
Shih chi 史記
Shihekian Mochō 四壁庵茂蔦
Shihōgin 四寶銀
Shijimi 蜆
Shijimi-gawa 蜆川
Shikidō ōkagami 色道大鏡
Shikikai 色界
Shikiri-gin/gane 仕切銀
Shimabara 島原
Shimanouchi 島ノ内
Shimenawa; see (Mi) shimenawa
Shimmachi 新町
Shimonoseki 下關
Shimo-onago 下女
Shimpa 新派
Shinchō bunko 新潮文庫
Shin enseki jisshu 新燕石十種
Shingin 新銀
Shin gunsho ruijū 新群書類從
Shinjū 心中
Shinjū Kamiya Jihei 心中紙屋治兵衛
Shinjū Kasane-izutsu 心中重井筒
Shinjū mannen-gusa 心中萬年草
Shinjūmono 心中物
Shinjū niharaobi 心中二腹帶
Shinjū nimai ezōshi 心中二枚繪草紙
Shinjū ōkagami 心中大鑑

Shinjū-shi 心中死

Shinjū Ten no Amijima 心中天の網島

"*Shinjū Ten no Amijima bōtō no kayō ni tsuite*"
　心中天の網島冒頭の歌謡について

Shinjū Ten no Amijima shōkai 心中天の網島詳解

Shinjū yaiba wa kōri no tsuitachi 心中刃は氷の朔日

Shinjū yoigōshin 心中宵庚申

Shinke 新家

Shin kokinshū 新古今集

Shinrui 親類

(*Shinshaku*) *Nihon bungaku sōsho* (新釋)日本文學叢書

(*Shinshaku sashizu*) *Chikamatsu kessaku zenshū* (新釋
　挿圖)近松傑作全集

Shintaku 新宅

Shironushi 代主

Shi shi no ikkan roppyaku me 四々の壹貫六百匁

Shōbai no o wa misenu 商賣の尾は見せぬ

Shōgun 將軍

Shohōken 書方軒

Shōji 障子

Shōmon 蕉門

Shōyō senshū 逍遥選集

Shōzon 正尊

Shūishū 拾遺集

Shunkan 俊寛

Shuo yüan 說苑

Shūshōken 秀松軒

Shusse Kagekiyo 出世景清

Shuzui Kenji 守隨憲治

Sodegoi hinin 袖乞非人

Sodesaki Miwano 袖崎三輪野

Soga Kaikeizan 曾我會稽山

Sōgō Nihonshi taikei 綜合日本史大系

Sonezaki shinchi 曽根崎新地
Sonezaki shinjū 曽根崎心中
Sonoda Tamio 園田民雄
Sōrinshi 巣林子
"Sōrinshi to yōkyoku to no kan; 'Shinjū Ten no Amijima' chū no
 'Nagori no hashi-zukushi' " 巣林子と謡曲との關・心中
 天の網島中の「名殘の橋づくし」
Ssu-hsien shu-chü 思賢書局
Ssu-ma Kuang 司馬光
Ssu-pu ts'ung-k'an 四部叢刊
Sue; see Osue
Sugawara no Michizane 菅原道眞
Sugi 杉
Sugihara-gami 杉原紙
Sugimori Nobumori 杉/椙森信盛
Sugu ni jōbutsu tokudatsu no (chikai) 直に成佛得脱の(誓)
Suji 筋
Sukiyare-gami 漉破紙
Suma 須磨
Sumiyoshi 住吉
Suō 周防
Suzuki Yukizō 鈴木行三
Tahei 太兵衞
Ta hsüeh 大學
Taihei-bashi 太平橋
Taiheiki 太平記
Taiko-mochi 太鼓持
Taira no (Akushichibyōe) Kagekiyo 平(惡七兵衞)景清
Taishaku ten 帝釋天
(*Taishō shinshū*) *Daizōkyō* (大正新修) 大藏經
Takano Tatsuyuki 高野辰之
Takaragura 寶藏
Takeda Izumo 竹田出雲

Takeda Manjirō-za 竹田萬治郎座

Takemoto Gidayū 竹本義太夫

Takemoto Masadayū 竹本政太夫

Takemoto-za 竹本座

Takigawa Masajirō 瀧川正次郎

Takimoto Seiichi 瀧本誠一

Tama 玉

Tamba Yosaku 丹渡與作

Tamba Yosaku matsuyo no komuro-bushi 丹渡與作
待夜の小室節

Tamuke no mizu 手向の水

Tanaka Kagai 田中香涯

Tanaka Minoru 田中稔

Tango 丹後

Tango fudoki 丹後風土記

Tanka 短歌

Tankei 短繋

Tantō 短刀

Tao-te-ching 道德經

Tayū 太夫

Teimon 貞門

Teki 敵 ; *-sama* 様

Tembatsu kishōmon no koto 天罰起請文の事

Temma; see following entries

Temma-bashi 天満橋

Temma-gu 天満宮

Temma-gumi 天満組

Temma Ōsaka sangō 天満大坂三郷

Temma Tenjin 天満天神

Temmō kai-kai so ni shite morasazu 天網恢恢
疎にして漏らさず

Tenjin 天神 (deity) ; see Temma Tenjin

Tenjin 天神 (prostitute)

Tenjin-bashi 天神橋

Tenjinki 天神記

Tenna 天和

Ten no ami 天の網

Ten no Amijima shigure no kotatsu 天の網島時雨 の炬燵

Ten no ami ni kakaru 天の網に罹る

Terajima Ryōan 寺島良安

Tobi 鳶

Tobiume 飛梅

Tōkaidō 東海道

Toki 時

Tokugawa 德川

(Tokugawa jidai) Gengo no kenkyū （德川時代） 言語の研究

Tokutomi Iichirō 德富猪一郎

Tōrō ga ono de gozaru 蟷螂が斧でござる

Tōrō no ono o motte ryūsha ni mukau 蟷螂の斧を 以つて隆車に向ふ

Tōten gyōhitsu 楊鳴曉筆

Toyotake Wakadayū 豊竹若太夫

Toyotake-za 豊竹座

Toyotomi 豊臣

Tso-chuan 左傳

Tsubouchi Shōyō 坪内逍遙

Tsubouchi Yūzō 坪内雄藏; see Tsubouchi Shōyō

Tsuki hi no sekimori nashi 月日の關守なし

Tsuki hi no seki ya 月日の關や

Tsukimi 月見

Tsukushi 筑紫

Tsukusu 壺す

Tsunajima Ryōsen 綱島梁川

Tsuraki 辛き

Tsuru-gun 都留郡
Tsuta no ha 蔦の葉
Tung-fang So chuan 東方朔傳
Tzu-chih t'ung-chien 資治通鑑
Uchihadaka demo, soto nishiki 内裸でも、外錦
Udaijin 右大臣
Ueda Akinari zenshū 上田秋成全集
Ueda Mannen 上田萬年
Ue no machi 上の町
Ukiyoe 淨世繪
Ukiyo-zōshi 淨世草紙
Ukiyo-zōshi shū 淨世草子集
Umeda 梅田
Umeda-bashi 梅田橋
Ummon-kan 雲門關
Uramachi 裏町
Urashima nendaiki 浦島年代記
Urashima-no-ko 浦島子
Urashima Tarō 浦島太郎
Uryōko 右龍虎
Ushi mitsu 丑三つ
(*Uso to makoto*) *Sato namari* (虚實) 柳巷方言
Uta 歌
Utsumi Shigetarō 内海繁太郎
Uzuki no iroage 卯月の潤色
Uzuki no momiji 卯月の紅葉
Wada 和田
Wakamidori 若緑
Wakan sansai zue 和／倭漢三才圖會
Wakashū kabuki 若衆歌舞伎
Wakatsuki Yasuji 若月保治
Wakizashi 脇差
Waniguchi 鰐口

Wankyū-mono 椀久物

Wankyū sue no Matsuyama 椀久末の松山

Wan'ya Kyūemon 椀屋久衛門

Wan'ya Kyūhei 椀屋久兵衛

Warifu 割符

Waseda bungaku 早稲田文學

Wasure nokori 忘れ殘り

Watakushi no Chikamatsu kenkyū 私の近松研究

Wen hsüan 文選

Wu-chou T'ung-wên shu-chü 五洲同文書局

Ya 家/屋

Yabu 藪

Yado 宿

Yajiri-kiri 家尻切

Yamamoto Kyūbei 山本九兵衛

Yamaoka Genrin 山岡元隣

Yamato-gawa 大和川

Yamatoya Dembei 大和屋傳兵衛

Yanagawa 柳川

Yari no Gonza kasane katabira 鑓の權三重帷子

Yarite 遣手

Yarō bōshi 野郎帽子

Yarō hyōbanki 野郎評判記

Yarō kabuki 野郎歌舞伎

Yashiki; see *Kura-yashiki*

Yashima 屋島

Yaso no okina mukashi banashi 八十の翁昔話

Yatsu to nanatsu 八つと七つ

Yodo-gawa 淀川

Yodogoi shusse no takinobori 淀鯉出世瀧徳

Yokkai 欲界

Yokuichi 欲市

Yōkyoku 謡曲

Yōkyoku kenkyū 謡曲研究

Yōkyoku sōsho 謡曲叢書

Yōkyoku taikan 謡曲大観

Yomiuri 讀賣

Yorobōshi 弱法師

"Yosaku odori" 與作踊

Yoshida Hambei 吉田半兵衛

Yoshino 吉野

Yoshino Shizuka 吉野靜

Yoshiwara 吉原

Yoshizawa Ayame 芳澤あやめ

Yotsuhōgin; see Shihōgin

Yotsu sankamme 四ツ三貫目

Yüan Shao chuan 袁紹傳

Yūgiri Awa no Naruto 夕霧阿波鳴渡

Yukata 浴衣

Yuna 湯女

Yuya 熊野

Yuzawa Kōkichirō 湯澤幸吉郎

Za-gashira 座頭

Zeami 世阿彌

Zenshaku Chikamatsu kessaku shū 全釋近松傑作集

Zōho matsu no ochiba 增補松の落葉

(Zōho) Rigen shūran (增補) 俚言集覧

Zōho Ten no Amijima 增補天の網島

Zoku enseki jisshu 續燕石十種

Zukin 頭巾

-Zukushi 盡し

Zuri 掏摸

Index

Page references in italics are the more important ones